C000291657

Cł

Stronger Than You Look

Copyright © Charlotte Ruth Clark 2020

Cover Design by Charlotte Ruth Clark

All rights reserved. Any portion of this book
may not be reproduced or used in any manner whatsoever
without the express written permission of the author
except for the use of brief quotations.

ISBN: 9798648887787

15% of author royalties will be donated to support
Cyclical Vomiting Syndrome Association UK.

For all inquiries:
Email - chikarastory@gmail.com
Instagram - @chikarastory

Chikara

Stronger Than You Look

Charlotte Ruth Clark

For Ruth, my grandma

Wherever you go, I'll go. I'll never leave you. I'd swim the South China Sea for a glimpse of you, run through the mountains of Hokkaido to see you wave goodbye, I'd starve myself for days and nights to feel your arms around me. Wherever I go, I move a step closer to you. Every sunrise is a day closer to seeing you. I won't stop fighting until you are beside me again, until your hand is on top of mine, where it should have stayed. Some days I wish I had never left, I should have waited for you, done it all with you. I should have done everything with you, because without you, I have fallen out of love with life.

CONTENTS

INTRODUCTION

My name is Charlotte, Cece to my friends. I'm twenty-three and suffer from Cyclical Vomiting Syndrome (CVS), *which I like to think makes me a 'CVS Warrior'.*

Now I want to point out that CVS is not my defining feature, it is just something I have. Unfortunately, the condition decided to join me for a considerable proportion of my journey through Asia and so before you read on, I think it's important I explain what exactly CVS is, based on my experience of the condition. *I'll make it brief as I know you haven't picked up this book to read a page from a medical journal!*

My CVS Story[1]

For me, CVS presents itself in the form of an 'attack', a bit like a stomach migraine. Attacks usually manifest early in the morning so I wake to waves of stomach cramps, which get progressively worse throughout the day. If I eat or walk around the pain intensifies, so I'm resigned to lie flat on my back in a dark room. After about six hours the nausea kicks in, leaving me unable to read, watch films or even talk to anyone. When the pain is at its worst, I'm often sick. I'll feel better for a few moments until the pain starts to build up again - the cycle begins. Attacks normally last between twelve to forty-eight hours, any longer than this and I'm admitted to hospital.

The recovery is slow and I'm restricted to my bedroom for a few days due to exhaustion, dehydration and strained stomach muscles. It takes me a little time to get back on my feet, but otherwise, I'm back to normal. That is, until the next attack comes along, and then the cycle begins again.

---

[1] *It must be understood that there are many people who suffer from CVS far worse than I do, in fact they probably make my condition seem mild in comparison, which gives you an idea of just how vicious this illness can be.*

It all started when I was thirteen. Doctors initially thought it was a bug that I couldn't shake; but as I grew older, it only got worse. At sixteen, attacks had increased to three - five times a year and by the time I reached my second year of university, they had rocketed to once every two weeks. This meant that I spent more Friday nights bedbound than at the student night club. My days were ruled by four-hour paracetamol cycles and each month was riddled with hospital visits - *not exactly the life of a university student I'd imagined.*

CVS affected my life tremendously: impacting my grades, straining relationships and dramatically reducing my quality of life. If I wasn't cramped up in pain or throwing up, I was recovering from the last attack; forever in the CVS cycle. Invitations were declined, moments were missed and memories unmade, as I lost more of my life than time would let me keep.

As a last resort, my parents found a private gastroenterologist, via the CVSA UK Charity Support Group, which I started to visit at the beginning of my final year of university.[2] I was prescribed a suitcase load of pills and put on several strict diets. This pushed attacks to once every three - four weeks, a huge improvement from the previous year, allowing me to re-claim my life.

Nowadays, my attacks are more sporadic than they used to be and, in general, I like to think I'm improving. So, following university and having just finished two years of teaching mathematics, I decided to reclaim lost time. Despite friends' reservations and doctors advising against it, it was time for me to travel.

The Journey Begins

I began to think seriously about travelling two years prior to my departure date, although I really think I'd been

---

[2] *"Welcome to CVSA UK". Cvsa.Org.Uk, 2020, http://www.cvsa.org.uk/. Accessed August 2020.*

planning it since childhood. I'd store photos from holiday scrapbooks in my mind and memorise relatives' stories of their adventures in foreign lands so that, one day, I could do the same.

Every night I'd rush home from work, pull out every travel guide, magazine and book I owned and spend hours looking through the pictures of these wonderful places, places that were so different from anything I had seen before. Places where the water is bluer than sapphires, where the jungle is the country's orchestra, where women paint their faces the shade of moonlight and where mountains rise so high the cloud turns the ground to ice with a single touch. My heart was set on Asia.

Knowing that most of my friends, including my boyfriend Alex, were restricted by work commitments, I planned to go it alone. Alex hoped to visit me at some point, but for the most part, it was to be a solo trip.

I tried to keep the route vague, with only the start and finish plus a few key flights booked: fly out to Singapore, then head to Borneo, spend a month in Japan, a month in China and use the rest of the time to work my way through Mainland South East Asia. My trip would span almost five months. It would be long, but I was ready.

This was my project, my escape. When I suffered from an attack, these glossy magazine photos and guidebook descriptions helped me pull through the pain and pass the time during recovery. When the pain became so intense, I'd imagine myself somewhere along my route, *where will I be in a few months' time? Hokkaido? Kota Kinabalu? Or maybe Shanghai?* This was my escape, I was missing out now, but I wouldn't be very soon. This was my time.

A few months before my planned departure date, however, my grandmother was diagnosed with cancer, terminal cancer. They didn't know how long it would be, but as far as we knew she still had some time. As my outbound flight beckoned, her health declined and she became bedbound. In quick succession, she was forced to move in with my parents, transferred to a nursing home and then finally admitted to a hospice. I didn't want to miss the last few months with her, but she was adamant that I continue with my trip. I loved my grandma very much and wanted her to be happy, so when she said I should go and travel for her, I made it my mission to do so.

CVS has taught me a lot about resilience, determination and quite frankly, just how to endure. It doesn't define me, but it has made me who I am today. I knew those closest to me, in particular my grandma, believed this too and knew I could complete my journey. It is their words of kindness that motivated and kept me going throughout the many months and challenges that lay ahead. I remember receiving a card from one of my closest friends before I left, the final line stayed with me the entire trip and gave me courage when I had nothing left, 'Remember Cece, no matter what happens, you are *stronger than you look*.'

The Journal

I invite you to read my personal journal, written during my travels, in the hope that it may provide a small help to those who have experienced illness, grief or pain in their lives. If nothing else, I hope it makes you laugh and smile as I recount the many situations and acts of kindness I experienced in Asia.

Please note for the purpose of this journal, all names have been changed for the sake of anonymity. I appreciate there are many characters in this story, so I've included a name list *(pg331)* in case you lose track. Everything I write is aimed to represent the truth. In some instances, details may have been changed for the structure of the journal or have simply been remembered or recorded incorrectly. Every entry was written on the day stated between the months of August – December 2018.

This is a true story, a story taken from life.

CURRENCY CONVERSIONS[3]

Country	Currency	Currency Code	Local Currency Equivalent to £1 (GBP)
Singapore	Dollar	SGD	1.78
Malaysia	Ringgit	MYR	5.30
Japan	Yen	JPY	147.17
Hong Kong	Dollar	HKD	10.24
China	Yuan	CNY	8.76
Thailand	Baht	THB	43.53
Cambodia	Dollar (US)	USD	1.30
Vietnam	Dong	VND	30077.44

MY JOURNEY THROUGH ASIA

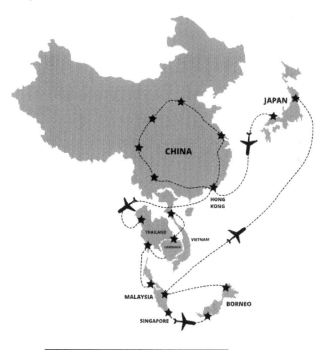

---

[3] *"August 2018: Monthly Exchange Rates - GOV.UK". Gov.uk, https://assets.publishing.service.gov.uk/government/uploads/system/uploads/attachment_data/file/728079/exrates-monthly-0818.csv/preview. Accessed August 2020.*

PART ONE

Malaysia and Borneo

ONE

If I'd have known what was to come, would I ever have left?

1ˢᵗ August (the night before I left for Asia)
Oxfordshire
8:50p.m.

'Charlotte, how on earth are you going to fit all this in your rucksack?'

'Ummm, by squashing it? Really tightly…the dry sacks will help?'

'I may just be being a mum but I think we should have started this earlier. Look at your room, you can't move in it!'

Mum was right, large archive boxes covered the floor, pill boxes littered the carpet and huge containers of laxative sachets towered upwards, barricading the doorway.

'Wow, it's drug city in here!' Dad commented, peering round the doorway.

'Yes Dad, we know.'

'How are you going to fit all that in your rucksack?' he exclaimed.

'That is just what we are trying to figure out Paul,' my mother snapped. 'Okay…what if we take the pills out of their boxes, flatten the boxes and write the month on each one, and then combine them together with an elastic band?'

'Ahh good idea, then if I get stopped at Customs it should be fairly obvious I have a health condition,' I replied.

'Well, Charlotte, I think you should declare the items at the airport *before* you get stopped. Did you research each country's allowance?' Mum enquired.

'Yes, Malaysia permits three months' worth, but most other countries only allow one month's supply…which is where it gets a little trickier.'

'Okay, so you definitely need to declare them at each airport.'

'I think it will be fine.'

'Charlotte – you don't want to end up like Bridget Jones in some Thai prison do you?'

'No.'

'I don't want to have a phone call from airport security explaining to me that my daughter has tried to import ten kilograms of drugs into their country.'

'But it's for my illness.'

'Yes, but they don't know that.'

'True.'

'Okay then, you declare the medication at each airport. Right, you start opening the boxes and laying out a month's supply of each drug and I'll write the labels.'

'I'm on it. Mission travel meds has begun!'

Having the condition CVS for over a decade, I had been to numerous hospital appointments, completed dozens of tests and after seeing a gastroenterologist in London acquired a hefty pill intake: twenty-plus daily medicines and vitamins. There was no way I could carry a five-month supply with me. So only the crucial meds were packed.

After a few hours of unboxing, counting and fifty elastic bands, I had packed a ten-kilogram supply of meds that would last me the first few months, or at least until my boyfriend came out to visit.

'Well, I'm certainly going to be popular at parties!'

'Charlotte!'

'Just kidding! Anyway, who wants to fall asleep at 7.30p.m. thanks to amitriptyline?'

'Right, it's quarter to midnight, I think we're finally done,' concluded Mum. 'We have to be up early tomorrow to see Grandma before we head to the airport, she's going to smile so much when she sees you with your huge rucksack!'

I didn't want to go to sleep because, when I woke, it would be my last chance to see Grandma before the trip began.

2nd August
The Cotswolds
10:30a.m.

That was hard. Saying goodbye to Grandma. A woman who shaped my childhood and helped me become the person I am today. I held it together when I left her room. I made sure the very last thing she saw was me smiling. Because deep down, I knew that this might be the last time I'd see her, the last time I could say goodbye. And that, that was hard to imagine.

Gatwick Airport
3p.m.

With the squeeze of Mum's hand, a little metal angel was placed into my palm.

'Just stay safe, Charlotte, promise me you will?'

'I promise,' I whispered, giving her a tight hug.

They all came to see me off, my little family: Dad, Mum and my younger sister Jemima. I proceeded to passport control, waving back to them for as long as I could until they were out of sight. Through the doors, a ripple of fear and excitement pulsed through me. From now on, it was just me on this adventure.

Even though Grandma wasn't at the airport, I would remember our goodbye at the hospice forever. I would always see her smiling, her little never-ending wave, wishing me to go, to see the world.

So that's just what I did, I went to see the world. I went to Asia.

Stopover
11:52p.m.

I was alone, alone in a sea of people. People lying on benches, queuing for drinks, midnight snacking, women praying and men in white robes speaking in tongues I did not understand. Duty Free was filled with shiny boxes of Turkish delight, I nibbled the corner of a sample; the sweetness of pomegranate and pistachio brought me to my senses. *I'm in Istanbul.*

1:00a.m.

Not entirely sure what to do with myself. With no one to talk to, I remained fixed in front of the large screen displaying flight times, switching from Turkish to English. I had taken my meds by this point and, as a consequence, was feeling the sluggish drowsiness amitriptyline induced. I remained standing, trying to avoid the overwhelming desire to sleep.

Somewhere over Malaysia

Nine hours into the second flight, I woke and thought of my grandma. I had to turn to the window, to prevent my eyes from becoming glassy. *She is still alive, Charlotte, you will see her again.*

Beyond the glass, I saw a tiny island, followed by the coastline of a continuous stretch of land. I had hit Malaysia, Singapore (my first stop) was in fifteen minutes. *Once this plane lands, you'll be in Asia, solo.* I promised myself that I would see everything I could. See it for Grandma, for my family and for all the CVS sufferers.

'I will do it for them,' I pledged silently.

3rd August
8:00p.m.

Singapore: a busy, hot and clammy city, but beautiful nonetheless.

The subway system was a ribbon of colours, a network of opening and closing gates, ticket offices and slippery escalators. Emerging from the cool carriage into the street's hot air felt like entering a greenhouse - the complete opposite to moderate London. It was a little intimidating walking through the dark streets alone. A small, curly-haired

English girl hobbling through Chinatown with a bright blue rucksack wouldn't exactly be a difficult target.

Thank God for mobile offline maps...made it to the hostel! I checked in and hauled my heavy rucksack up to the twenty-four-bed dorm. Finding only a few travellers in the room, I sat quietly on my top bunk. Looking around, everyone was either asleep or fixated on their phones. *Welcome to Singapore, the fun starts here!* The silence was claustrophobic. *Well, this is a bold welcome to hostel life.*

My internal monologue filled the silence. *Well, I guess I'll sort out my rucksack then, pyjamas, clothes for tomorrow, ah which dry bag did I put my underwear in?* It sounds silly but I guess when you are in a totally unfamiliar place, if you can carry on with familiar routines it makes things a little easier to process. *Anyway, today I made it to Asia. That is a small success in itself!*

10p.m.

Lying down for my first night, I recalled walking through my grandparents' garden, just as my mother and I had done a few days prior to my departure. This was the last place I had seen my grandfather, standing confidently at the gate, waving a fond goodbye as my sister and I walked further away across the meadow. We were younger then and didn't know it would be the last time. *Sometimes it's better not to know when it will be the last time.*

My grandfather invested so much of his life in this once beautiful garden. Now nettles and weeds fought in an upward tangle for the sun, while the flowers and vegetable plants lay solemnly below, almost accepting their gardener's absence. The forlorn look on my mother's face had shadowed the heavy sadness, not about the weeds themselves but at the unintentional ruin that had become her parents' garden.

TWO

In my little existence so far, she was such a special person.

4ᵗʰ August
First full day in Singapore
9a.m.

I love walking and felt that walking, as opposed to the subway, was a great idea! I strode through the city, but it was hot, sweaty, and unfortunately thanks to my map-reading failure, mostly along main roads which wasn't the most cultural experience.

Too many hours after 9a.m.

Following hours of navigating the Singaporean road network, I saw a glimpse of Gardens by the Bay's centre piece, the Supertrees. I remember seeing them on television, a fine example of urban structures cohabiting with nature. The beautiful towers stretched up to fifty metres high, entwined with rich exotic flora, creating enchanting vertical gardens. Some even featured photovoltaic cells to provide solar energy, lighting up the Supertrees. The distant silhouettes ignited a spark of excitement in me, a spark that had long been extinguished ever since Mum had broken the news of Grandma's terminal illness to me.

Grandma's cancerous shadow had sapped all the joy and excitement from me, I couldn't possibly think about enjoying myself when she was in so much pain. The only reason I left was because I knew she had wanted me to go but, despite this, guilt and sadness remained the heaviest items in my rucksack.

The gardens
1p.m.

Navigating around huge commercial complexes and rows of air-conditioned shops, I made it to the garden; and there before me were the Supertrees, standing confidently like the garden's guards. Little orchids and strands of ivy created intricate patterns that ran up the iron trunks, until the towers opened into hollow funnels, like flowers in mid-bloom. It was a beautiful garden and I enjoyed a few hours there being a tourist.

I sat by a fountain for a simple lunch from a cute café that served toast-based meals. I tried a Singaporean delicacy of kaya toast. A thick layer of coconut jam, kaya, and slabs of lightly salted butter were sandwiched between thin slices of multigrain toast. I spent the afternoon at the ArtScience Museum, browsing a temporary exhibition which displayed impressive structures made of natural materials that moved purely powered by the wind. *Pretty cool.*

Evening

During breakfast I'd met an Argentinian lady in her forties. She was an experienced explorer, reeling off countless tips and hidden gems of Singapore to eager-eyed travellers who were fresh to the city. A little nervous about going for dinner by myself for the first time, I arranged to meet her at 6p.m.

Romping back to the hostel, after yet another map reading failure, I arrived dead on six and sat patiently in the lobby, excited to make my first friend of the trip. I spent the next twenty minutes listening to the air con and rising hopefully every time the door went. *I think you've just been stood-up Cece. Fabulous. Right, plan B.*

There were a few people sitting on the sofas of the hostel lobby, so after a few minutes psyching up the courage, I asked each traveller their plans for the evening. I sat back down feeling defeated. Everyone was busy or looked away

13

dismissively as they carried on talking to their friends or partners. *This is not what I thought backpacking would be like. Everyone said 'it's super easy, you'll make loads of friends.' Do I have a massive sign on my forehead saying do not go out with this English girl, she's clueless and has zero travelling experience? No, pull it together Cece, this is just your first attempt.*

There was one other girl who sat quietly on her phone. Approaching with a huge smile, I asked if I could sit beside her. The girl smiled back and moved her things. *Win number one.* I asked if she was travelling alone and she was. *Yes, this is promising.*

'Do you fancy seeing the light show at Gardens by the Bay this evening?'

Her eyes lit up, 'Why yes, I was going to see it by myself anyway.'

Okay this is even more promising!

'Great, do you want to go together and perhaps we can grab some dinner too?' I responded.

'That sounds great.'

Yes, finally my first reliable travel friend. I felt like I had just built the first step on my bridge to becoming a successful traveller.

Walking to a food court nearby, we chatted about our journeys so far. Marianne had recently turned twenty but, despite her age, she was already an experienced traveller, having worked in Iceland, Australia and Bali for the past year. Before returning to her home in Germany, she had planned a long weekend in Singapore to finish off her trip.

7p.m.

The food court was unlike anything I had seen before. Dishes were on the floor, tables were made of flimsy plastic and stands displayed faded laminated photos of noodle meat dishes. I had been warned that the best places would probably look the worst, so judging by appearances this could have been the Ritz! We saw strange delicacies of shark, turtle and crocodile stewed in curries and sauces.

'Thank God I am vegetarian!'

'I know, I just swam with turtles, the last thing I want to do is eat them!' giggled Marianne.

Despite appearances, the people were friendly and Marianne sweetly put up with my quest to find some veggie food. We settled for a simple rice dish with some vegetables tossed in a hot wok with soy sauce and garnished with some shreds of red cabbage. After the successful local dining experience, we ventured to explore the light show back at Gardens by the Bay. With the sun shining its last rays several hours ago, a blanket of darkness had covered the garden. The Supertrees were even more impressive by night. Illuminated by blueish turquoise lights, the climbing vines were transformed into plankton, glowing in the sky. Iridescent turquoise globes lit the humid air, turning the garden into an oriental fantasy land.

5th August

Today was a sightseeing day! I bought a metro pass, minimizing road walking and maximizing exploring time. The botanical garden was first on our list because a special orchid garden was on show. Beautiful blooms were intricately arranged in an exotic fashion. We had never seen orchids so big; each curved petal was pigmented with a small cloud of colour, a drop of ink on a silk canvas. We spent the time taking close-up photos and admiring the abundance of flowers.

Around midday we took a brisk tour around little India, China and Arab Street. We browsed colourful buildings, temples and eyed up local delicacies. Despite feeling a little out of place in the local Chinese food court, we enjoyed watching the lunchtime rush as countless parcels and packages were purchased. Interesting pearl coloured doughy spheres were piled high in bamboo baskets as the steam wafted over the counter; we took the plunge and tried one dollar steamed buns for lunch. Sitting down in the sun, resting our hot feet, we sunk our teeth into the warm dough before quickly looking at each other and laughing.

'It tastes of...nothing, what does yours taste like?' Marianne exclaimed.

'Umm, definitely not purple sweet potato.'

'Well at least we tried them!' Marianne jested.

The evening

After stopping back at the hostel to freshen up, we headed back into town for a drink at the towering Marina Bay Sands Hotel, to celebrate the end of Marianne's travels and the beginning of mine. Glammed up in floral playsuits, bum bags and trainers, *the highest of backpacker fashion*, we strolled past designer shops and expensive restaurants, pretending to be millionaires waltzing back to our hotel room. *Which would probably cost per night the amount we'd spend on our entire trip!*

Entry to the rooftop bar cost twenty Singapore dollars, pricey but it did give us credit for a drink, which were also very pricey, so a good deal. A rapid lift, lit by blue lights, carried us up to the top floor with an infinity pool which, to our disappointment, was only for hotel guests. We headed to the bar, overlooking the city, and admired the glittering city lights of Singapore. Tall glasses, topped with little white flowers, dried pineapple and filled with juices the shade of a sunrise, were ferried on silver trays to glamourous guests.

'Oh Charlotte, you must order a Singapore Sling, it was so wonderful,' I heard my grandma's voice.

It wasn't Raffles, where she had fondly implored me to visit, but I saw it as the modern sky-high version with a view. As I took my first sip, I felt like Grandma was right next to me smiling. A little later, we managed to sneak to the west side of the bar to watch the Gardens by the Bay light show from above, which looked more like fairy lights dancing on Christmas trees from the height. We watched in awe as the sea air cooled our cocktail warmed skin.

6th August

Marianne and I parted this morning, exchanging Instagram names before moving onto the next stage of our adventures. I was sad to leave my first travel friend but confident I could now make many more.

11a.m.

I made it to the airport, just about. I was ten cents short of a rail ticket, but out of the kindness of his heart, and what I think was slight sympathy at my forlorn face, the ticket officer gave me one of his silver dollars, allowing me to complete my journey. I smiled for the rest of the ride, reflecting on this act of generosity. *The first of many I would encounter in Asia.*

THREE

Terima kasih.

6th August
Kuching, Borneo
Afternoon

I'd booked a mixed dorm again but this one had twelve beds as opposed to twenty-four. There was more space between each bunk and it seemed a little less busy. The hostel backed onto a chipped painted wall with a small waterfall flowing down beside it. The fallen water formed a pool on the ground floor where terrapins basked in the small slice of sunshine that shone through a crack in the wall. A tree branch, encasing a little table and chairs on the balcony, appeared to be growing through the building making it seem more of a watering hole for travellers than a hostel. The tree branch continued to cradle the common room which was open plan, with only a few bamboo mirrors hanging from the ceiling to create a divide between the bathroom and kitchen.

Walking into the room, I was greeted by two friendly Malaysian women who complimented my curly hair, a rare sight in Borneo.

'We never see this kind, ours always black and straight.'

'Ah well it's very lovely, I would love to have Malaysian hair,' I replied.

The Malaysians giggled, 'Aw you sweet, where you from?'

'England! Have you been?'

'England, naa, too far, but nice place.'

'Thank you, well, if you get the chance you can come and stay with me, I will be in London, so it's very easy to get to.'

'Yes, maybe one day sweet girl.'

'Here, your room key, locker key, breakfast seven to nine, doors close at ten so remember the code. Enjoy your stay!'

'Thank you, wait, please could you tell me how to say "thank you" in Malaysian?'

'Terima kasih.'

'Tera, um sorry, how do I say it?'

'Teri ma ka sih.'

'Terima kasih.'

'Yes perfect, you got it,' the Malaysians giggled.

'Well terima kasih for terima kasih!'

After paying the small price of forty ringgits, equivalent to eight pounds (under half the price of Singapore's hostel), I entered the dorm to find an excitable young man welcoming me from underneath the far-right bunk.

'Hello there, my name is Dalir, I'm from Pakistan.'

He had a broad smile, tanned skin and dark eyes from what I could observe in the doorway.

'Hi, I'm Cece from England,' I responded matching his enthusiastic tone.

He explained rapidly that he was just completing his fellowship as a pediatric surgeon and was in Kuching to take an exam to allow him to practise in England.

'I'm already qualified in Pakistan you see, so this is to see if I can treat patients in your country. Ah this is going to be so good you are from England, I may need to ask you a few questions later, I am studying you see.'

'Wow, that's awesome, yes of course, if I can be of any assistance please let me know!'

'Really? Oh wow, you have no idea how helpful that would be!'

'Well, I'm just travelling so if I can help you it's a good use of my time. Right, I'll start unpacking and let you get back to your reading.'

'Okay, very nice to meet you, Cece.'

'Nice to meet you too Dalir. That is a very English phrase, you are doing well!'

19

'Oh really? Thanks Cece, you are going to be very helpful to me I can just feel it!'

He carried on studying but the conversation continued in broken segments as I unpacked. His positive energy and politeness made me feel at ease. Even if he was an exception, I felt I'd be very happy in Kuching now I had found someone with as much enthusiasm as myself.

'Cece, are you hungry? I'm going for some food if you want to join?'

'Sure, I had lunch on the plane but I'll come along for an explore, you can show me around!'

We talked non-stop while walking along the riverfront. It was a peaceful town in comparison to Singapore, boats trickled along the river, little stalls were lit up with fairy lights and locals smiled as they walked by. It was a nice change from the city, my first glimpse of Borneo.

'Okay KFC, we're here!'

I tried to hide my disappointment, I was hoping for my first experience of Malaysian cuisine to be something a little more authentic. *I haven't come all this way to see a fast food chain frying its way across the globe!* Dalir looked at me and spoke before the reaction appeared on my face.

'I know, I'm a surgeon, but during exams I eat fast food...and smoke. I know it is bad but it's only for a little while, then the job makes me stop with thirty-six-hour shifts!'

I smiled 'I get it; people do different things when they are stressed. For me it's exercise and unhealthy amounts of chocolate.'

Dalir laughed as he collected his chicken and fries.

Walking back to the hostel I spotted an impressive bridge-like structure, it reminded me a little of the Millennium Bridge in London except the sides of the bridge spiraled upwards with grand supporting cables extending in opposite directions.

'Ooh, can we walk up it?'

'Sure, I could use a half hour study break.'

When we reached the bridge, Dalir placed his arm on my shoulder and pointed across the river.

'See that huge, gold spired, circus tent-like building? A guy from the hostel, Saris, said that it's a shopping mall, want to check it out?'

'Sure, it's the fanciest shopping centre I've ever seen!'

Waltzing up the small driveway, we nonchalantly entered the building.

'It seems a bit quiet doesn't it? I don't see any signs, oh wait there's a man over there; I'll ask what time the place closes.'

Before phrasing my question, the security guard waved his arms and hastily escorted the pair of us out the entrance.

'No entry lady, restricted building. You no come in.'

'Oh, we're really sorry, this isn't the shopping mall?'

'No, no, this is government building, very important. You not allowed in.'

'Okay, we're going right away.'

I made wide eyes at Dalir, out of slight alarm but mainly at the hilarity of the situation.

'Oh damn I forgot to buy socks, we'll have to go back in again,' Dalir shouted.

I burst into a fit of giggles trying to pull him away before we got into any more trouble!

'So Saris said it was a shopping mall, huh?'

'Ah man, he must have been drunk when he saw it; he's always drunk or high.'

'Perhaps he said it as a joke, and we embarrassingly believed him?'

'No! No way, man he can't have done, or maybe he did. Ah Saris, I'm going to get that dude when I see him!'

Just when I thought the afternoon's exploration was over, Dalir proposed another idea. 'There is a small white fort over the other side of that hill, want to try and find it?'

'Why of course, I love an adventure, but let's try and get there without using our phones for an extra challenge.'

And so the 'no-maps' quest began, across grassy fields, concrete ruins, logs and jungle. Normally I was confident in this kind of terrain, yet in slippery flip-flops it proved to be quite a challenge. Sweetly, Dalir offered his hand like a big brother at each crossing.

'Where are we going, we've been walking for over an hour now?'

'It was right next to the official building when I pointed it out to you, where has it gone? You saw it right Cece?'

'Yea, well, I thought I did.'

As I got out my phone to check the map, one of Kuching's standard afternoon rain showers began, drenching us within a minute. A black car came to a standstill beside us.

'You guys okay, need a ride?'

It was tempting to hop inside the dry vehicle but, loving the spontaneous adventure and finding the rain a little home comfort, I thanked the driver and refused.

'We're going to soldier on in the rain, terima kasih.'

The car drove on. *People in Malaysia are so nice!*

'Aha I like your style English girl, nothing can stop us,' Dalir said.

'Oh hell no, we have committed an hour of our lives to find this ancient fort, so we're going to damn well find it!'

'Haha, well after you, expedition leader!'

'Okay then, onward!'

Eventually, we made it to the fort just as the guard was closing the gate. Dalir explained that we'd walked for hours to find the place; the guard was quickly swayed and let us in. We spent a while taking photos beside the castle, doing funny poses and a few selfies. I learnt all about his life in Pakistan, how his entire family were surgeons and that he had no choice in his future career; 'the parents always choose the son's profession'. *It was a different kind of life.*

'It's either a doctor or an engineer, they are the only two respectable professions parents want for their son.'

He had had a very strict upbringing, being forced to study all the time. Television was limited to thirty minutes a day and even that was only the news.

'Wow that must have been tough?'

'Yes, and he beat me too if I tried to copy the answers to my homework!'

'Well serves you right for cheating!'

Watching Dalir's surprised face, I quickly followed up the sarcastic comment with an apology. 'I'm sorry that was meant to be a joke but it came out really insensitive.'

'It's okay, I found it funny,' he replied with a smile. 'Yes, I am the stupid one of the family; I have to work really hard.'

'Don't worry, I'm the same, I'm not naturally good at maths I just worked damn hard. I think that's what counts.'

'I couldn't agree more.'

Dalir had exams to pass the day after next, one of them being patient diagnosis. So, keen to help in any way I could, I agreed to be the patient so he could diagnose me. Medical role play was quite fun, my extended experience of hospitals made the pretend appointment easy; I knew exactly what questions he'd ask, making it quite a challenge for the young surgeon.

He sighed saying 'you keep answering the questions before I have asked them, you are too good!'

'Haha, sorry! I've had way too many hospital visits.'

After a few more rounds of 'guess the prognosis', we sauntered back down the riverfront, the only way to get onto the pier was a well-used half-broken ladder. 'Hey, do you think this will hold? It looks like it's been rusted into the pier!' I asked.

'Yes, I'll go first and test it out, so don't worry if you are nervous about heights.'

'No, no I rock climb, so heights don't bother me, I'll go first. Then at least if I fall there's a surgeon around.'

'Rock climbing, ah nice, I have never done such a sport before, very interesting,' he replied hauling himself up the creaking ladder. 'Hey, have you taken the water taxi to the other side yet?'

'I just arrived a few hours ago so everything is new to me. Let's give it a go, it's only two ringgits, right?'

The boats were old, narrow painted vessels that lay so low in the water that you could feel each one of the river's ripples. Thin planks of wood covered the boat so passengers were forced to sit a little hunched over, clutching their knees.

Dalir did not immediately follow me into the boat. He seemed to be discussing something with the old Malaysian sailor, several ringgit notes were folded in his right hand. When he appeared to have made a deal, he thrust the notes towards the sailor, who received them with a sleepy smile and nod. The engine started to splutter and Dalir ventured inside to join me. The boat's captain pushed away from the pier, crossing his hands to other passengers implying the boat was full. But it wasn't full. *What arrangement had Dalir made?*

Crouching under the boat's makeshift roof he sat down beside me. We started to move, floating gently across the water, the lights on the bridge had just started to glow as dusk approached. I felt a little uneasy as the boat started to detour towards the bridge.

I whispered to Dalir, 'Aren't we supposed to just go straight across?'

'I paid him extra to go to the bridge and back.'

'Aw, thank you, that is very kind of you, I'll split the ticket with you.'

'No don't be silly!' he said firmly, ending the conversation.

'Okay, well thank you, this is really pretty.'

By the time the boat docked, it was nearing 7p.m.

'Do you fancy going for more food, perhaps after a little more studying this evening?' I waited nervously for a response, concerned that he may have had enough of me for one afternoon.

'Yes sure, can you give me one more hour?'

'Of course, that would be great!' I was relieved that I wouldn't be eating alone.

'There is a food market not far from here if you want to try it? Saris told me about it.'

'Yes I'd love to, thank you…just as long as it isn't another one of those shopping centres!'

'Haha, no no, I went with him and a bunch of others from the hostel last night, it was really good!'

'Okay, tried and tested, sounds perfect then.'

8p.m.

After a long walk circling a roundabout several times, as Dalir tried to navigate the market from memory, we eventually arrived at a huge arena of endless white marquees. Flood lights lit the market, illuminating large printed menus of Thai, Malaysian, Mexican, Vietnamese and other cuisines. It was packed; the place had a wild buzz of hungry locals and tourists eyeing up each tent's delicacy. A little worried about finding something vegetarian, I confessed to Dalir it may take a while.

'Take your time, we can look at all the stations.'

Dalir was kind, thoughtful and very attentive, making sure I fitted through the crowds by lending his hand for me to follow. There were noodle soups, Khmer burgers, hot curries, bubble tea, even an alligator in a tank. *Only in Malaysia!*

'Ooh let's go there, it would be nice to try something local, no?' I asked.

'Yes, I love local food!'

'I thought you said you'd only eaten fast food since being here?'

'Well, I like anything you like!'

'Okay, I'm veggie, are you sure?'

Again, being very thoughtful, Dalir made sure the noodle dish I liked was meat-free, quizzing the staff even after I had checked it myself.

'It's okay Dalir, I think it's fine.'

'No, I want to make sure it is suitable for you, I don't want you getting sick. It is my job to protect you.'

'Haha, it's not your job, you've only just met me!'

'Yes but as a pretty woman like yourself, I do need to protect you.'

Unsure whether he was still talking about the noodles, I made light of the comment. 'Haha, trust me, I'm sassy enough to protect myself! Ah, here we go, our first local dish, mee goreng mamak! Let's head to the river to eat.'

The mee goreng resembled a Malay version of pad Thai, a sweet orange spicy sauce with egg noodles, beansprouts and spring onion. We sat watching a sweet, yet raw, choir of local women who as Dalir put it, 'should only be heard in the shower!'

After the spicy dish, I spotted a refreshing stand which sold coconut bowls filled with ice cream and topped with young coconut curls.

'Oh Dalir, that looks so yummy, I'll get us both one. I owe you for dinner, plus the boat!'

'Sure.'

But when we got to the stand he admitted he didn't want one, leaving me a little disappointed and indebted to him. 'Okay, well let me pay you back by more surgical quizzing?'

'Yes, that would be brilliant, thank you. You are so nice Cece! In fact, this is a little embarrassing to ask, and please feel free to say no if you feel uncomfortable, but could I practise a physical examination on you back at the hostel?'

'Ah ha, um yes, but er what kind?'

'Oh, just a knee examination, nothing too intimate.'

'Oh well, yes of course then.' *First night in Kuching and I receive a free knee examination, that'll be one to remember!*

Back at the hostel

'Cece, you have no idea how helpful you are being! I'll get Saris to be your chaperone.'

'A chaperone, what does this knee examination entail? I am over eighteen! Okay, Saris apparently you're my chaperone. Nice to meet you by the way, I'm Cece! We should probably know each other if you're going to be my chaperone for the examination!'

'Haha, nice to meet you too, don't worry, I'll watch your back, or knee. You know what these doctors are like,' raising his eyebrows and flicking his eyes at Dalir.

As I lay down on the bench I felt a little strange, I had never imagined a knee examination would involve lying down, but then again, I had never experienced *this* kind of procedure before. I did as I was told, extending my leg, flexing this way and that while Dalir explained what he was doing, asking me questions about pain or discomfort every now and again. It was a little odd having a man I had only just met slide his hands up and down my thigh, but I suppressed my nervous thoughts, chatting to Saris with the occasional giggle as a distraction. After the exam was over Dalir thanked me sincerely.

'You've been a great help to me Cece, and I am eternally grateful.'

'Ah, it was easy, I just lay there!'

'Yes, but not many girls would let me do that.'

I paused considering what he meant, 'Well I'm just trying to help you pass your exam, that's all, you are a pediatric surgeon after all, and that's awesome, why would I not want to help you? Anyway, I'm off to sleep now, night guys!'

I left the boys smoking on the little table and chairs in the warm night air. *What a bizarre, but amazing, first night in Kuching.*

FOUR

If only I had known the situation I was creating for myself, I may not have taken that table by the riverside.

7th August
Morning

Dalir was studying, so I got up early and decided to brave some yoga by the riverside. Rising quietly at 6a.m. I aimed to leave the dorm undisturbed and hopefully find the riverside empty. It was nice to have a proper stretch by the water, I felt alive under the warm Borneo sun; the rays of which only a few early birds of the dawn experienced. My presence however, wasn't entirely unnoticed. While practising Downward Dog I saw a pair of shoes beside me. I tried to ignore them, hoping they'd walk on, but they remained there for the next minute. Moving into a plank, a little unnerved, I looked up and smiled innocently. *Maybe this was a bad idea after all.* The shoes belonged to an older Malaysian man in uniform who had been patrolling the area as a local policeman. *Oh lord, please don't arrest me, maybe yoga isn't allowed in public, oh how could I have been so naïve?*

'Yoga,' he said with a thumbs up. 'Where you from?'

To my relief, the old policeman smiled warmly.

'England, you're a local?' I replied.

'Yes, Kuching, my home. Where England?'

'Oxford, two hours from London.'

'London, very nice. Yoga very nice.'

'Terima Kasih, you do yoga?'

'Me, no! Ha ha, but me, my friends we know yoga, very good for body. You keep going young girl.'

'Ah, yes very good for the body! Okay, I will. Have a nice day.' *Oh that was easy Cece, he just wanted to know what kind of exercise you were doing!*

The policeman continued to watch as if it were a game of bowls, commenting on each stretch I performed from Cobra to Child's Pose. When I finished my routine, I gave a quick wave and walked back to the hostel. *A quaint encounter but perhaps I won't do yoga in public again!*

I spent the rest of the day looking at old court houses, various Kuching cat statues, Chinese temples and little stores selling Malaysian clothing and wooden carvings. Taking a long walk over the river, I arrived at a shop selling traditional layer cake native to Sarawak, kek lapis. Layer cake is famous in the region due to the time and skill needed to make it. One cake can take up to six hours to prepare, as each fine layer is cooked individually and a cake often features up to twenty different layers. Entering the cool air-conditioned bakery was a blissful escape from the midday heat. Shelves upon shelves were lined with different kek lapises: watermelon, tiramisu, durian and 'Sarawak' (a local favourite, featuring an array of different colours and flavours condensed into a single slice). I settled for an attractive purple and cream striped cake, labelled blueberry cheesecake. Expecting a simple slice for ten ringgits, I was surprised when the lady packaged the whole cake in my bag! I nibbled a few slices by the riverside and saved the rest for a very grateful Dalir back at the hostel. He had, after all, been stuck inside studying and I wanted to repay him for his kindness the previous day.

Back at the hostel

As Dalir ate a slice, he asked me a question I wasn't expecting.

'So tell me, if you don't mind of course, what *is* your condition?'

I took a deep breath. I was hesitant about explaining my condition to him. I was scared that he wouldn't view me in the same light, view me as equal; a girl who carries around ten kilograms of medication is a liability. No one wants a travel partner who could become bedbound every other week. I longed to be like everyone else with an unlimited supply of energy, but that wasn't the case, and it hadn't been the case for the past twelve years. But for some reason, I trusted Dalir, I looked him directly in the eyes and began.

'Well, I have a condition called CVS, Cyclical Vomiting Syndrome. Now don't look at me like that. I am completely fine when well. But every few weeks or so I have an attack where I get really bad stomach cramps. They are debilitating, I can't do anything but lie down in a dark room, they get worse throughout the day and sometimes I am sick a lot of times. Attacks last between twelve to forty-eight hours and I've been hospitalized several times in the past few years. I take over twenty pills a day and half my rucksack is filled with medication.'

'Wow, that was an efficient description!'

'Sorry, I've had to explain it to countless doctors over the past decade; I know my medical history by heart!'

'That sucks.'

'I know but there are worse things. People have CVS way more severely than I do, longer attacks more frequently, daily hospital visits and life on a drip. At least I can go to work and have been able to come on this trip, even if it is a challenge.'

'Are you seeing anyone?'

'Yes, I've seen many different gastroenterologists over the past few years but, unfortunately, little is known about the condition, so it's a challenge to treat.'

'What about investigations?'

'Well, I've had a few: MRIs, barium swallows, endoscopies, hundreds of blood tests - you name it. Have you heard of it before, CVS?'

'No I haven't, but it sounds very interesting.'

'Yes, it's a weird illness, they have no idea what causes it.'

'No idea, at all?'

'Well there is a list of triggers, but they are all the triggers under the sun, temperature, stress, fatigue, light, diet, noise, blah blah blah. I think stress, tiredness and diet affect me the most, hence the strange dinner request last night!'

'Ah Cece, that is tough.'

'Well as I said, there are people way worse off than me, you have to live life with what you have, so that is simply what I am trying to do, even if it is a little difficult.'

I was relieved to have told someone and appreciated his sincere interest. At least now if I got sick in Borneo, someone would understand.

Evening

Walking along the riverside looking for a dinner spot, we stumbled upon a sweet waterfront venue which appeared to accommodate half the city. We were lucky to get a table right beside the river. It seemed a little romantic, but it was a nice evening and he was a good friend so, *why not?* Despite the fact that our acquaintanceship could be counted in hours, we were already tight friends, I trusted him. We drank from coconuts and I chose another Malaysian style rice dish with anchovies and a spicy sauce.

'Dalir, aren't you going to order anything?'

'No, I'm not hungry.'

'Oh, you shouldn't have come out to dinner with me then, I feel bad if you're not eating!'

'It's fine, I wanted to come with you.'

After we had finished, he clicked commandingly, violently jabbing his hand in the air for the waiter to come over, which in my view couldn't have been more embarrassing.

'Dalir, that is so rude! You can't do that!'

'You can't tell me what to do, this is what we do in my country.'

'Oh, I'm sorry, but in England this is very rude, well, I think it is anyway.'

He replied with a smirk, 'I promise I won't do it around you again then.'

With the blunt way he spoke to the waiter, however, I wasn't convinced. I pulled out my purse to find Dalir's hand in my face, shunning my appeals to pay my own way. I looked pleadingly at the waiter, trying to hand him my ringgits, but all the waiter did was giggle as he accepted Dalir's money.

'It's okay lady, he happy cos he get woman, he he!'

'Dalir, I can pay for my own things. Thank you, it is sweet of you but, honestly I've had a job for two years, I can pay!'

'This is pennies to me. Put your purse away woman.'

I just looked at him, frustrated and put off by his sudden arrogance. Not wanting to cause a scene and trying to remain calm, I agreed to walk along the river while helping him do some final practice before his exam tomorrow. I was to be the terminally ill patient and he was to break the bad news to me, enabling him to practise consoling in English.

'Welcome, madam, please have a seat.'

'Thank you, why am I here? I thought all the treatment was over?' I replied.

'Well madam, if you would just listen to me.'

'*Out of character...*wait this sounds a little patronizing, just say "I appreciate you are worried madam, you are here because..."'

'Ah okay, thank you. *In character...*well madam, I appreciate you are worried, you are here because we have received your test results.'

'Test results, what did they say, oh my gosh what have you found?'

'Well, I am afraid it is not good news.'

'*Out of character...*no, go straight to the facts, "bad news" scares people, madam will freak before she knows what's going on.'

'Okay, *in character...*I am afraid there is evidence of a growth in your left breast.'

'No, no I am only young,' my eyes filled with tears as the worry spread across my face. I rather enjoyed hysterically acting and even burst into tears, perhaps a little too convincingly as people around started to stare. '*Out of character*...okay, I think people are watching Dalir, we should do this somewhere a little less visible.'

'*In character*...I agree madam. Wow, Cece, I didn't expect you to be such a good little actress, you're really convincing, this is perfect. You know they bring in real actors for this exam, the best, they will be as convincing as it gets, so you are doing perfectly.'

'What kind of a doctor compliments his patients on their realistic crying when they have just found out they have breast cancer?'

'Cece, I was out of character then.'

'Dalir, I know, sorry it is just my English sarcasm.'

'Ah, yes, this is good practice for me too.'

We burst out laughing and continued the melodramatic exam practice in a more secluded area by the port. I interrupted occasionally with a few phrases and mannerisms that would perfect his English response. After several hours of practising, we returned to the hostel to find a new group of four French girls who we chatted to for a while before bed. They called themselves les filles françaises: Feeca (Fee), Liba, Amelia and Mini.

11p.m.

I can't get the restaurant scene out of my head. Feeling intimidated by this new side to my friend.

FIVE

'Freedom and opportunity are dependent upon your place of birth.'

Having a British Passport makes the world more accessible – up until now I had gone through my life naively unaware of this privilege. I learnt that on an average Malaysian salary, you'd have to save up for a lifetime to be able to afford a plane fare to the UK. Most of the people I'd met would never get the chance to visit my country. They did not have the same opportunities as me, just because of the location and society they were born into. How is this fair in today's world?

'I wish one day we will all be considered equal regardless of our passport and I will be free to visit you, as you are free to visit me.'
- Delima

8ᵗʰ August
Kubah National Park

I took the local bus to Kubah for my first day of jungle trekking. Tackling public transport was easier than I imagined, following the advice of the two Malaysian receptionists; I walked to the bus station and jumped on the number twenty-one to Kubah National Park. *Four ringgits (less than a pound), not bad for a forty-five-minute journey.* I was a little nervous, attempting a day trek alone in a foreign terrain posed many potential problems. I knew little of pitcher plants, snakes, tree frogs, scorpions and other poisonous creatures. Although I had no phobia of these small animals, an encounter with one worried me, but not enough to curb my excitement for the adventure that lay ahead.

I was greeted by two officers at the park boundary. They scrutinized me, looking me up and down from walking boots to the tight ponytail that held back my messy curls.

'Alone you go?' barked the male officer.

'Yes, is that an issue?'

'Ah, no but you be very careful.'

'Oh yes I will.'

'There are several trails, waterfall, frog pond, summit, circular walk.'

'The waterfall sounds pretty, but so does the summit. Is it possible to do both?'

'No, no way. No time do both, you must be fit but also know the ground, you English, first time?'

'Yes, but I do a lot of walking.'

'Good, but still choose one. Park close four.'

'Oh, okay.' I had heard the waterfall was meant to be nice but a little easy. The summit trail was more appealing; I wanted to feel like I had accomplished something by the end of the day. 'I'll try the summit then, thank you for your help.'

'Good luck, remember park close four, everyone need be out.'

'I will, don't worry,' I called back with a smile.

Tugging at the straps of my rucksack, I set off at a pace. I loved a challenge and despite the advice of the officers, my determined mind couldn't be deterred from trying to complete the waterfall and summit trail in a day. *Challenge accepted - let's try and complete them both!*

The jungle created its own music, the whir of flies and screech of cicadas, the hollow call of birds, echoes of branches swaying and tree top leaves quivering as the southerly wind rattled through them. I felt alone but never lonely. Consumed by the surrounding beauty, this exotic terrain welcomed me as I followed the deeply rooted pathway the jungle had created for its explorers. Gathering speed the higher I climbed, the curiosity and thrill of being in a jungle fueled my increasing pace, I reached the summit in an hour and a half, half the expected time the officers had predicted. Wiping the sweat from my face I looked out to the expanse of tree covered mountains that made up the deep green landscape ahead. *You did it Cece, solo.* It would have been nice to share it with someone. However, victory seemed sweet enough alone, alone in the loud silence of the jungle.

On the descent, I met a lovely Malaysian couple who were both at university and spoke pretty good English. As much as I prided my new-found independence, it was nice to make some friends and they seemed just as delighted to have made a new acquaintance. After a few photos together they asked if I wanted to join them on the walk back.

'Oh, thank you but I would quite like to see the waterfall on the route back.'

'We are heading to the waterfall too, come along with us?'

'Oh really? That would be wonderful, thank you!'

We chatted for most of the walk, comparing our cultures, languages and cuisines, as well as discussing the kind of life Delima led as a female Muslim and the implications of wearing a hijab.

'I like them, I have several and they go with all of my clothes, like an accessory.'

'I like it on you too,' her boyfriend, Hatar, replied.

'Yes it's really cute, it suits you,' I chimed. 'Does everyone have to wear one?'

With an air of pride at his extensive knowledge of a woman's coming of age, Hatar responded. 'No, only if you want to. Once a girl has her first menstruation, she is then given the choice whether to wear one or not.'

Delima smiled admiringly at him. 'Yes, that's right, in Malaysia, Islamic culture is more relaxed, we have more choice, there are rules but they are not compulsory - one of the many misconceptions about our culture.'

Making it to the waterfall, we bathed our feet in the cool river and chatted some more, laughing at Hatar jumping and squealing every time a small fish came to nibble his unsuspecting feet. On the final leg of the trail, the couple suggested we get coconut milkshakes - a Malaysian specialty.

'They are the best things ever, creamy coconut, sweet, rich but refreshing. You haven't tried them yet? Oh, we *have* to get them! We'll give you a lift back home too; you won't have to get the bus back to Kuching then.'

Aw these two are so sweet! 'That would be amazing if it doesn't trouble you too much?'

'Nonsense, we like the company, it's made our second-year anniversary much more exciting!' Hatar grinned.

'What? I've been crashing your anniversary this whole time? I should give you some privacy; this is your special day!'

'Nonsense, it's far more fun with other people,' Delima smiled.

'Well if you insist, but I'm buying you both as many coconut milkshakes as you like!'

'Yes!' Hatar's face glowed even brighter, 'I'm getting five!'

Delima tugged his arm sharply and leaned in to whisper a few curt words. 'Hatar, it's rude to ask for this much.'

Turned away, but still in earshot, Hatar replied, 'But she said as many as we like?'

'I know but this is greedy,' Delima eyed him.

As an attempt to relieve Delima's embarrassment at her boyfriend's open love for the coconut milkshake, I quickly responded. 'Honestly, you have both been so kind to me, I will buy as many as you like, please, it would be my pleasure and anniversary gift!'

'Okay five coconut milkshakes!' Hatar announced.

'Fab, I'm on it.'

'Five, Hatar? There are only three of us,' Delima questioned.

'Yes two for you and two for me.'

'No Hatar, what did I just say?'

'Okay fine, one for you and three for me.'

'Five it is!' I announced before any more dispute could occur.

They taught me how to ask for five coconut milkshakes in Malay, although now I can only remember a jumble of words, *lima,* five, and *kelapa shake,* coconut milkshake. I repeated the phrase while the couple laughed hysterically at my accent, but by the time we got to the roadside shake shack, I'd just about nailed it. The vendor had to do a double take when he witnessed a little English girl spouting near perfect Malay, bringing Delima into another fit of giggles. I carried the five icy plastic cups back to Hatar's jeep, where we sat resting our weary feet and contently sipped the sweet coconut nectar.

Just when I thought my time with the couple was up, Hatar pulled into a traditional local seafood restaurant floating on wooden planks above the sea. Flies were buzzing around hot fish dishes and locals sat around plastic tables. They looked up as I entered, possibly staring at the first English girl they had ever seen, at least in this restaurant. We had a plate of Sarawak green vegetables fried in shrimp paste, plenty of rice and a bowl of shrimps, razor clams, a whole crab, cauliflower and corn swimming in a deep scarlet chilli sauce.

I had never tried crab or anything on my plate with eyes, claws or a shell, but thought it was time to give it a go. After I got over the initial horror of breaking its shell and violently jabbing the claws with my spoon, it was actually quite nice - a sweet soft meat that went well with the chilli. Hatar even taught me how to eat with my hands; I watched as he compacted the rice then shovelled it into his mouth. Delima laughed at my slightly awkward face.

'Haha, don't look so scared Cece, this is how we do it.'

'I know, sorry, I'm not scared, I'm just so used to eating with cutlery. It's actually really fun now I try it. I'm practically a local.'

'Haha you sure are!' Delima giggled.

They were two gems. As we got up to leave, I offered to pay but Hatar said it was already taken care of. On the drive back they wanted to take me to a special palm sugar ice cream place, but due to an early closure from the afternoon's rainstorm, Delima and I returned soaking and empty handed. Instead, they gave me a tour of Kuching and their favourite places to go: malls, bowling alleys, late night diners and coffee houses. Our day came to an end when they dropped me off outside my hostel. We exchanged Instagram names and bid each other a fond farewell. *What a surprising encounter, now I am starting to see how travelling solo can be so awesome!* They were so openly kind, in England this sort of kindness would never be shared between strangers; perhaps to them I was no longer a stranger, but a friend.

SIX

'I need you.'

9th August (Flashforward)
Kuching
0:01a.m.

> *Oh, how wrong was I.*

8th August
4p.m.

I couldn't wait to see Dalir to share our stories, about his exam and my awesome day with Delima and Hatar. *I wonder if any of the scenarios we practised came up. Did he encounter any hysterical patients or perform any knee examinations?* We were meant to be having an evening out in Kuching with les filles françaises to celebrate the end of his exams. I was excited and had been keeping up with my meds, so hoped my energy levels would hold out for a bit of dancing.

When I returned no one was around, so I took the time to shower, epilate my legs and put on my blue floral playsuit for the evening. It was nice to wear a pretty piece of clothing after sporting sweaty tops and shorts all day. This piece was special to me; it was my grandma's favourite item out of my travel wardrobe. She loved shopping but, now bed bound, simply leaving the room was impossible. So before I left, Mum and I brought the shops to her hospice room. I changed into each outfit and did a little fashion show, strutting from the door to the window, twirling in front of her. She praised every item I wore, her kind words always made me feel cherished but at this particular playsuit, her eyes lit up and her little hands clapped together, thrilled at the sight. *'Now, doesn't she just look wonderful?'* I smiled at the memory but the thought of her in that bed made me sad. I had messaged as often as I could and had already sent a postcard that was propped up by her bedside, where Mum had placed it.

I shook out my curls, trying to dispel my watery eyes from forming tears until a voice downstairs made me stand. I could tell it was Dalir before he entered the dorm. His cheerful bursts, articulated in a thick Pakistani accent, resonated through the wooden floorboards. By the sound of it he seemed pretty happy, recalling the entirety of his day to the receptionist downstairs. As soon as his face poked round the corner I ran towards him.

'So? How did it go, any hysterical women?'

'Cece, I nailed it, nailed it. There were eighteen sections, eighteen and I nailed them all but one!'

'Wow, that's grea…'

'I breezed through the counselling because of you! A woman came rushing in screaming, "Where is my son?" But I kept calm, like you said, and kept repeating the instructions. Because of *our* role play, I had it under control.'

'Ah, I'm so pleas…'

'Everything else was fine except I ran out of time to diagnose the final two patients. I had four teenage ones, four, can you believe it? Ah but I did it well, I even had three minutes to spare on one part, what do you think?

'Well, I thin…'

'Ah but I did so well, I aced those rounds!'

'That's great y…'

'I did so well, I just aced it.'

It carried on like this for a while, a constant stream of questions and comments without a pause. It was more of a conversation between Dalir and Dalir. I got it, he was happy and relieved, but still, it would have been nice to squeeze in a congratulatory line. Eventually I had to tell him to pause so I could actually answer his questions and advise him to take a breath!

We went out for dinner as usual. Dalir thoughtfully ordered a special veggie roti for me. It was a kind of doughy flat bread which came with curry sauce, pretty tasty. He continued talking and talking about what an amazing surgeon he was and boasting about his incredible career.

'Cece, you'll never understand the kind of level us surgeons are at.'

'Aha well I never said I did but I can appreciate it, with teaching.'

'No, it's completely different, surgery is demanding, there is nothing like it, you just wouldn't get it.'

Table talk became more of a lecture and a didactic one at that. He even had the audacity to tell me how to deal with children. I burst out in a half laugh. 'Um, hello, who is the teacher here?'

'Oh yes, but I know how to deal with them, I'm a pediatric surgeon you know.'

I swallowed my frustration, retaliating wouldn't get me anywhere but it was getting harder to contain. At one point he did this horrible pose where he leant back on his chair, arms bent behind his head and looked around as if he were God, in control of the world and everyone in it, including me. He spoke appallingly to the staff, ordering them around, not saying thank you and dismissing them when he had finished. I was embarrassed to be with him. I tried to smile at the staff to soften his harshness but it was useless, I was in his shadow. I felt like an obedient wife following her husband. This was not what I had signed up for. When we eventually moved on from the exam and his surgical greatness, I told him about my amazing day with the Malaysian couple. For anyone looking at the pair of us they'd have thought I was reciting pi. His eyes flitted around the room; he asked no questions and seemed agitated at having to listen to me talk for a change. In the middle of a sentence, he got up abruptly and on return ushered me to leave quickly.

'Dalir, don't we need to pay? I'll get this, you've bought everything else!'

'No, come Cece I got it already.'

'What? Dalir, I need to pay for something, you can't keep getting everything.'

'Stop it, or I'll get annoyed.'

This is really strange; no guy pays for a friend every time, in fact not even if they are dating.

'Well thank you again but I am going to pay you back.'

'I need liquor, lots of it, come we need to buy some,' Dalir ordered.

Our quest for alcohol was a mad hunt from shop to shop. Due to the high Muslim population, liquor was sparse. Each shop we left unsuccessful, the more aggravated Dalir became, almost as if he was addicted to the stuff and couldn't last any longer without it. He marched ahead, waving his hand, ushering me to keep up like I was his dog.

'Cece, come on.'

Finally we found a few bottles of whisky, but even then he seemed unsatisfied.

He growled at the staff, 'This one, no this one. Here can't you see where I am pointing. Get me this one.'

Snatching the bottle off the poor shop assistant, he headed for the till. I stood watching at the sidelines, mortified by his rudeness.

Back at the hostel I was relieved to see les filles françaises; I couldn't stand another minute alone with Dalir. He poured drinks for everyone, he was very generous I'll give him that, although didn't seem to understand the word 'stop' or 'that is enough!' Before we knew it, our plastic cups were filled with a brown sugar-coloured liquor topped with a splash of cold cola. *It was going to be a heavy night*. I took a sip of the strong mixture; it burned my lips and tongue so I put it back down quickly. At the same time, Dalir had downed his and was pouring himself another one. *It was going to be a very heavy night*. I had hoped a drink would satisfy him and he'd return to the person I met on the first day. This wish soon vanished as the omnipotent surgeon bullshit started again.

'J'ai une idée, tu parles en français, et je parle en anglais donc nous pouvons pratiquer.'

Feeca had sat opposite me. I was relieved to start a new conversation with her.

'Oui oui, j'ai eu la même idée!'

Great, this is a perfect escape, I can use my French and Dalir won't understand a word I'm saying. I chatted to Fee for most of the evening. She was interesting, wanting to be a GP but still have a life outside of work, she romanticised about London and I about Paris, we got on well. Our discussion, however, was interrupted by a brewing argument in the corner of the room. Dalir stood opposite a Malaysian guy who had recently joined the party. It was funny at first, until the tension grew and we realised it wasn't a joke. Fierce words were being shot at each other and arms cut violently through the air as each savagely tried to make their point.

'Listen to me, listen to me!' Dalir shouted.

'No man, you listen,' the Malaysian responded.

'Man I swear I'm gonna...' Dalir interrupted again.

'Guys, guys, listen. Attends, Let's pause here,' asserted Fee.

She had come between them, trying to calm them down but they only spoke over her.

After ten more minutes, the boys eventually slowed down as Liba (Fee's friend) and Fee had taken a boy each to calm. I tried to help initially but whenever the Malaysian spoke to me, Dalir barked back at him. My presence wasn't going to make the situation any better. I snuck off into the dorm and changed back into my pyjamas, lying as quietly as I could on my bed until they'd all left for town. I didn't want to play any part in Dalir's night. Five minutes passed before some footsteps shuffled loudly up the stairs, hands slapped the door frame and Dalir drunkenly stumbled into the room.

'Cece? Cece, where are you? Why aren't you with me coming out?'

'I'm tired, Dalir, I don't feel like it anymore. I'm sorry.'

'No, you have to come. Is this because of me and that guy? Cos we're cool now. Is all good.'

'I'm glad but I am tired. I already took my meds, they make me really sleepy, you should know more than anyone.'

'Cece, I will make sure you are okay, I need you to come out.'

'Dalir…' He pulled my arm and led me outside the room. Clumsily swaying, he held my shoulders in the doorway and spoke to me face to face.

'Cece, listen to me.'

'I am listening to you Dalir.'

'Cece. Listen to me,' he said swaying slightly.

'I am,' I replied.

'I'm a bit tipsy.'

'I can see that.'

'Listen to me woman. I'm a bit tipsy and I need you.'

'Okay, you don't need me, you go have fun with the French girls, you need *them*. I'm tired, I'm staying here.'

'No, I'm a bit tipsy and I need you.'

'Just have fun without me, I'm going to sleep.'

'No I need you there.'

'No, you really don't.'

'Yes I do, I can't have fun without you. I need you.'

'I'm in my pyjamas, I'm going back to bed.'

'Please Cece just half an hour, I need you to come, I really really need you.'

Crickey, what was this guy's problem? We had known each other for less than forty-eight hours! Annoyed for letting him change my mind, I reluctantly slipped back into my playsuit I had been so keen to put on earlier.

'Turn around I need to change. No turn around! I'm not dressed yet.'

'Oh sorry sorry, Cece I'm a bit tipsy.'

'I know, you said.'

'I'm a bit tipsy and I'm not trying to get into your pants, I just really need you.'

'Okay stop talking, I'm ready, let's just go.'

So back down the stairs I went, met by a cheer from les filles françaises.

'Cece you come now, bravo!'

I gave a sheepish smile, pleased to be out with them but ashamed it was Dalir who had made me change my mind. We dawdled slowly to the bar. Everyone else had a beer in hand, except Dalir who had half a bottle of whisky. We seemed to have picked up a musician in a long black coat with dreadlocks, clutching a guitar. Les filles beckoned him to play, I hung back by Fee. We came to a standstill outside a bar. It was occupied by drunken locals and tourists alike, speaking loudly and thrusting their drinks into the air. Dalir appeared with his arm around the guy who he had previously been fighting with.

They mumbled simultaneously, 'Look we're good, we're sorry we upset you Cece.'

'I love him now,' said Dalir.

'He is my brother,' the Malaysian smiled.

'We're all good,' they replied, swaying slightly as a pair.

'Okay great,' I said coldly.

As if I cared, the fight had happened and I had seen a horrible argumentative side to them both, all over nothing, hot headed young men who needed to get their priorities straight. After a while of standing around and chatting, I'd had enough and whispered to Fee that I was going home. Fee looked me in the eye to check I was okay and smiled, 'Je te verrais demain, bonne nuit Cece.'

'Bonne nuit Fee, merci, à demain.'

I stepped up the pace, rocketing away before anyone else could notice, but as I reached the hostel stairs, I heard his footsteps.

'Cece where are you going? I need you.'

'I'm tired Dalir, I came with you, now I am going home.'

'But I'm a bit tipsy and I need you.'

Oh bloody hell not this again.

'No you don't, go back and dance, have fun, you did the exam, now celebrate!' I whispered loudly, reaching the top of the stairs.

Dalir pushed me to the wall before I could reach the dormitory. His body was pressed closely against mine and I could feel his hot alcoholic breath on my cheek. He'd drunk a lot. He was beyond drunk. I squirmed, trying to move away, but he pushed his weight onto me, holding my arms to the wall. His bloodshot eyes stared into mine. His body was warm and I could feel a strong pulsating heat below, pushing into my waist repeatedly.

'But I need you, you are way more than a friend to me.'

Shit, what was happening. A sudden rage came over me and I pushed him backwards. 'Dalir, I said no! I'm not coming back out with you! I am going to sleep.'

'But I need you there.'

By this point I had leapt into bed, using the sheets as a barricade.

'Dalir, you need to go now, I am going to sleep.'

'Fine!' he moaned before shuffling out of the dorm, stumbling into everything in his path.

I heard the chink of the whisky bottle as he left the room. It all went quiet, *he must have left*, I closed my eyes.

'Cece, Cece wake up I need you, please Cece.'

He hadn't gone, oh please don't get into bed with me. I lay motionless, praying he would leave.

'Cece, Cece? Cece? Woman wake-up!'

After a while I heard the creak of the floorboards, he had moved away. I lay still for the next few minutes not wanting to give any sign of life. Ten minutes passed before I dared to look up, he had passed out on his bed, his intoxicated mind still swirling around the room. I couldn't settle after that, afraid he would come back again.

SEVEN

When travelling, time is blurred - a few hours can seem like years and friendships rise and fade as quick as sunsets.

9ᵗʰ August
The morning after
6:45a.m.

I sat up and looked around. Everyone had made it back, including Dalir whose body hadn't moved after face planting the pillow six hours ago. He had asked me to wake him up for jungle trekking in Bako, before the drinking started that is, but oh how I just wanted to run away. I tapped him very lightly before flinching back. No sound, thank God, the drunken beast continued to slumber. I went over to Fee and shook her hand gently.

'It's Bako time!' I whispered.

Sleepy eyed, she smiled, 'D'accord, je me lève.'

The word spread and each of les filles started to stir, some more reluctantly than others.

'Bah, je suis trop fatiguée.'

'Tais-toi Amelia, nous sommes toutes fatiguées!'

'Quelle heure est-il?'

'Sept heure quinze.'

'Merde.'

'I think that Amelia had too much to drink last night, but she will be okay, eventually!' Fee giggled.

I really wanted Dalir to sleep through the whole day, for it just to be a girlie trip, but this would never happen. Still wearing the orange t-shirt from last night, he stumbled into the living room. He looked rough, his eyes were half open and bloodshot, and his hair was flat and greasy from the night heat. I muffled a quick 'morning' and hurried past to prepare my bag for the day. *Damn it, he was coming to Bako.*

The more time I spent with him the more I seemed to dislike him. Without even a 'good morning', he immediately started firing questions at me.

'Where are we going? What bus? What time?'

'Um it's the number twenty, which leaves around eight.'

'No, exactly what time? You need to be precise.'

'Well, depending what time everyone is ready, the 08:03.'

'Oh, that's just great Cece, for God's sake.'

I continued to pack my bag in silence. We made it to the bus just about, Dalir running behind in his jeans and flipflops, a plastic bag in hand. If it weren't for Fee and I stalling the bus, he would have missed it. *Who was this guy who seemed so knowledgeable yesterday, but now seemed to be utterly clueless about anything in life besides surgery? Who comes to Kuching, jungle capital of Malaysia, without a backpack, trainers or even shorts?*

The hour bus journey was awkward, we said few words to each other.

'Are you hungover?'

'Yes, but I had breakfast so I'm okay.'

'Did you have a good rest of the night?'

'No!' he responded aggressively, looking at me as if I was a pile of vomit. 'I came back with you remember and you didn't come out!'

'Oh, okay,' I said quietly.

And that was it until we reached the port.

As soon as we arrived, I leapt off the bus and stood next to Fee. For the rest of the morning I stayed close to her. I didn't want to be associated with Dalir.

Next was the speed boat to the island. We jumped on board and of course I ended up next to him again. We put on our life jackets in silence and listened to the driver warning us about the crocodile-infested waters. As soon as the boat started, the silence was drowned out by the hum of the motor.

Bouncing across the waves was amazing, the wind whipped through our hair as we passed pale blue shadows of mountains and grey and sandy rocks protruding from thick green jungle in the distance.

The boat slowed as we arrived at a small stretch of beach scattered with shells and three wild boars trotting across the sand. We had to take our shoes off and wade through the remaining waves that separated the island from the ocean. After a few group photos posing in jungle paradise, we went off to register and find a map. We agreed on seeing the sea stack first and then, if we had time, attempt the jungle trails after that. I took the lead, regaining control. Dalir tried to take over, but in his jeans and hungover state he couldn't keep up, so Fee and I carried on ahead. Mini had a crippling fear of *les serpents*. She took slow anxious steps and needed several rests to compose herself. It was clear from the sweat beading on her forehead that she was terrified, there was no way we could complete two trails this morning, in fact we'd be lucky if we completed this one.

'Cece si tu veux, tu peux continuer? We are quite slow.'

'Non merci, tu es gentille mais j'aimerais bien marcher avec vous. Mini is doing really well, nous allons compléter cette marche en équipe!'

I also didn't want to be alone with Dalir.

After tackling steep ant-covered stairs, tree root ladders and hanging tree vine curtains, we surfaced from the deep green to a vast granite rock which provided an arena to view the beautiful coast below. The light blue water lapped against the island. Palm trees curtained the sandy stage while monkeys and insects produced the jungle whir. I loved walking with the girls but had promised Alex to find some proboscis monkeys. With the slow pace, I wasn't sure les filles would manage another walk. I quietly explained to Fee that I would go on ahead to try and do another walk, but a walk alone.

'Bien sûr Cece, it's fine. I imagine you want some space…le garçon?' I was glad she had noticed. In French I quickly explained the whole story, that Dalir had crossed the line last night and I didn't feel comfortable staying with him alone anymore.

'Woa, yes I completely get you Cece, but you better sneak off quietly without him noticing.'

'Oui, bonne idée, oh and if he tries to come after me…'

'Don't worry I'll make sure he doesn't!'

'Merci beaucoup Fee. À toute.'

And I was off. Roping back up the rock, over the boardwalk, through the hanging tree vines, down the ant covered ladder, across the puddles and back into the jungle shade. After fifteen minutes I turned, the path was empty. I had escaped, I was free, once again a solo traveller. *Let mission monkey begin!*

My plan was to complete the jungle walks that crossed mangrove territory as, according to a guide, that was where the monkeys lived. I almost trail ran the first route, enjoying the freedom, jumping from rock to rock, whizzing past slower tourists and turning whichever way I pleased. I think I was still in escape-from-Dalir mode. It was one o'clock but still no sight of the monkeys. I had two more hours before the boat left so jumped straight onto another route.

Ten minutes in, I turned the corner to find two girls looking up, camera in hand, whispering. 'C'est les singes, oui, là-bas.'

'Regarde, là-bas.'

Coincidentally, they were French too. I strained through the treetops, desperately hoping for a glimpse of the funny nosed monkey. Suddenly a branch rustled, a tail curled quickly against the contrast of the blue sky and then a creature jumped off the tree. *Wow, I'm in Borneo watching monkeys, practically David Attenborough!* I tried to capture the experience on camera, but we were so far away that they only showed up as little brown smudges in the trees. Regardless, I knew that I had seen a proboscis monkey. Eventually we carried on, leaving them to swing in the trees alone.

As I neared the end of the trail, I passed by a murky looking pool. Intrigued, I headed towards it straying from the path. Ducking my head under a branch, my eyes met a little orange face. He was just as surprised as I to encounter the unexpected company. He cocked his head to the right like he was looking at his own reflection, inquisitive eyes widening. Just when I realised it was a baby proboscis monkey, he vanished.

'Little monkey, thank you,' I whispered.

Turning back to the pond, a dark leather strip zigzagged across the black water. A cold chill whipped through my body. *Shit, a huge snake, shiiit!* But as it emerged, its sides expanded to form hands and feet resembling a reptilian dragon. Its thick black tongue slipped in and out, tasting the air as his beady eyes scanned the ground. I watched silently in a terrified awe, before scurrying back onto the path, hoping to escape unnoticed. I later learnt, from a passing guide, that it was a monitor lizard.

'But a baby one, as they can grow almost as big as crocodiles,' the guide smiled.

'Oh, well I'm glad I saw a baby then!'

She laughed, 'Yea, they're pretty calm animals just don't get in their way!'

Walking back to the beach, I caught up with a lady who had retired and was using her savings to travel. So far, she had been on the road for three years, *talk about life goals!* Just as we returned to the sand, the tree branches started shaking. I looked up expecting a few birds, but only five metres away hung three proboscis monkeys - they were so close! They used their long arms to swing from branch to branch, catapulting themselves onto a crash pad of leaves, before sliding down the tree trunk. After each monkey had completed the sequence, he waited for the next to follow; they were a real team. We followed them along the path, as if we were part of the pack too. Seeing these little monkeys roam free in the trees was humbling and well worth the entire day's search. I even managed to film a snippet of their gymnastic display to send back to Alex, I knew he'd be thrilled.

Les filles, Dalir and I all met at the jetty, sharing stories of our afternoon adventures while waiting for the boat home. Back on the coach, I was positioned next to Dalir again. When he closed his eyes, I turned to look at him realising I'd booked the whole day tomorrow in a double kayak together. An experience that initially I'd been so keen on, but now couldn't think of anything worse. His dark sunken lids suddenly rose and met mine.

'Cece, why the fuck would you run off like that? When I am with you, you need to stay by my side.'

'Dalir, listen I wan…'

'No, I've had enough, tonight you are with me. No running off.'

'No, Dalir, you can't…'

He grabbed my wrist, twisting the skin and yanked it towards his torso. I let out a silent whimper, 'Dali...'

'No, you played games with me last night, it's not happening again. You hear me?'

'Yes,' I whispered.

'Now I'm going to sleep, when we get off this bus we're going into the hostel together, then we'll go out for dinner like we have done every other night, okay?'

I just looked at him, his dark eyes piercing through mine. I hadn't been scared before, but now I was. I felt real fear, fear of my own kind.

'Okay? Answer me!' he implored.

'Okay,' I responded.

What was happening? This was not the person I had first met, not the person I knew before. He had transformed, transformed into an unkind, controlling and possessive being. I was no longer in control. I didn't own my own actions and I feared soon I wouldn't own my own body. I had to escape.

Using the fleeting signal on the coach ride back, as Dalir slept next to me, I searched escape routes for that evening. By the time we were back in Kuching, I'd booked a fifteen-hour night bus up to Miri *(a coastal city just over 700km north-east of Kuching)*. It was my only option.

As the others were chatting in the common room, I rushed into the dorm, grabbed my rucksack and with shaky hands crammed all my possessions into it. I couldn't be seen, questions couldn't be asked. It was too risky. If I was seen or questioned, he would know, and wouldn't let me go. This was my one chance.

Hauling the bags quickly onto my back to leave, I almost toppled over from the weight and crashed into the doorway.

'Cece, tu nous quittes?' Fee asked.

Oh shit.

'Cece, quoi?' said Mini.

'Cece?' said Liba.

I stared blankly at them. I didn't want to leave them, les filles, my friends.

Dalir rose 'Cece, Cece what are you doing?'

Then I remembered I had no choice; my chance was disappearing fast.

'I'm sorry, je suis desolée, je suis tellement desolée, I'm sorry. I must leave, je dois partir.'

Before I could hear them respond I turned and fled down the stairs, bashing the banister with my rucksack.

'Cece, turn around, look at me,' Dalir's footsteps chased me like a shadow down the stairs. 'Cece, wait, hold up.'

'I'm sorry, I must go.'

'But why, Cece wait!'

I'd loaded my bags into the taxi and was opening the car door when he grabbed my shoulder, causing me to jolt to the side and face him.

'Cece?'

He looked directly into my eyes, gripping my arm tightly. I looked back into his, I felt so small.

Seeing my fear for a moment, his grip loosened, and the anger dispersed from his eyes, leaving the person I knew from that first night in Kuching, the old Dalir. A boy with an open enthusiasm for life. Now he looked hurt, on the edge of losing something dear.

'Cece, you're leaving?' he said quietly.

I looked at him for a few seconds, a blanket of emptiness seemed to cover us, all anger and frustration washed away.

'I'm sorry, Dalir…' I replied turning to the car.

'Cece, no, how will I contact you? You can't go!'

'Goodbye Dalir.' I closed the taxi door.

He began to run, chase after the taxi, like a boy running for his life. I opened my mouth to speak but we turned the corner, leaving him behind. So off I fled into the darkness, fleeing Kuching by night and escaping control, but leaving the dear girls and who I thought would have been my travel soulmate for Malaysia.

One hour into the bus journey
North of Kuching

The adrenaline abated, and the sadness hit me. I missed Kuching already.

EIGHT

Better the devil you know.

9th August
The night bus
9p.m.

It was a long and grotty journey. Fifteen hours to be precise. The driver pulled my backpack off and threw it into the compartment, almost taking me with it. The bus was filled with old locals who looked at me as if I were a piece of meat, the drivers chuckled dirtily to each other every time I returned to my seat and there was always a pair of eyes tracking my movements. Sleep was poor and broken by stops at seedy gas stations and dirty food courts filled with fat commuters and fried food. Stale durian and mouldy fruits were laid out on dusty boxes pinned with '5RM' signs and the toilets were just grim. I reminded myself why I had taken this voyage. I reminded myself about the way he had spoken to me, grabbed me and held me to the wall.

I was better off alone.

11:30p.m.

Oh, why have I taken this miserable journey? I loathed to admit it...but a small part of me missed Dalir, I missed his protection. *Better the devil you know?*

10th August
1a.m.

Sleep took over as I closed my eyes, praying that when I woke I'd be in a safer place, far, far away.

Miri
9a.m.

After arriving in the early hours of the morning, I made my way to the hostel. I was disappointed to find my dorm of twelve completely empty and the rooms further down the corridor as equally uninhabited. I appeared to be the sole traveller in the entire hostel. It seemed my time in Miri would be lonely.

10a.m.

I headed towards the beach, a long, hot and dusty walk through town only to find oil ships and rubbish clogging up the coastline. I cut through a Malay garden to find a neighbouring beach. It wasn't amazing, the water grey, the sand grey, but it was clean and open. Locals stuck large poles into the sand hunting for seafood, while little children chased the bubbling waves.

As a child, Grandma and I looked for mermaids along the coast, running along the sand searching for their shell jewellery. I picked up a shell and held it to my ear. I wished I could have placed it in her hands. She'd have put it to her ear and smiled as she listened to the sound of the sea.

'Can you hear the mermaids sing Charlotte?'
Yes Grandma, I can hear the mermaids.

Evening

I took a Grab, the Asian version of Uber, to an LED light show at a nearby dock. Large white roses, fabricated from synthetic satin, illuminated the sandy banks, walls and even formed a tunnel, creating a small wonderland in this silent city. The smell of rice, fried fish and coconut milk drifted from the large array of food stalls, clustered to the right of the twinkling garden. I sat down with rice and greens in a carved-out bamboo boat, content at watching excited faces lit up by the lights.

You're not lonely, just alone.

9p.m.

Returning to the hostel, refreshed with new faces and experiences, I decided my time in Miri would be brief and booked a flight to Gunung Mulu National Park. I wanted to be in the jungle once again. Everything was simpler in the jungle.

11ᵗʰ August
Mulu

To get to Mulu from Miri you have two choices: a thirty-minute flight or a six-hour voyage on a cargo ferry. After my fifteen-hour bus experience, I took the plane. The airport looked more like an enlarged bus shelter. The entire building consisted of a bench, toilet and baggage chute. The same man who guided the landing and delivered our baggage was also the security officer and airport owner. *An impressive one-man show.*

Just about managing to stay on my feet as the rucksack returned to my shoulders, I noticed a smiling Malaysian lady holding a sign: *'Charlotte Clark, Mulu Homestay'.* It was a nice relief knowing I wouldn't have to wander around trying to find the place myself. I jumped into the back of her jeep, alongside a Japanese guy, before we headed along the dusty track to the hostel.

An elderly lady from the local tribe appeared, welcoming us to her homestay. She'd transformed her wide garage into an open plan living space with a bar and long communal table partitioned by bamboo shutters. It overlooked a pretty garden, riddled with pink and red blooms, that stretched all the way down to the banks of the gentle Paku river. Far in the distance, the light green silhouettes of the Mulu mountains outstretched into the sky. It was beautiful.

I paid for three nights, handing her husband 150 ringgits. He noticed me waiting patiently for the change and looked a little alarmed, moving his eyes slowly from me to the notes in his hand. His wife hurried over searching for the thirty-five ringgits change and handed it to her husband with a quick kiss on the cheek.

'Thirty-five,' she said knowingly as her husband passed the crumpled notes back to me.

I gave him a sympathetic smile; *education's availability is relative to its location.*

The dorm was basic, a room with metal framed beds lined up like an old hospital ward. There was no aircon, only a few fans attached to a pillar in the centre of the room which rotated at night, giving each bed a three second waft of mild air; in the humid evenings it was worshipped like a tribal totem pole.

4p.m.

Collapsing onto my bunk, a perky been-everywhere Chinese student with an American accent, suggested we head to the park.

'Thank you that's really nice of you to ask but I'm good for now, maybe later!'
Once bitten, twice shy.

5p.m.

An hour later, I headed down the dusty mud road to the park. Crossing a suspended bridge to the entrance revealed the humid Mulu rainforest. Fauna glowed a warm green from the evening sun as lizards lay on leaves, absorbing the last rays of the day. Heading towards reception, I followed the boardwalk maze that misled me to several park bungalows. *Maybe Center Parcs have branched out to more exotic locations.* While registering, I was handed a numbered wristband for the days I would be staying and told that anything worth seeing had to be booked and paid for in advance. 650 ringgits for the famous Gunung Pinnacles! *Wow, I really should have researched this more beforehand.* It was so much more commercialised than I'd imagined.

Unsure whether I liked the touristy vibe or not, I headed out for a short walk. *Hopefully you can still walk through the jungle without paying to go down every path!* From the Chinese travel know-it-all, I'd heard the Deer Cave was meant to be impressive so headed to the entrance, hoping to get one site ticked off my list.

'No Entry' I read. 'Damn it, of course you have to pay to go inside!' I muttered.

Oh well, back to the booking office it is then. I turned to leave to find three dozen people sitting on wooden benches that formed a kind of arena. There was even a shop to buy beer and snacks like a nature cinema! They were waiting for the bat exodus.

6p.m.

I sat staring at the vast cliff face, made up of grey and white chalky limestone, for about an hour. I'd spent so long studying the cave entrance I could paint it from memory; mossy plants and ivy crept their way up the rock until some parts were so green it looked like a vertical forest. The bats probably thought it bizarre having all these humans waiting hours every evening to watch them come out of the cave. *I doubt they'd ever waste their evening nibbling on a mosquito watching the tourist exodus, aka rush hour at Mulu Café.*

Within a moment the chatter dulled and a synchronized 'three, two, one' was called. Black dots streamed out of the cave, spiraling upwards like a double helix. It was amazing, a little like birds flying together in murmuration, racing through the sky but never touching. I asked a Spanish family sitting next to me how they knew when the bats were coming.

'If you look really carefully, you can see the bats rising against the white rock, the contrast makes them visible,' the dad replied.

It was quite subtle, but you could just about see them migrating north up the chalky cliff. They came out in packs every few minutes, the last group stealing the crowd's applause as they shot out in a long trail, spanning the sky's canvas above. It was simple, but beautiful. Nature can be so elegantly spectacular. This certainly made up for the *pay for everything* vibe earlier!

9p.m.

Showering was interesting. There was only a dribble of water, so it took a while to wash the sweat, sun-cream and insect repellent off my sticky skin. I was just drying off when a huge, green wasp-like bug flew into the cubicle, buzzing angrily. It convulsed as it zig-zagged sporadically, clashing into each side of the shower.

'Shit shit shit.'

Ah it's coming for me, I need to get my clothes on, shiiit.

I almost fell over, trying to shove both legs into one trouser leg. Practically falling out of the cubicle, I darted into the dorm without looking back to see if the night monster had followed.

9:10p.m.

All is good, back in dorm. Green monster stayed playing squash with itself in the shower.

12th August

The next two days were a combination of cave discovering, long boat rides, river swimming, trail trekking and watching geckos scale the roof of the hostel during thunderstorms.

8:30a.m.

I tried my first Malaysian breakfast. A nice change from the floury white toast with spreadable yellow grease and red goo previous hostels had provided. The sweet old lady brought out a plate of stir-fried rice noodles with soy sauce and little strips of sweet fried bread, a bit like a yum yum.

An hour later, I joined the Clear Water Cave tour, it consisted of a lot of walking up and down the arches of the cave, tracing the paths of stalagmites, stalactites and helictites. *To this day I'm still not entirely sure of the difference between them.* After bathing in the clear waters of the Paku river, we visited the local village where Mulu women sold bamboo bracelets and wooden carvings of hornbills.

3p.m.

This afternoon I decided to fit in a bit more exercise and tackle the Paku loop trail, an eight kilometer walk which circled the entire park. I liked the feeling of unguided walking, being free like I was back in Bako, going as fast as I could.

3:14p.m.

My feet slid off either side of a tree trunk I'd cockily attempted to hop over. I landed heavily in the damp undergrowth. Within seconds I was back on my feet, not wanting to know what creatures I'd disturbed. For the rest of the walk I slapped my legs every thirty seconds checking for scorpions and mosquitos, I must have looked like a mad cave woman by the end of the trail!

13th August
9:30a.m.

I spent Monday morning with a Belgian guy called Elias; he'd been at the park for ten days already. He had completed nearly all the tours and spoke very highly of each one. He was in love with Mulu and his enthusiasm was infectious but, after the third time of hearing his story about the Racer Cave being 'so cool', it got a little old.

'Why don't you become a tour guide and just live in this "UNESCO world heritage site?"' I joked.

'Haha, Cece you are funny. I really like it, it's amazing but I should leave and continue my trip, there are so many things to see. I am spending too much time here already!'

I managed to steer the conversation to fresher topics and we had quite a nice morning, taking our time reading the signs along the botanical walk. We learnt all about palms, insects, flowers, soil, rainforest layers, canopies, extending trees, vines and how coconut seeds drop into the sea, so they can float to another location to grow. *That explains why they are always on the beach*. With information overload, we settled down for lunch overlooking the river. We both had the roti canai, crisp on the outside and doughy in the middle with a mild curry sauce, it was so yummy!

3p.m.

The afternoon was spent exploring the Deer and Llang Caves with a rather cheeky older guide. He laughed at my youthful face and couldn't believe I was travelling alone.

'See that one bat Cece, up there in the cave?'

'Yes, I do.'

'Well, that's you Cece, the lone bat.'

'Haha very funny!' I giggled sarcastically.

He patted me on the back and gave me his headtorch so I could see the millions of bats clustered in the dark spots on the roof of the cave.

'Just watch out for the bat poo,' the guide smirked. The teenage Chinese girls all screeched and ran back to their parents, the guide rolled his eyes and winked at me.

'Come on Cece, lead the pack on.'

'Okay, right you are, cave leader!'

We chatted most of the way, waiting for everyone else on the tour to catch up after selfie-taking in the pitch black. *Black squares make a great Instagram*. On the three kilometer walk back to Mulu headquarters, the guide described his training at Mulu and more interestingly his life before cave tours. He had worked as a pastor where he helped tribal people get medical help in the larger cities.

5:30p.m.

After a day of walking, I sat down for an early supper at Mulu Café and munched my way through pan-fried fish, BBQ aubergine and rice. Then took a gentle sunset saunter back to the hostel for my final night in the rainforest.

NINE

I will climb it for her.

14th August

I was excited to wake up this morning; I couldn't wait to head to Kota Kinabalu (KK). Mulu had been a good outdoor escape, but I was starting to feel a little lonely and missed Alex. Despite the park being filled with people, most were couples and kept themselves to themselves, or were Mulu fanatics and only talked about the *insane Racer Cave* or *life-changing Pinnacles Trail*. Don't get me wrong, it was nice to hear about their experiences but after hearing the description of the Racer Cave ten times, conversation got a little repetitive.

10a.m.

Last night I spoke to a nice guy from the Netherlands. He was flicking through the guest book when he noticed everyone had written about the amazing pancakes they'd had for breakfast.

'Pancakes! I've never had the pancakes! Have you had them yet?' he asked.

'No, but I love them!'

'Let's pray for pancakes tomorrow then, haha?'

Low and behold, this morning we woke to find plates of pancakes for breakfast.

Thrilled, I took one big bite until a familiar pain in my stomach prevented me from swallowing. The dread dawned as the ache at the top of my stomach strengthened - the cramps had begun. *Fuck. CVS. Urgh why do you have to come on travel day?*

Trying to stay calm and manage the attack, I took all the meds I could to dull the pain but not make me too drowsy to travel to KK. *It's okay, you can deal with this, you've dealt with it before. This is just another attack, but in Asia, and you're alone...Okay just ignore the part about being alone.*

'It's just one flight,' I exhaled finding my ticket.

Shit, no you idiot Cece, you booked a flight to Miri then another flight to KK. Oh fab, and they are in the evening. What the fuck was I thinking when I booked this? I'll never make it there before passing out and throwing up everywhere. I hobbled to the little building that called itself an airport, praying that they had computers to change the flight.

10:30a.m.

Turns out the airport was better than I thought. I changed the flight to an earlier one for a ridiculous price that I chose to forget immediately. I made it to KK for 3p.m. just in time for the cramps to really kick in.

I shuffled, bent over from the pain and the crushing weight of my rucksack, pathetically trying to find my way. I made it to the hostel and upgraded to a private room, enabling me to writhe in pain in peace. I was scared, scared of being alone. *What if the attack gets really bad and no one will help me? What if I need to go to hospital?* I missed my family and I missed Alex. The thought of lying ill in bed made me cry as it reminded me of my grandma. I switched the light off, took some more painkillers and lay whimpering in the darkness, praying the pain would be gone by the time I woke up.

15ᵗʰ August
8:45a.m.

The cramps had dispersed. My tummy hurt when I walked, but the attack had stopped and I was grateful for that.

I should have had a bed day to recover, considering how weak I was, but in the back of my stupid determined mind I knew that if I wanted to climb Mount Kinabalu, it had to be soon. Alex would arrive in a few days and my chance would be gone. I slowly made my way into town, helplessly looking for travel agents, tour operators or any building for a matter of fact that displayed a picture of a mountain. After the fifth rejection I walked into the final shop, my energy was running low but I was determined to organise a plan.

'We have a place tomorrow madam,' the tour operator confirmed.

This is great, I can do it before Alex arrives and have a day to spare!

'How much does it cost?' I asked.

'1069 ringgits madam.'

'Ah okay.'

'This price does not include mountain fees. You need to pay for these separately madam.'

'Oh, okay, so how much all together?'

'About 1590 ringgits madam.'

Yikes, that's expensive, almost 300 pounds!

'Thank you, would you mind holding it while I think about it?'

'We can only hold it for up to an hour madam.'

'An hour would be very helpful, thank you. I'll be back in an hour.'

Unsure what to do, I sat at a local café and drank a coconut hoping its healing powers would help my achy post-CVS stomach. I was lucky to have this last-minute chance but I could barely walk, let alone climb a fricking mountain. *This is stupid, you'll get ill again Cece, you shouldn't do it.* But I'd been longing to do this ever since I began planning the trip many months ago. I was determined not to give up before I'd even started. *I'm doing it!*

12p.m.

Feeling pleased that I had made the decision, I hobbled back into my hostel with a smile. The owner's eyes widened when she saw the price I had paid. She explained to me that this was only accommodation and that I would have to organise the rest myself.

'That's entrance fee, guide fee, mountain permit and transport there and back. You should have booked it with us; we do it for 850 ringgits, all inclusive.'

Fuuuudge, what have I done?

'Wow it is tomorrow, you need to get there tonight my dear, otherwise you will miss it!' she added.

I must travel tonight? I'm exhausted, what have I done? She saw the panic on my face.

'It's okay, we can sort this, I will help you with everything, don't worry.'

And true to her word she did, giving me instructions as to which bus to get to Kinabalu National Park, a hostel to stay at tonight and even recommended a mountain guide. I was so grateful, I bought her biscuits to say thank you!

Thanks to my sporadic decision making, I had to leave within the next two hours to get there in time to climb the following morning. Hunched over from an achy stomach I packed as quickly as I could, then took a taxi to the bus station and found a minibus destined for Kinabalu. I was nervous and half tempted to jump out; *this is probably the stupidest thing you've done right after an attack Cece.* I was still very weak and this mountain was going to be tough. My thoughts were interrupted when my phone rang. It was Mum. Her usual cheery voice seemed a little dry.

'Darling, how are you feeling?'

'A little better thanks.'

'Where are you now?'

'Aha...well you'll probably tell me off but I'm in a minibus on the way to climb Mount Kinabalu.'

'Charlotte!'

My voice started to waiver as the stress of the challenge ahead dawned on me.

'Charlotte?'

'I'm fine, I want to do it.'

'Charlotte, get off the minibus.'

'No, I'm fine.'

'Charlotte, can you get out please?'

'No I'm...'

'Charlotte please get out...Charlotte I have...I have something to tell you. Charlotte, I want you to be somewhere safe, it's about Grandma.'

My heart sank. Mum's voice trailed off, I could tell she was fighting back tears.

'She's no longer alive, is she?'

'Charlotte, Grandma passed away on Monday.'

I felt I had sunk to the bottom of the ocean; my heart was so heavy, unable to breathe from the suffocating realisation. This was not how it was meant to be.

'No, she was...she was meant to stay alive, at least for a few more months!'

'It was peaceful. We were all with her. Charlotte?'

I couldn't process it. I'd just sent her another postcard. A postcard she would never receive.

'Charlotte get off the minibus, I don't want you to be upset, I didn't want to tell you like this, especially now you are about to leave, but it is Wednesday and I couldn't keep it from you any longer. It happened on Monday and we couldn't get hold of you. Don't worry about the money you paid for the trip, just get out.'

I couldn't speak. If I spoke, I would break down completely.

'Charlotte? Charlotte? Darling say something.'

'I'm going to do it. Going to...going to climb the mountain for her.'

'No darling, you've been ill, please get off the minibus and just be somewhere safe.'

'I have to do it for Grandma.'

'You don't have to.'

'Yes I do. I will do it for her, in her memory. It will be really hard but when I get to the top I will be closer to her.'

Salty droplets ran behind my sunglasses as I fought back the urge to wail and cry out.

'It was peaceful, you were there, we put a photo of you by her bedside. You were always there with her.'

But I hadn't been there, I'd been here.

'Charlotte please don't go, you'll get ill again, you should get off the minibus.'

More tears splashed from my eyes as it became harder to contain my sorrow.

'Mum, thank you for telling me.' I pulled, myself together and used whatever strength I had left to steady my voice, 'I'm going to climb this mountain for her. I will do it for Grandma.'

6p.m.

I have no recollection of the journey to Kinabalu after that. All I know is that when I left the minibus I was numb and drifted through the next few hours, my mind consumed on the words my mother had said on the phone.

I found the seedy looking hostel outside the park, checked in and opened door number three to find two smiley roommates. Neither of them were climbing tomorrow but they did invite me out that evening. I gratefully declined.

Sitting alone in the room was suffocating. *Cece, it's okay, you are doing this for her. Come on, it's time to get your game together. You need to do this for her!*

I gathered my things and started to pack, anything to distract my mind. After reading several Kinabalu blogs, the general consensus suggested packing light but taking warm clothes for the top. By elimination I reduced the number of rucksack items to a bare minimum. I didn't have many warm layers with me so decided to pack all the thin layers I had, hoping it would be enough.

7:30p.m.

I went to the restaurant next door and ordered veggie fried rice and a small side plate of mixed veg. I wasn't hungry but I had barely eaten anything over the past forty-eight hours and knew that I wouldn't get up the mountain without some energy. Despite the food, I felt empty. I felt nothing and everything. I wanted to scream. Scream as I had done back home, scream as I drove down the A21 to the coast after finding out she had cancer, scream out into the sea when the cancer got worse, scream as I ran through the fields when she was taken away, scream after every visit she became weaker and scream silently after our last goodbye. Each of these times, no one had heard my cries, I had wailed in private. Now I didn't care. I felt so hopeless that screaming seemed like the only thing left to do. I wanted to scream, scream so loud that everything on the mountain heard and understood my sadness. But there was no one there to listen. I was alone. I lay down in bed and cried until it stung to keep my eyes open.

16th August

I checked my phone. It was 5.28a.m. I lay in a state of drowsiness, coming to terms with the world. There was a moment of sweet ignorance before the pain hit me, before I realised she was no longer alive. She no longer lay in her bed, my family were no longer by her side holding her hand and the photos I had sent her remained on her table, never to be looked at again. *No, not today Charlotte, today you are going to be strong. You are going to climb this mountain for Grandma and you are going to do it with pride and determination. You will not give up, or let grief or CVS take you down.*

7a.m.

I headed to the gate and paid for my entrance fee, climbing permit, and what felt like a million other fees. I looked around hoping to find another solo climber to share a guide with, it would halve the price and double the experience. The last thing I felt like doing was smiling and making friends, but I had no choice if I wanted to climb with someone. *You need to find someone Cece, just get on with it.* To my right a girl was signing up, I instantly smiled and asked if she was hiking with anyone; to my delight she was alone too.

'Do you want to share a guide then?' I asked hopefully.

'Yes sure, I'm Chesa, from Philippines.'

'Nice, I'm Cece, from the UK. Chesa and Cece, we'll make a good climbing duo.'

The first day was forest hiking, dusty steps and trails - essentially six kilometres of stairs. It was hard but I enjoyed the mind-numbing monotony. I didn't have to think, only focus on putting one foot above the other. A kilometer in, Chesa stopped and bent over panting, she was struggling to keep up with our guide's pace. He took her rucksack from her.

'Wooa, heavy,' the guide laughed in disbelief, 'what you bring Chesa?'

Chesa gave a sheepish smile, 'I come straight airport, everything with me.'

No wonder she was struggling bless her, she'd packed the whole kitchen sink and enough battery packs to power a small house.

'Here Chesa, let me take something,' I gestured, 'we can share the load, my rucksack is super light.'

'Oh, no Cece, it heavy.'

'Honestly Chesa, mine is so light, just give me a few things like the power banks,' I smiled encouragingly.

She gratefully handed over the small weighty items and relief washed over her face when the pack was returned to her back.

'Okay, I keep going now,' she smiled.

We continued onwards, ploughing up the steps, through leafy jungle riddled with pitcher plants and skittering lizards. As we ascended higher, the air cooled and mountain ground squirrels dashed and darted over tree trunks, playing hide and seek with passing climbers. We made a tight team, the guide, Chesa and I. We climbed together, pausing every so often to look at the view which eventually became just a blanket of clouds. Despite their English being very basic and my Filipino and Malaysian being non-existent, we became good friends, understanding each other's strengths and weaknesses along the trail.

Our guide was an interesting man. Old, but kind with a wicked laugh. At every break he stopped for a cigarette, even at the high altitude, and wore tatty Converse rip-offs on his feet. This wasn't unusual, all the guides were poorly equipped and the porters were in an even worse condition, some with no shoes at all. Despite their attire, they carried tens of litres of oil, water, rice and sacks of potatoes on their backs and still overtook us. Their fitness was incredible, they were the souls of the mountain. They were probably doing more exercise than a professional footballer, yet getting paid a fraction of their salary. If their income couldn't afford them a decent pair of shoes, then how did they support their families?

'Are there many women who do this?' I asked the guide.

'Oh yes, but only about ten. It's a very tough job, but I know a few strong female porters and even guides who climb the mountain.'

Reaching the halfway point above the clouds, we stayed in wooden lodges at Laban Rata. The food was being laid out for a buffet dinner and the common room had a warm and cosy feel. We were greeted with hot ginger tea. I took it gratefully but felt guilty; someone had spent their entire day carrying this water up the mountainside, just so we could have a hot drink. Chesa went to sleep shortly after finishing her tea, having flown to Borneo from Manila the night before. Amazingly there was phone signal, so I rang my mum. We had a long conversation. We spoke about how it happened, how she had passed away that is, and how they had all been together at the very last moment. Silent tears trickled down my face. I felt faded, and felt my face was so tear stained that the salty water had carved out rivers in my cheeks. I dug my nails into my thighs to suppress the urge to cry out, trying to deflate any emotion, but the pain continued to rise.

17th August

We woke at 2a.m., had a quick breakfast of French toast and marmalade and began the hike again. It was freezing but the climbing was good. The top of the mountain was made up of steep slabs of granite; we tugged ropes and pivoted on our tiptoes to trudge up the slope in the pitch black. It was a slog and I was in a lot of pain from the wind and the cold. My Reynaud's flared up, my hands and feet were numb and my body was chilled to the bone. *If I fall, I'll smash like ice and break into a million pieces.* The only good thing about the cold was that my mind went numb too.

At 5a.m. we summited. We reached the highest point on earth either of us had ever been in our lives, 4095 metres. We were too cold and exhausted to speak, but no words were necessary. For a moment, the mountain steals your words and your thoughts, it numbs your mind and body and strips all emotion. It cleanses you of pain, grief and anger, and for one brief moment at the summit, you feel free; content with the fact that you are on top of the world. We gave a frozen smile to each other, our cheek muscles barely able to move, before starting the descent.

I was proud of myself for completing the trek after everything that had happened, but the person I wanted to tell the most was no longer on this earth. But I knew she knew. *Today I climbed Mount Kinabalu for my grandma and she was proud.*

TEN

I couldn't have wished for him to come sooner.

18th August
Kota Kinabalu
8:30a.m.

Returning to KK, I met Elias again who had arrived at the hostel the evening I left for the mountain. I smiled at him, relieved to be greeted by someone I recognised.

'Elias, hey, what are you doing here?'

He looked distressed, 'Hey Cece, I've come to climb the mountain, you've just done it right? But listen, we cannot stay here, this place is filled with them, disgusting things.'

'What, you're kidding, I was here for a night before I left for the mountain, I didn't see anything.'

'Oh dear, you'll need to be careful, they'll have got into your things, come with me, I'll show you.'

He pulled me into his room to reveal a traveller's worst nightmare: bed bugs. Vile brown bugs scurried over the mattresses and to our horror came crawling out of our backpacks and clothes! After panicking for a good hour, we trawled the shops for toxic sprays, fumigated everything we owned and moved hostels. But even then, the bugs followed. Elias suggested putting everything in the freezer, including ourselves *(it had got pretty desperate),* but the new hostel owner looked at us as if we were mad and didn't seem too pleased at the thought of having two infested travellers lying next to his ice creams. In a desperate final attempt, we lay our belongings on the rooftop in the hope of frazzling the pests. To our relief, it worked. *Thank God for the hot Malaysian sun, nature's very own frying pan and pesticide.*

Afternoon

The afternoon was much better. We met a kind Malaysian man called Che who, having ample time on a business trip, took it upon himself to be our tour guide. We visited KK's port, the popular shopping mall and chatted over lunch at the mall's rooftop food court that overlooked the sea. He took us to several local markets, taught us about local fruits, vegetables and baked delicacies. We tried three types of mango, rambutans, mangosteens, green coconut roles and glutinous palm sugar rice cakes.

Evening

We dined at a hectic fish market. Large, once-white tents contained a small village of stands, kitchens and tables trapped in an unbearable humidity. Vendors called out prices as they tried to auction off their catch to passersby, fish were tossed from scale to scale and loaded plates were served in a continual stream to hungry locals. It was quite a show. Huge yellowfin tuna lay rigid on briny table-tops, live crabs crawled in boxes and sea slugs wilted out of their shells. Che chose our fish, a small grouper, requesting it to be cooked with garlic and ginger. It arrived splayed on the plate, looking slightly scary with contorted fins and sunken eyes. I stared at the poor creature and then looked up at Che's smiling expectant face. *You've eaten a crab Cece, you can eat a fish!* Despite appearances, it was the best fish I had ever tasted. *Cultural experience no.37 - complete.*

10p.m.

I returned to the hostel, content from the afternoon's excitement. But when I closed the bedroom door I felt completely alone. Grief filled my mind and I sank to the floor. The room started to cave in on me as my mind projected memories onto the grubby white walls, memories of home, of Grandma and of the week before I left. Tears fell as I cried louder and louder into my hands, trying to stifle my sobs. I closed my eyes but the images remained, I couldn't escape from the pain, from the sorrow or from the grief.

'Alex, Alex please come, come and save me from this place.'

19th August
8a.m.

My eyes were sore from crying but I woke with a smile. *Alex is coming today!* Picking up my phone, my smile grew even wider.

[19/08, 06:16] Alex: Cece! I've landed in Kuala Lumpur earlier than expected so have just bought a new flight to KK so I can have an extra 8 hours with you...I figured you were worth the extra £150. Can't wait to see you soon!!

I loved him. With this news I could get through the morning. I picked up a watermelon kek lapis, Alex's belated birthday cake, from the Gaya Street Sunday Market, before heading to the airport.

I arrived several hours earlier, just in case he was there. I didn't mind waiting, in fact I quite enjoyed it, knowing that every minute I waited was a minute closer to seeing him. I stood for forty-five minutes in front of the arrivals gate, not wanting to move. Every time a pair of trainers came through the gate, I raised onto my tiptoes in anticipation. After what felt like hours, I recognised the smiling face and ran as fast as I could. I collided into his chest and swung my arms round his neck, staying there, pressed tight to his body for a good minute, not wanting to reveal the tears of relief that had welled up in my eyes. After a final squeeze, he tipped my chin to his face and kissed my lips softly.

'Hello you.'

'Alex, I've missed you so much, I'm so glad you're here.'

'Me too Cece, me too. Now let's explore Borneo!'

20ᵗʰ August

Snorkeled for the first time with Alex on Sapi and Manukan island. It was incredible seeing the clown fish, coral reefs, and even spiky black sea urchins clustered on the seabed. The islands were beautiful, white sand and crystal waters made for stereotypical paradise beaches. Well, a paradise beach featuring huge monitor lizards if you ventured inland. Hours were spent swimming, jungle exploring and sipping chilled coconuts under the palms. We left the islands content that we'd found Nemo *(and Gill)*.

21ˢᵗ August

Inspired by our boat tour yesterday, we ventured on another snorkeling trip to one of the closer islands. The variety of fish was much more limited due to the depth of the water, so, in search of the supposed 'hidden' beach, we decided to hike to the other side of the island. After getting tangled in branches, sliding down mountainsides, being chased by a monitor lizard and attacked by mosquitoes, we eventually made it to the hidden beach. We floated in the sea, soothing our cuts and scrapes from the epic hike, before heading back to the boat. As we started to scramble back up the mountainside, a couple explained that the pier was just around the corner if we simply clambered over a short stretch of rocks. Turns out the beaches were connected after all - *talk about coming full circle!*

22ⁿᵈ August

We spent the morning at a cooking class, frying up curries and soups with shrimp paste, bitter jungle berries and oyster sauce. An interesting array of flavours that perhaps won't be repeated at home.

Afternoon

Returned to the hostel feeling exhausted and just, very sad. We hadn't spoken about my grandma passing yet but I couldn't contain it anymore. I sat solemnly on the bed for a while before breaking down and crying, turning my face into the pillow to muffle the noise. I missed my grandma. Alex held me for a long time, stroking my hair.

Evening

We went for a long walk along the seafront and ate rambutans while watching the blood orange sunset melt into the sea. Heading sleepily back to the hostel, tears no longer stained my face but grief remained heavy in my heart.

ELEVEN

Sandakan - a stopover city.

23rd August
Sandakan
Early afternoon

We took a Grab from the airport to, what was marketed as, a nearby crocodile sanctuary. Unfortunately, 'sanctuary' seemed a rather optimistic translation of the word 'farm' – quite the opposite end of the river for the poor crocs! The 'sanctuary' was a slightly dodgy looking place which ripped off tourists, charging them five times the local price. *I guess some smart owner had looked up the exchange rate and decided to charge English prices.* We hesitantly left our bags behind the counter, unsure if they'd be eaten by the crocodiles or the fat locals loitering in reception (who looked like they'd eaten a croc for breakfast). The reptiles were huge beasts with algae coated skin and dark yellow eyes spying from beneath the murky leather-black water. They remained statues until feeding time, which turned them into ferocious predators. Launching into the air, they snapped their jaws producing a tremendous gulp as they swallowed the rotting chunks of meat lobbed their way. Impressive if not terrifying. Despite the fear the beasts instilled in their observers, you couldn't help but feel sorry for the soon to be handbags or belts.

4p.m.

From there we travelled into the city, a city which scarcely welcomed tourists. Whichever street we ventured down, heads turned, eyes rolled and a wave of whispers and calls echoed like an urban rainforest.

'Hello, hello my best friend.'
'Hello lady.'
'Hei, how are you?'

'Whas your name?'

It was funny at first, feeling like minor celebrities, but after a while it got a little draining, we just wanted to walk freely along the seafront without an entourage chasing our heels. To lose our fan club, I suggested we search for the famous floating village: a cluster of houses made of rusty blue walls, wooden beams and flowerpots suspended over the sea. In true Cece style, we headed off without a map or even a concrete idea about the direction we should be walking in. After half an hour we ended up on an estate filled with tower blocks and, before we knew it, what felt like a hundred observers watching from their windows. I looked at Alex, his agitated expression said it all.

'Um, do you feel like we should be here Cece? I know you like to go without maps but this doesn't feel right.'

'Yea, it's definitely not the water village, but I think it will be fine. Malay people are really nice.'

He looked at me, plainly pissed-off now. I rarely saw Alex grumpy, so it was almost a novelty.

'I think it should be fine Alex, if we keep going we'll get there eventually.'

'Is this the kind of place you've been going to by yourself?

'Well, not exactly like this.'

'Cece, I think we should go, this isn't safe.'

'Come on, it's fine, live a little Alex.'

'Ey pretty lady, my best friend,' was hollered from above, 'you come, I see you from the road, I show you good time, your friend, he don't need come, Sophia take care of him.'

'Yea, you wan good time ladee, come wid me.'

We both looked at each other.

'Okay let's go, you were right, I take it all back!' I admitted hurrying out of the alleyway.

Back down the dusty path, back through the locals' market and back past the coconut vendors we ran, returning to the hustle and bustle of the seafront restaurants. When we finally stopped, it was a little tense between us. I knew I had pushed the situation too far.

'Shall we eat?' Alex suggested.

'Yes, good idea,' I said sheepishly.

We sat down quietly and waited in silence before the waiter came to take our order of two mee goreng mammaks. Alex's orange juice was brought to the table, he took one sip and his eyes widened in mild horror.

'Not good?' I asked.

'That's powdered water,' he replied, stirring the granules that had resided in the bottom of the glass.

'Euhhhh, who has powdered orange juice?' I responded, 'I think even my laxatives taste better than that!'

We both burst out laughing.

'Alex, I'm sorry for insisting to carry on, it didn't feel right, I don't know why I continued.'

'It's okay, although I admit I did start to worry about the rest of the trip if that was the kind of place you considered a highlight!'

'Haha, no trust me, Asian brothel isn't really my style! I should have realised sooner we were heading in the wrong direction...or just listened to you!'

'Yeah, oh well, I guess we'll never find the floating village but to be honest I think I'm done searching for it!'

He rolled his eyes, we laughed and all tension was sent out to sea. We spent the rest of the evening munching on stir-fried noodles and debating plastic pollution in the ocean, looking out across Sandakan's poor coastline. It was a nice evening until my stomach started to cramp up, so we headed back to the hostel. Luckily, they weren't CVS cramps and after a while the pain lessened. I was left to lie in peace with Alex, we dreamed of the orangutans and rainforest creatures we hoped to see tomorrow.

TWELVE

It was beautifully wild.

24ᵗʰ August
The Kinabatangan River

I woke with a slight pain in my stomach, I turned over and it became fiercer.

Alex turned to me when he realised I was awake and said in an excited whisper, 'It's rainforest day!'

'Alex, I think I have CVS.'

I sat up slowly, trying not to aggravate the cramps, reached for my medicine bag and swallowed as many pills as I could.

'Oh Cece, what if we tried to move the trip to tomorrow? It's okay.'

I checked my watch, it was 8:30a.m. We had just over two hours until pick-up, there was no way they would move the date with two hours' notice. Realistically I had two choices, I either stay here in the comfort of the hostel where the bathroom is clean and we have a private room, or I go to the rainforest where there might not be any of that. I pictured myself lying on a muddy bed of ferns, dripping with sweat as cramps and nausea tormented me. Then I looked at Alex, at his sympathetic face, he was so good to me when I was ill. I felt safe with him; I knew he would look after me. I couldn't deny him this one chance to see the orangutans, I had to go.

12:30a.m.

The bus spluttered to a stop and coughed us out. Our rucksacks followed shortly, flung to the ground by a small sharp man wearing lodge uniform.

'You all get in boat. Over there, get in boat!'

We looked at each other a little confused; no one had mentioned anything about a boat being part of the journey.

'It just get to accommodation, on other side of river.'

'Ah, okay thank you,' another tourist replied.

We bundled our hefty rucksacks into the long boat, which sunk further into the dark river as more members of our group stumbled onboard. Alex carried my bags and helped me ease myself into the boat. The combination of the rocking boat and strong motor fumes were nauseating, I just wanted to lie down.

The Kinabatangan Lodge

We were greeted with an orange welcome drink and given a brief orientation before arriving at our rooms. The place was nice, board-walk paths, old lodges made of dark wood and exotic flora everywhere you looked. We were in one of the dorm rooms with a decked balcony that ran around the entire building. A blast of cool air invitingly washed over our hot, sticky bodies as we entered. *Air-con - a blessing I was grateful for.* We were matched with another Northern couple who had been travelling for a few months already. They were down-to-earth, very easy to talk to and the guy also looked like a blonde Ed Sheeran.

Just as we'd claimed bunks, a gong sounded signaling teatime. *Or perhaps we'd accidentally booked ourselves onto a Buddhist retreat?* A mug of hot water, small pineapple biscuits and a warm bowl, containing the local porridge of coconut milk and green mung beans, were passed to me. The little sugar burst stopped me from fainting, even if it made my cramps worse.

The river cruise
4p.m.

We were told to fish out a wet life jacket, damp from tourist sweat and muddy river water, along with a dark leather cushion to sit on. The boat rocked from side to side as everyone crowded on, seeming to ignore the 'one at a time' rule. The boat lurched away from the bank, rolling to the side and slapping the water as a German, beer-bellied Indiana Jones wannabe barged through. His sense of urgency seemed a little unnecessary considering the boat would go only when everyone had boarded. We were the last to get in, filling the two back seats next to the driver. He was a dark-skinned man in his late twenties with a big proboscis monkey-like belly, around which he'd wrapped a leather belt, hiding a small machete style knife.

'Hallo everyone, my name Kairo, Kairo with a K, not a C, like Egypt. I am your Kapitan, your guide, and your ranger,' he winked with a crooked smile.

'I take you on two-hour tour of river; we see monkeys, maybe orangutan, elephants if lucky or even crocodile.'

A quiet shrill of excitement rippled through the boat as each passenger turned to their neighbour, eyes wide at the hope of seeing an animal along the banks.

The engine revved and we were off, for a moment I forgot I had cramps as the cool air whipped through my hair and we sped along the water. The dim light of dusk threw pastel pinks into the sky and the dark silhouette of trees lined the riverbank. It was beautifully wild.

Before long, the boat engine reduced to a purr as we approached the overgrown banks.

'Here, over here, look. Baby crocodile,' Kairo whispered.

The small crocodile's head bobbed just above the surface with its jaw open a fraction, making his tiny teeth visible. He was fighting to keep afloat which was becoming increasingly difficult with the muddy waves the boat was making. Cool, but I was relieved to move on, mummy croc wouldn't be too far behind!

The cruise continued upriver for the next hour and a half, we saw several long and short tailed macaques and our favourite: the proboscis monkey. They're funny looking creatures with their large noses and golden coats. We observed a male perched proudly on a branch with his big belly thrust forward and a comic looking spiky red penis sticking upright, like a red felt-tip pen, between his gangly legs.

'Okay so proboscis monkey, yeah guys, come in two groups:

1. Harem group, fam-i-ly group, one male many wives: the playboy monkey.
2. Bachelor group, all male, no woman no cry, gay club.'

Kapitan Kairo – outrageous but flipping hilarious.

On our way back to the lodge we passed a patch of long thick grass where a few boats were stationed, the drivers of which were waving frantically. Kairo quickly muttered something and immediately cut the engine, our boat slowed to a stop.

'Elephant guys, quiet yeah,' Kairo whispered, ''tis da pygmy elephant.'

I turned quickly to see a flash of a small trunk and flappy ears before it vanished back into the grass.

'Oh wow,' I whispered to Alex.

We steered back to the other side of the river to avoid scaring them off and waited. After about ten minutes the long grassy blades parted as a shy pygmy elephant slowly appeared, munching away to clear its path. We watched in awe and couldn't believe our luck when a tiny little trunk belonging to a baby appeared between its legs.

'We're seeing real elephants; I can't believe it, real elephants in the wild!'

'I know it's amazing! I've heard rumours from other travellers but never expected we'd actually see one!' Alex replied in a whisper, putting his hand gently over mine.

According to Kairo there are only 250 along the river, that's less than one every two kilometres; these two metre giants are few and far between.

Back at the lodge
Evening

After those amazing sightings we headed back to the lodge. The excitement had distracted me from the cramps but now we were back on land and the evening approached, they were getting worse again. I sat on my bed, head drooped in determination not to let CVS defeat me. I flicked on my phone as a distraction and saw a message.

[24/08, 18:23] Mum: I have some flowers for Grandma and a card from Jemima, Daddy, you and I. Perhaps you could write something inside to lay at the funeral? I have also placed a few things to put with her for cremation like your shells that were beside her bed, the poem you wrote for her when you were nine and a few photos of you and Jemima. Is there anything else you would like to add? She loved all of them xx

By the time I read the last line my eyes had filled with tears and I could no longer see clearly. I remembered the last time I saw her, I remembered placing the shells into her hands. And then, I remembered she was no longer here. Alex came in and looked alarmed when he saw my face, I showed him the message.

'Aw Cece.'

I burst out crying as the cramps became even worse, 'I'm not going to dinner. I'm in pain.'

I lay down and Alex stroked my hair before he left for supper.

Alone in the darkness I cried out quietly, 'I miss you Grandma, but I will never see you again.'

I lay whimpering in the dark, minutes felt like hours as the cramps got worse. I longed for Alex to return, to return and lay by my side. I felt bitterly sad. I closed my eyes and willed sleep to come; come and take me away from the pain.

25th August
Grandma's birthday

I woke at 5:30a.m. Thankfully the cramps had stopped, the attack must have passed away in the night. I was weak but happy the pain was over. Alex popped his head down from the top bunk to check if I was awake.

'Cece, how are you feeling?'

'It's stopped, I'm alive!'

'Oh that's great! Do you think you'll be able to make it onto the cruise?'

'I'm super weak so I may need your help but I don't want to miss it!'

'Yes, okay that's really great, we'll get you onto that boat. You'll be right next to me, so I'll look after you!'

'Okay I'll do it!' I gave him a smile.

6a.m.

I watched each passenger sleepily board the boat and sink into their seat, only half aware of Kairo's cheery morning banter. Despite the exhaustion, I felt alive. Everything seemed incredible just after an attack, I saw and appreciated every detail life had given me and took nothing for granted. A day without pain was a good day, and today was a good day. We drifted with the current for the first half hour, monkey spotting, until the boat stopped abruptly. Silently, Kairo raised his arm and pointed to a large brown patch in a distant tree. A long gangly arm covered in orange brown hair stretched to grab a nearby branch, its body followed swinging like a pendulum until it was comfortably repositioned. It was an orangutan! A wild orangutan! We ogled at the tree, watching it effortlessly swing from branch to branch, I couldn't believe we were seeing one. I was so grateful to have made it onto the boat.

Returning to the dorm, I pulled out my phone, eager to message Mum that I was better and tell her the news, but she had beat me to it.

[25/08, 08:52] Mum: I hope you're feeling better darling. Just to remind you, it would have been Grandma's birthday today xx

I hadn't forgotten but reading the words 'would have been' felt like I'd been dropped a thousand metres. But I didn't let a single tear fall, because I knew Grandma had sent the orangutan for her birthday; she was watching over me.

'Happy birthday Grandma and thank you!' I whispered, looking skywards.

Afternoon

We hired yellow gumboots for a short walk, plodding through the rainforest. The mud was surprisingly deep from the elephant footprints and heavy rain. At one point I even got my foot stuck in the mud and Alex had to pull me out! Kairo pointed out plants and trees used for local remedies, explained a few rainforest survival tips and, my least favourite part, showed us the leeches. They were horrible, especially the tiger leeches which were wiry brown things with red stripes. They moved around like a bendy magic wand, sensing your heat and trying to latch on. Some got stuck to my trousers, but Alex quickly flicked them away before they could latch onto my skin - I hated them!

Evening

I chatted to the couple in the dorm until Alex returned from the night walk (my energy reserves were too low to join). He arrived back into the dorm, dripping wet from the tropical rain.

'Was the walk good?' I asked.

'Not really, we didn't see much. Oh and I dropped my watch and now the bottom has fallen off. I tried to hit it back into place, but it didn't work.'

'Oh.'

'But I did find this!'

With a hopeful smile he produced a huge hammer from behind his back.

'Dude, why the fuck have you got that?' the blonde Ed Sheeran exclaimed.

'The back came off my watch, and I can't get it back on.'

After five minutes of loud banging, a little less enthusiastic Alex returned, sheepishly uncurling his palm to show a watch that had been turned into a compass - the once-second hand now spun when you tilted it. We all fell into a fit of giggles.

'Well, when else are you going to get hammered in Borneo?' he sighed.

From then on, I was the timekeeper.

THIRTEEN

We were chased by the man of the woods.

26th August
Sepilok
9a.m.

The bus dropped us off outside the orangutan sanctuary, we agreed that nothing could beat seeing one in the wild, but it would be nice to see them up close.

'You've missed feeding time, no point going in now, you won't see anything,' said the ticket vendor.

'Oh, um okay,' I replied.

'But if you want, you can go in just to have a look and then come back for the second feeding time.'

'Okay why don't we just go in to have a look, Cece?' suggested Alex.

'Sure, we're here so why not?'

This happened to be the best suggestion Alex made during the trip.

Wandering along the jungle boardwalk, it wasn't long before we heard a rustle in the trees. We stood like statues; an orangutan was contentedly munching on some leaves, sitting in a tree a few feet away!

Leaving him to enjoy his second breakfast, we carried on along the path. A mere five minutes later, we encountered another. This one traversed through the trees and slid down the trunk to rest on the boardwalk fence. It was only when she sat down that we realised she had a small fluffy baby clinging to her belly. They were so close, only a metre away, we stood in awe watching one of the animal kingdom's wonders. Awe, however, quickly turned to unease as she started to strut on all fours towards us, increasing her pace to match our retreat. Alex turned immediately while I, slightly mesmerized, held on a little longer to watch the beautiful creature. Her eyes were wide and set on mine, it was almost as if she was communicating with me. Unfortunately, I didn't speak orang, so the protective mummy took a more physical approach, galloping in my direction. I turned and ran! Half in disbelief and half in fear, we sprinted as fast as we could to take refuge inside the first building we came to - the orangutan nursery. At the entrance, the female slowed to a stroll, expanding her chest and walking off proudly.

'*Yeah, f-off out of my territory tourists,*' was what I imagined she would have said. To be fair, I probably would have done the same if someone took photos of me straddling a tree.

Once out of sight, and relieved we weren't stripped of our clothes, we both let out a nervous giggle of relief.[4]

'I can't believe how close she got to us!' Alex said.

'I know, we were practically given a private tour by an orangutan!'

'I'm not sure "tour" is exactly the word I'd use, I think we were escorted out by an orangutan security guard!'

From the safety of the nursery

Behind the nursery glass, we could view the toddler-tangs from a distance, shielded from any protective parents. One curious youngster was trying to high-five a little girl through the glass and another was playing tag with a friend. They were cheekily clever, more like humans than I'd imagined, especially the way they used their hands.

We had a short lunch break, tucking into a plate of fried rice and trying the local specialty, red bean and coconut ice cream (an interesting texture, one I'm sure will appear in a flashy vegan café in Brixton next year).

---

[4] *The Visitor's Centre had warned us of previous tourists being stripped of their clothes and belongings by orangutans if they got too close.*

Afternoon

Returning to watch feeding time in the afternoon was a mistake. It was horrible. Tourists were shouting, grabbing onto fences and worst of all taking photos with flash! I'm surprised the poor apes hadn't developed epilepsy! We left after five minutes.

Evening

Arriving at our hostel, disappointed was too weak a word. Our room was a small hot box with a broken fan, no air-con, grubby bedsheets and ripped mosquito-nets infested with geckos. We were also dangerously in the middle of a construction site. Annoyed and a little frazzled, we returned to reception explaining that this was clearly not what we had booked online.

The receptionist was so laid-back it was hard to get the message across, 'We are not happy with the room, we would like to change please?' I repeated.

'Okay, but you booked it,' he replied.

'Yes, I know but this is not what you showed us online.'

His face looked bemused.

After a few more rounds of question and answer, the young lad brought over his manager to deal with the situation. At the far end of the office they discussed in whispers, shooting us a suspicious glance every ten seconds; *anyone would have thought they were on 'Who Wants to Be a Millionaire?'* Eventually they came over and, to our delight, upgraded the room for no extra charge! *Is that your final answer?*

Upgrade to paradise

And wasn't it an upgrade? A double bed instead of two singles, air-con, an ensuite, tiled floors, kettles, towels, toilet paper and soap! Now, anyone who has been living in hostels for a while will know very well that toilet paper and soap are basically the hostel version of a mini fridge.

I jumped around and squealed, wrapping my legs around Alex's waist as he spun me in a circle.

'Did we do well or what?'

'We did, good job!'

'This room is like something from "Pimp My Crib" - hostel style!' Turning to a pretend camera I continued, 'Welcome to Alex and Cece's house, on tonight's show you'll see how simple touches make a hostel a home.'

We celebrated our one night in backpacker luxury with crispy roti and veggie curry in the hostel's 'rustic' outdoor restaurant. We watched the thunder and lightning rage while keeping an eye on two stray cats that kept jumping onto our table to steal our dinner. It was less fun running back to our room, but thankfully we had those free towels!

27th August

We visited The Borneo Sun Bear Conservation Centre, a rehabilitation centre for the world's smallest bear. They'd become endangered from poaching and greedy humans keeping them as pets. After seeing the scratch marks on the trees, I did wonder how people thought it was a good idea to take one home. We met a sweet English girl who was living in Sepilok for eight months, studying sun bear personalities for her dissertation at university. She spent all day recording the bears and observing their behaviours, needless to say we learnt a lot from her. I admired the girl for spending all day at the sanctuary, the bears were cool, but I couldn't imagine spending each day of the week just observing and filming. I'll give it to her, she certainly made the most of the travel opportunities for her dissy project, I think the furthest I ventured was the Victorian Library on campus.

After pineapple fried rice for lunch, we visited The Rainforest Discovery Centre. It had a cool canopy walkway, thirty metres off the ground that allowed you to see the rainforest from tree level, making monkey spotting a lot easier. The forest stretched for miles, each tree contributed to this vast kingdom, housing thousands of creatures. It was breathtaking to see an expanse of land covered in endless shades of green. Although from the thousands of palm oil plantations we'd seen on the bus journey here, I was left hoping that this green empire's days were not numbered.

Towards the end of the trail, we encountered a few of the king's men who weren't prepared to let us leave without a fight. They growled in the bushes, scampered above our heads and barked like dogs each time we took a step: an ambush of short-tailed macaques! It sounds ridiculous to be scared of such a small creature, but these were more like vicious baboons with razor rows of teeth than playful monkeys. We must have looked like a low budget Karate film with nothing but sticks to defend ourselves with. I think we'll leave the close-up 'Life of Apes' to Attenborough in the future!

FOURTEEN

Did we really have our first argument over two pounds?

28th August
8a.m.

I am so annoyed.

We needed to get to the airport to catch our flight from Sandakan to KK. Due to the remoteness of the place, it was difficult to get a Grab. Alex, too anxious to wait a few minutes, ordered a taxi from reception. I guess it was a good idea at the time, but I was wary of the price. It's not stinginess; it's the principal of these things. I'd rather support the people who provide a fair service than a rich taxi man who bumps up the price every time he sees a traveller.

The driver seemed chatty enough, but I noticed he didn't have a meter in the car. When I questioned this, he claimed they didn't use them in Sandakan. *Bullshit.*

'How much is it going to cost?' Alex asked.

'Fifty ringgit my friend,' the driver replied with a smarmy smile.

'Fifty!' I blurted out, 'Fifty, a Grab only costs fifteen! Alex this is over triple the price, this is ridiculous!'

Alex, a little embarrassed at my protestations, looked uncomfortably at me.

'We just need to pay it to get to the airport; it's our only option Cece.'

'Okay, but I'm determined to get that ridiculous price down,' I replied curtly. *There's no way I'm paying fifty ringgits!*

I spent the rest of the journey compiling an argument while Alex googled fees per kilometer, I wasn't getting ripped off by another taxi driver. Upon arrival, the driver started talking some crap about the government charging for insurance and then the hostel charging him twenty ringgits for calling him - no way would the hostel charge him that much! I decided to hold my ground and boldly held out a fan of three ten-ringgit notes.

'I'll give you thirty, that's double what a Grab would have charged, that should cover insurance and hostel.'

He looked at the notes and repeated the same malarkey again, so I explained my reasoning once more. He then lowered his fee to forty ringgits.

'Now I get twenty, hostel gets twenty'

There was no way the hostel would get half of his money, he was still bluffing.

'Thirty,' I replied.

'Cece, where are you getting this figure from? Let's just pay forty,' Alex stressed.

I turned to look at him, I couldn't believe he was now challenging me, I was the one trying to flipping get us there for a decent price! I kept up with my thirty offer and just when the driver was about to give in, Alex, feeling incredibly uncomfortable, caved and handed him the extra money.

Frustrated and very annoyed I smiled politely until the taxi drove off. Then all daggers turned to my supposed boyfriend. The same boyfriend who was meant to support me.

'Why did you do that, I had him at thirty?'

'I felt bad,' he replied quietly.

'He was going to charge us fifty ringgits Alex, that's ridiculous for a short drive in Malaysia!'

'But his cost breakdown made sense.'

'That was a load of bullshit, I can't believe you gave him forty, I had him at thirty!'

'No you didn't Cece!'

'Yes I did!'

'We should have paid him in full; he probably has a family to support.'

Sometimes, Alex had such high morals it was annoying, I was about to protest but thought better and checked myself. Causing a scene over ten ringgits would not be something to be proud of.

'Okay, let's just leave it at that shall we?'

I walked off sulkily into the airport; he followed looking pissed off and chucked his rucksack down to the floor with a loud thud. We both strapped them up in silence ready for bag drop.

It was weird, seeing a different side to him put me on edge, I had never really been in a proper argument with Alex before, he was always so calm and easy-going.

When we got to the bag drop, Alex broke the silence.

'I need to empty my water bottle, shall I do yours?'

'No thank you, it will be fine, they let water through on domestic flights.'

Ignoring my advice, he went off to do it anyway. The anger that I had just calmed, flared back up again. *Why did he not listen to or trust me?* He returned thirty seconds later just as I was pulling my bag through. Surprise, surprise the water was fine.

When he followed, I spitefully replied, 'I told you so.'

From the look he gave me, I knew I shouldn't have said it, but he bloody well should have listened to me!

Side by side in the departure lounge, we waited in silence.

'I'm going to the bathroom before we board, I'll meet you on the plane, okay?'

Alex replied curtly, 'Fine, see you on it.'

I knew I was making things worse, digging myself an even deeper hole, but I couldn't stop, I couldn't crawl out.

Alex was already seated on the plane by the time I came out, he looked up briefly without smiling and then looked back down at his phone. A few minutes later, as I was struggling to push my rucksack under the chair in front of me, a voice commented, 'Rucksack troubles too?'

I looked up to find a bronzed, curly haired Aussie had sat next to me.

We started chatting about rucksacks and our various travels so far. I learnt he was actually from England but had moved to Australia six years ago as an electrician. He was a 'live in the moment' kind of guy, where every penny he earnt went into his travel fund.

'My life is basically work, travel, work, travel. The day I got my Australian visa I quit my job and buggered off out the country, haha.'

He had had the same issue with the taxi in Sepilok too.

'I wasn't paying fifty ringgits to get to the airport! So, I got out, waltzed up to another Malaysian guy in a car and offered to pay him for giving me a ride. He asked for thirty, so I brought it down to twenty and he seemed more than happy.'

He seemed reckless, spontaneous and with his visa story in mind, didn't sound like he played by the rules either. He was the polar opposite to Alex and, at that very moment, I found his attitude pretty refreshing.

We continued to chat and it turned out he was heading to a hostel close to ours in KK, so he offered to share a taxi.

'Great, well I'm ready as soon as we get off this plane.'

'You have no hold luggage?' I asked.

'Yeah, got all I need right in here. You donna need much to travel.'

'Yes I suppose, I have another rucksack.'

'Whatcha carrying in there girl?'

'Well I have a long-term illness so need lots of meds, plus the yoga mat takes up a fair bit of space.'

'Ohh okay so what you're saying is you're actually a drug dealer, got it!'

'Haha no, they're all for me.'

'Shh, don't worry sweetheart, I gotcha, and I guess that yoga you do is some kind of code?'

'What?'

'You know, Downward Dog…that's how you carry the hard-core drugs isn't it?'

'Oooh, nooo!'

'Yes, I gotcha, and just checking out your Insta, you have all these emoji's in your bio. Is the watermelon like code for something else?'

'I just like fruit.'

'Oh yeah sure, it's code for drugs.'

'No!'

'Sure sure, if I ever get a message from you with a watermelon, I'll know what you mean.'

I giggled, he was outrageous, but funny.

'Is this your boyf, is he in on the drugs act too?'

Alex turned from looking grumpily out the window, 'Haha no, I'm just travelling with Cece for a few weeks.'

I smiled sheepishly, another person in the mix eased the tension between us a little.

'Alex, nice to meet you mate, I'm Jason.'

After sharing a Grab to KK centre, he suggested we meet up for dinner.

'Sure I'll message you, we'll take you to the seafood market near the beach,' I replied.

'Sweet, sounds good, catch ya guys later!

Hostel in KK
12p.m.

The hostel was an upgrade from our last place in KK - simple, clean and with air-con included. Finally, a nice place that lived up to its online description.

Alex lay on the bed and curled his arm around my waist, pulling me down to his level. I'd embarrassed myself over such a petty thing that, at the time seemed important, now seemed so stupid.

'This is the closest we have come to a proper argument isn't it?' I admitted.

'Yes, I'm sorry for being grumpy at the airport,' he said quietly.

I was relieved to hear the words, the past few hours had been tense and unpleasant.

'I guess we both wanted the same things, but we were willing to go to different lengths to get them. You have a higher moral regard for rules, I'm not as good as you,' I said sheepishly playing with my hands. 'Alex, I'm so sorry. At the time it seemed so important and I was annoyed you didn't support me, but now it just seems silly. He probably was telling the truth and after all, it was only two pounds. It all seems so petty now, falling out over two pounds!'

'Yes, it's okay, you bend the rules far more than I do. Oh, but when you said "I told you so", that was so annoying,' Alex laughed.

'Haha, I know,' I giggled, 'but I was right about the water!'

'Right miss, that's it,' he said tickling my waist.

'Stop, stop! I'll buy us coconut milkshakes to call it quits!'

Afternoon

We walked around for a little bit in town and stopped off at a cute coffee house to escape the afternoon heat. The interior was decked out a little like a mountain cabin with wooden beams, tables and carpets to sit on. We sat upstairs on a little balcony that overlooked the entire café, nibbling on slices of chocolate ganache and passionfruit layer cake that Alex had treated us to.

I caught up on my journal while Alex wrote a few postcards. It was nice to have time to gather your own thoughts. *I do like travelling with Alex, but sometimes I think my stubborn mindset and temptation to bend the rules doesn't fit in with his calibrated moral compass. I know he is such a good person, he makes me slow down and appreciate things, but, I wonder if, when I am with him, I take the same risks and opportunities as I would on my own?*

Evening

That evening we met up with Jason and his Swiss friend. We patrolled the fish market looking for somewhere to eat. Jason named me the 'boss' because I had suggested the market, meaning every eager restaurant owner we passed was directed to me.

'She's the boss mate, don't look at me, ask her.'

'Madam, please.'

'Lady here.'

'Pretty lady.'

'Madam over here.'

'Girl, nice fish you like?'

I was bombarded by tens of owners shoving dead fish in my face and trying to place crabs in my hands.

'Cheers Jason,' I said giving him a sarcastic smile as he laughed behind.

Finally selecting our chef, we ordered two grouper, one steamed in ginger and the other fried in three flavours, with mixed garlic veggies, sweet ginger kalian and plain rice. It was a nice meal, sharing the food and chatting, or mostly laughing at Jason's outrageous stories.

When the bill arrived, everyone stopped laughing.

'188 ringgits!' Swiss exclaimed as he passed me the bill.

Things got a bit awkward. Everyone looked at me as I read through the bill. I looked at Alex. *Shit, I recommended this place because it was meant to be cheap.* I re-read the hand-written receipt, scanning it desperately, I tried to decipher how they had overcharged us. The vegetables and rice only cost a few ringgits and the fishes were larger so admittedly more expensive, but only a little. Then I spotted that Jason and Swiss had ordered calamari and tiger prawns, which on their own came to eighty ringgits!

'Oh guys, I'm sorry I've never ordered them before so I didn't know.'

'It's okay Cece, we'll pay for them separately and split the rest,' Jason said.

'Are you sure? We don't mind,' I replied.

'Yeah it's fine,' agreed Swiss, but he looked particularly miffed about the prawns.

'Hey mate,' Jason commented, 'maybe you could take a prawn shell back to your girlfriend instead of a postcard, it's worth a lot more!'

In search of a bar, we passed another food market to pick up dessert. We each bought a one-ringgit crispy pancake from a young man who worked like he was on speed; his hands moved so fast you could barely see them as he flipped each one. He poured batter over an enlarged cupcake pan, let them cook for a minute, folded and filled with kaya jam before wrapping in a little brown paper bag. I held mine preciously in my fingertips, nibbling away as the salty butter marked the brown paper. We all had one except Swiss, he couldn't stomach anymore food after devouring two twenty-five-ringgit prawns.

We continued to wander through KK's busy covered craft market, displaying exotic goods from ornate bags to dried seahorses. There was a particularly funny moment when, amongst the vendors shouting out prices, we heard a thirty-year-old British male's voice shouting.

'Mummy, Mummy where are you? Mummy? Mummy are you there?'

The incredibly posh accent combined with the language of a five-year-old was cruelly comic. We started to giggle shamefully and tried to pull a straight expression, all except for Jason who responded by mimicking the poor guy.

'Mummy, Mummy.'

'Jason!' I whispered sternly.

'Mummy dearest,' he carried on, 'ah man, British people sound so dumb.'

'You are British, Jason!'

'No, I'm Aussie.'

'You're a wannabe Aussie!'

'Shut up shorty,' he sassed back.

The night ended at a touristy bar before we headed our separate ways back to our hostels. We were flying the next day and the guys needed to be up early for a morning hike, so it was farewell for now. Jason was a funny but outrageous guy; I liked him and hoped our paths would cross again.

FIFTEEN

Just a girl in love with a boy on the rooftop of Kuala Lumpur.

29th August
Kuala Lumpur (KL)

We bought a KLIA Express card which took us smoothly into the city centre. From there we headed to our last hostel in Malaysia. Roadworks seemed to cover the few pavements giving us no choice but to walk along a tightrope of curb, trying not to fall off into the sea of bikes, beeping buses and angry taxis.

After the hot and heavy walk, we were pleasantly surprised to find a smiling hostel owner. He was smartly dressed in a black top and trousers, welcoming us in with a cool glass of lemongrass and brown sugar cordial. The building was very modern, with bare installations, a clean grey brick kitchen, huge rainfall showers and plants hanging down the sides of the walls, making the place seem like a hidden urban temple. With an edgy coffee shop and free movie theatre, this place was definitely worth the extra ringgits.

We completed the usual routine of contract signing, passport scanning and key deposits; before being taken to our room. Our names were chalked onto the blackboard door, '102, Welcome Charlotte and Alexander!'

'This place is so cute!' I whispered to Alex.

We both jumped onto the big white double bed, feeling satisfied we'd found a good place for the last few nights together.

Eager to make the most of the evening, we headed out to a food court in Chinatown and ordered plain rice, sticky garlic kailan and spring rolls. We shared our simple meal under a plastic tarpaulin, hidden from the evening thunderstorm and planned our next few days.

Afterwards we headed to a sky-high bar which was recommended to us by the hostel owner. Due to the metro's poor interconnectivity we decided to walk, using the opportunity to see the city. I stood in awe at my first glimpse of the Petronas Towers, they were so much grander than I had imagined. Gold and silver lights crowned the towers the king and queen of KL, with all the other skyscrapers cowering below as their humble subjects. Behind the towers we found a lake with hundreds of fountains and multicoloured lights. Huge jets of water were propelled into the air, leaping to the music, as droplets descended in all colours of the rainbow. It reminded me of my first night in Singapore with Marianne.

Entering the bar, a swimming pool glistened in the centre of the room, strobe lights flashed and ripples from the water's surface were projected onto the walls. Chart music blared from large speakers and groups of travellers, couples and sightseers clustered by the windows admiring the cityscape. Alex joined a queue of unimpressed guys to order drinks. Service was slow as it was ladies' night. They gave unlimited grapefruit cocktails (*probably just juice*) to women, meaning the staff were pretty preoccupied with the never-ending stream of women. Saving Alex from the fate of the other males, death by queuing, I took things into my own hands and ordered drinks from a waiter passing by who brought them right to our table. We sipped our lychee fizzes and made fun of girls pretending to be drunk on the grapefruit mocktail and flirt outrageously with other 'gap-yar' travellers.

'I just get annoyed,' Alex chimed up, 'when the guy at the bar is spending the whole time making free drinks for the girls in the low-cut dresses.'

'Aw, are you jealous Alex? Don't worry we'll get you a push-up bra next time!'

'Ha ha, very funny, I just don't see why it has to be only ladies' night?'

'Well I guess it's to encourage more girls to come, to make the bar more popular?'

'Yes, but why just the women? Everyone should get a free drink.'

'Then it defeats the point of ladies' night'

'And that is a bad thing because...?'

'Well perhaps they have a guys' night too? I just think it's a clever strategy to encourage more women into the bar, it makes it more accessible and welcoming for some.'

'More accessible, all they have to do is get in a lift and press number thirty-four!' Alex exclaimed.

'Okay I get your point, but if it works for the bar, it works. Speaking of gender equality, have some more of my free ladies drink!' I winked as we both burst into laughter.

Talking with Alex now made me realise he was my very best friend; no one knew me like he did. I couldn't understand how a few weeks ago I had even considered the surgeon as a good friend. Perhaps I was deluded by the freedom of travelling and seduced by the chance of new experiences, with new people that were far away from my world.

'Alex, when you were travelling last year, did you ever, I mean were you ever tempted?'

'What do you mean exactly?'

He looked at me, his eyes filled with intrigue and a little apprehension at the leading question.

'I mean, did you ever want to try a short travel fling, even if you didn't, did you ever think about it?'

'No,' he replied confidently, 'I'm not into that kind of thing, it's meaningless, and all I could think of was you. I just wanted them to be you. I won't deny that I saw other girls and could appreciate they were hot, but they just weren't you.'

I smiled gratefully.

'Why, what about you?'

'I think sometimes I miss you so much that I try and find people like you, but they never compare. I miss your friendship so much that I look for it in other people, and perhaps that means I get too close and guys get the wrong idea.'

Alex's forehead creased.

'But I only want you. Alex, I want you to know that I'll always have you in mind, wherever I go. And no matter how far away I am, I'll always come back to you,' I said squeezing his hand.

'I know, and I'll always be here for you. Come let's look at the view,' he said taking my hand.

I stood pressed against the cold glass with Alex behind me, his chin resting on my head. The top window was open, so I stuck my hands over the pane letting the air skim my cheeks. He put his arms around my waist and pressed his body into mine as our eyes followed the skyline in synchrony, jumping from light to light. I turned my head up to his and let our lips touch, the stubble on his upper lip brushed my skin as we kissed. In that moment I felt electric, as if I were a light shining brighter than any skyscraper in the city. I was just a girl in love with a boy on the rooftop of Kuala Lumpur, with the whole world to explore.

I know in life, time tarnishes even the strongest of lights, but I was content with being the brightest and happiest *that* night.

30th August

We woke for the first time in our new hostel. The light shone through the top window, illuminating the room. I shuffled back to Alex and he squeezed me tightly.

'Good morning Cece,' he whispered, kissing my shoulders, neck and cheeks.

'Morning,' I whispered back as I turned to face him.

His arms wrapped around my waist and he pulled me closer towards him. I kissed his lips softly and smiled. 'It's adventure time!'

Breakfast was laid out in the open courtyard: a big tray of pineapple and frozen watermelon, with freshly baked roti. We ate as we chatted about our plans for the day.

10a.m.

The world's largest aviary was first on our list.[5] It was clear when we arrived how it had earned its title. Giant nets were hung above towering rainforest tree-tops, covering tens of smaller netted aviaries filled with an emporium of birds: parrots, egrets, peacocks and cranes to name a few. Our main goal, however, was to find the hornbills; our new favourite bird since the river cruise. We found the oriental pied hornbill and the great hornbill, but no sign of the rhinoceros hornbill.

They were impressive birds, elegantly carrying their huge beaks as if they were fascinators at Ascot's Ladies' Day. Coming to the end of the aviary, I was desperate to see a close-up of the emblem of Borneo, the rhinoceros hornbill. I asked the cleaners, café staff and gardeners but with little success. On the fourth time of asking, I noticed Alex filming and giggling at me.

'What's so funny? Don't you want to see the epic bird?'

'Hehe I'm sorry, this is just so funny.' Mimicking my voice he exclaimed, 'We've seen the pied and the great but I want to see the rhinoceros hornbill,' his lips curled into a cheeky smile, 'I never saw you as an ornithologist Miss Clark.'

To be fair, the women I was asking could barely tell me what Magnum flavours were on offer, let alone anything about bird species.

'Well,' I replied defensively, 'I thought they might know, it's such a famous bird.'

'Yes, but not everyone knows the Latin names!'

---

[5] *Technically, Kuala Lumpur Bird Park has the title of 'The World's Largest Free Flight Walk-in Aviary', but I thought that that was a bit much to put in one sentence!*

I playfully pushed his arm, 'Urgh you've changed me, I'm now Cece the Borneo adventurer and hornbill spotter.'

'Well lead on Miss Hornbill Explorer, lead on!'

Pretty certain they didn't have the bird, we continued to look anyway, pretending we were in an episode of Planet Earth, *searching for the rare rhinoceros hornbill, in its natural habitat.*

Afternoon

Central market: a large container building filled with smaller market stalls, selling Malaysian pottery, durian chocolate, smoothies, batik paintings and traditional masks. Within one of the batik stalls, I spotted a stack of blank canvases.

'Look it's only fifteen ringgits for a small one, do you fancy it? I haven't painted since school but it's really fun!'

'Yeah, why not, let's do it!'

As Malaysia was the first place both of us had seen a clown fish in the wild, we chose an empty canvas with Nemo's outline. It was therapeutic to mix the paint and watch the ink spread onto the silk, like dye running into a river. We spent about an hour and a half carefully colouring our canvases, seeing who could get the best shade of coral.

8p.m.

We tried an amazing eatery for Laksa this evening. The restaurant was recommended to Alex by a local on his outbound flight. We had trouble finding the place, until we realised Alex had been pronouncing it wrong the whole time - it was 'Madam Kwan's' rather than 'Mumma Kong's'!

31st August

We savored our final morning in KL, slowly getting ready and munching on toast with thick layers of kaya and butter, before heading to the Batu Caves.

It was a public holiday so the place was packed, jam packed. People were coming and going in every direction, pushing and shoving, screaming and shouting, sitting on the muddy floor eating with their hands and then discarding the rubbish right beside them. You could almost say the place was polluted with people. Inside the cave wasn't any better, loud music shaking the stalactites, tacky religious relics on sale and macaques bouncing off the sides of the rock - terrorizing anyone with food in their hands. That said, there was beauty if you searched for it. Sequined saris glittered in the sun as visitors climbed the 273 rainbow painted steps to reach the mighty golden Buddha at the top. Still, it wasn't what I'd describe as a holy place.

To cool down after the hot and busy cave visit, we found the best place for ice cream in a shopping centre below the Petronas Towers. We each had a scoop of their specialty - *Coconut Ash*. A black flecked grey ice cream with a rich caramel flavour and a hint of vanilla, *amazing!*

Evening

To finish off our visit in KL we headed to the Heli Lounge bar, an exposed helicopter pad that turned into a rooftop bar with a live band at night. Waiters waltzed around in pilot's uniforms, carrying strong cocktails on silver trays. We chatted as the sunset cast ruby shadows throughout the sky. One-by-one, as darkness fell, each skyscraper's twinkling lights were illuminated. It was beautiful to watch, but neither of us wanted the sun to set on KL, for we knew that it would be our last sunset in Malaysia - our last sunset together for a while.

SIXTEEN

Turn around, one last time.

1st September
Morning

Warm and lying next to Alex, I became conscious. For a blissful moment I was unaware of time, unaware that in a few hours we would be separated between two continents once again.

5:30a.m.

Peace ended as the alarm blared out like an evacuation siren. I pulled his arms tighter around me, my sleepy eyes opened and stared into his. I willed him to stay, for the clocks to turn back, for the alarm to stop and to give us one more day. Without a word being said I knew he felt the same, he held me close, squeezing my hand and kissing my forehead lightly.

'I don't want to get up, I want to stay with you,' Alex whispered.

'Then stay, you have a flight to Tokyo, we booked it together last year before you got your new job. Just come with a me,' I replied softly.

I knew this ask was impossible, he had to return to work. For a long time now we had known it would be a two-week trip, no more. Those two weeks were up.

The sun was yet to shed its light on KL, the city was dull with only the glow of yellow streetlamps illuminating the roads. We had walked down this route so many times in the past few days, hand in hand, smiling and laughing, still freely enjoying the few days that time had granted us. Now we walked for the last time, silently, only our fingertips touching.

7a.m.

We arrived at the airport, a vast space of shiny floors, flashy stands and cafés containing sleep deprived passengers slowly sipping coffee. Eventually, our slow walk came to a standstill, neither of us wanted to step any closer. In my mind I was pulling Alex's hand back, like a child not wanting to go to school.

Alex started, 'I've had an amazing time Cece.' I hugged him tight, burying my head into his shoulder I didn't want to hear what he was about to say because I knew this was goodbye. 'It won't be long until we see each other again.'

'I know,' I replied quietly.

'You'll have an great time in Japan.'

Our lips touched one last time, before our bodies, hands and last of all fingertips separated as he walked towards check-in.

'I love you, Alex,' I whispered.

'I love you too, Cece,' he called back before turning.

I tensed my whole body and held my breath, it was painful. I felt like I was losing control. *I should be with him; I should be with him boarding the plane.* A wave of panic hit me as he disappeared down the escalator.

'Look back, look back, turn around, Alex let me see your face one more time. Turn your head to look back at me,' I whispered.

He continued down, soon to disappear. I stood on my tiptoes to see him turn, willing him to turn around one last time, I needed to see him smile one last time. But he didn't.

I wandered slowly, hoping that at some point he'd run back and tap me on the shoulder. My mind became empty and numb. My flight was in the other terminal but I couldn't bring myself to leave the building. I wanted to be in the same place, to share the same ground as him. I dropped my rucksack and sat slumped in a corner near the entrance. Every minute I was there was a minute that he could return, return and join me in Japan.

Just in case the plane hadn't taken off, I waited an extra twenty minutes after his departure. I then stood up to leave but waited another ten, so I knew for sure he'd be in the air. The building now seemed very empty, filled with people I didn't know, people that weren't Alex. He wasn't coming back; he was returning to London.

And just like that, I was alone again.

PART TWO

Japan

SEVENTEEN

The toilets had more buttons than my phone.

3rd September *(Flashforward)*
Tokyo

I'm sitting in the hostel lobby in Kawasaki, Tokyo. I am weak from a CVS attack and feel pretty low. Everything is new, it's overwhelming. I just got the hang of Malaysia, I knew the people, the language, the food and had just about mastered the travel. Japan is so different, I have to start all over again. I have to figure it all out by myself, but I'm so tired. I miss my adventure partner Alex, I miss my family and I miss my grandma. Every time I think of her I want to cry and have to focus really hard not to let tears well up in my eyes, a) because I'm in a public place and mainly b) because my eyes hurt. I've cried too much already over the past twenty-four hours.

2nd September *(Very very early...still 1st September in Malaysian time)*

Making it through the seven-hour flight, I arrived in Tokyo: a brightly lit city with a travel system that looks like the neural pathways of the brain. It's impressive to say the least, but I had no idea how to understand it. Luckily a kind assistant helped me buy a ticket to get to the correct station.

Walking through the streets at midnight I felt surprisingly awake, adrenaline counteracting amitriptyline's drowsy effects. I was alone so needed to be alert, it was time to return to the confident Cece I was at the start of the trip, a lone adventurer once again. My eyes lit up when I read the painted black letters on the side of a tall building, 'Kawasaki Hostel' - *made it*.

The hostel seemed more like a hotel from its clean and modern lobby. The receptionist handed me a metal ring with six keys on it.

'Haha, am I breaking into a bank?' I joked.

She replied staccato, 'Key for room, lift, locker, showers, floor and bathroom floor,' before gesturing to the door.

Needless to say, she didn't get my joke.

I was staying in a capsule room, basically a large shelf with a curtain separating my bed from the rest of the world. It featured a mattress, light, Wi-Fi and plugs. Sounds basic but it was the nicest shelf I have ever slept on (the added privacy of the curtain was a luxury). I wasn't sure if the bathroom was a washroom or a spa. I entered to find a long mirror with movie star lights, hairdryers, clean showers, plush white towels, slippers and fancy gels and hair soaps smelling of orange blossom and citrus. The toilets looked like they belonged in a spaceship. It had more buttons than my mobile phone. I sat on it nervously, the seat was warm, presumably from a button I had accidentally pressed. I stood up again as it started to hum, uncertain whether it was going to shoot water out of the basin or send me up to space. After five minutes I found the only necessary button, the flush. Eventually my head collapsed onto the fresh white bedding and, at 2a.m., I fell asleep.

What everyone else considers to be the morning

The alarm woke me at quarter to nine, the latest lie-in I could allow myself considering I was meeting my paternal grandparents' old-time friend, Nanami, at ten. They had met her thirty years ago when they lived in Tokyo for my grandfather's work. She had been a good friend, introducing them to new friendship groups and helping them get settled in a new country. When my grandparents returned to the UK, they had kept in touch by the odd email and phone call. So, when my grandparents heard I was to visit the city, they instantly reached out to her to show me around.

Lifting my body up slowly, *gosh I was exhausted*, I felt a slight pain in my stomach which I put down to tiredness. I got ready quickly, trying to look as presentable as I could from my backpacker wardrobe.

Entering reception, I saw an elderly, petite and very well-kept lady in smart grey trousers and a blue floaty top. She sat bolt upright and wore a purply red lipstick which contrasted with her serious pale face. As I approached, a smile warmed her face, she seemed pleased and eager to meet me as she gestured to the seat beside her. Her English was broken but we could just about get by; I felt ignorant only being able to say 'thank you' in Japanese.

Nanami was keen to show me many places, we started the day visiting the busiest crossing in the world, Shibuya Crossing. From a cosy window in Starbucks, we observed hundreds of people scamper over the zebra crossing like ants with shopping bags. Soon after, we hopped on a metro to the Meiji Jingu Shrine. A beautiful wooden torii gate symbolised the entrance to a green woodland park which housed the temple. We bowed to enter and then used sacred water to wash our hands and lips with a special wooden spoon.

'The left first, then the right, the lips and then wash the spoon handle for the next person,' Nanami explained.

It was nice to experience these Japanese traditions firsthand.

Walking back from the shrine, my energy levels were running low. I had a bite of my apple but immediately the pain in my stomach rocketed, it was a CVS attack. *Noooo, why CVS, why? This is such a nice day, why do you have to ruin it? Oh shit, I have no paracetamol with me.* I tried to explain to Nanami that I was ill and needed paracetamol. However, visiting a pharmacy, I learnt that paracetamol (or at least the name) didn't seem to exist in Japan. I put on a smile and tried to continue the sightseeing, but the pain got worse. The metro shook us from side to side, aggravating my swollen tummy. I leant forward to try and ease the pain, but nausea took its place. As we walked up the steps into the street, the pain became unbearable, I could barely stand and my face had turned grey.

'I'm sorry Nanami, I need to go back to the hostel to lie down, I am unwell.'

'Oh, Charlotte, okay, you need help?'

'I'll be okay, I just need to lie down, thank you.'

Before leaving me at the hostel, she squeezed my arm and handed me a paper bag with some plain traditional Japanese cakes inside.

'For when you feel well,' she said with a little smile.

I felt bad for cutting the day short, she had been so kind to me.

Back on my private shelf

I collapsed into my little capsule; I was relieved to be back but so sad that the day was ruined. I rang my dad in tears.

'It's such a waste to be in a new place and spend it inside in the dark,' I wailed.

'You're doing really well C, but you could probably do with incorporating a rest day into each week. Hang on in there,' he comforted.

I agreed; my body couldn't keep up with me. I lay down deflated. I missed Alex, I was in pain and I couldn't keep grief out of my mind. I wanted to go home.

3rd September

I stayed at the hostel, *what a poor start to a city that has so much to offer.*

EIGHTEEN

I felt we really understood each other; and for a moment, I felt at peace.

4ᵗʰ September
Tokyo sightseeing round two

I agreed to meet with Nanami again at 10a.m. She was waiting there like before, a sweet lady studying her tablet, sat bolt upright, immaculate hair, make-up and clothing. *She was post-sixty goals.* She greeted me with a warm smile and gestured for me to take a seat. Concern spread across her face when she asked me how I was.

'We get medication today, it Tuesday, pharmacy open,' she said confidently.

'Aw thank you but I am fine now, I'm okay.'

'You still sick?'

'No, I am okay, I rested, thank you.'

'You okay? Ah good. Very good. So today, what would you like to do?'

'I'd love to see a market and maybe exchange my rail pass if we have time?'

'Yes, very good, but first I show you typhoon.'

When she pulled out her tablet, I realised this wasn't a Tokyo attraction. Her face turned somber as she started describing the weather that would sweep across the city over the next few days.

'You must be careful Charlotte, stay inside,' she implored.

If I had known what was about to happen to this country in September, I would have felt the same anxiety, but at the time I nonchalantly agreed, 'Oh yes, I will.'

JR Station

I was relieved to get this bit of travel admin out of the way as I handed over my rail pass receipt.

'Arigato, passport miss,' the ticket officer asked.

'Yes, I will just get it.'

I unzipped the plastic bag where all my valuables were kept and reached around for the maroon booklet. My fingers flicked between a Kinabalu mountain pass, orangutan sanctuary tickets, flight reservations but found no passport. The officer looked at me indifferently, ignoring the mild panic in my eyes. After another thirty seconds of awkward fumbling in my bag, a wave of panic hit me. *Oh fudge, my passport was in the top pocket of my small blue rucksack. I must have left it there after my 2a.m. arrival and forgotten to put it back.*

'Nanami I'm really sorry, my passport is in the hostel.'

'You have no passport? Oh, you need passport,' she replied.

'I know, it's in the hostel, I'm so sorry to have dragged us all the way here.'

'You lost your passport?'

'No, it's in the hostel, I think I need to get it to get the rail card.'

'Okay we go get it. But first, sightseeing!' she said with a cheeky smile, unfazed by my act of carelessness. 'You buy day ticket for train now, then rail pass later, okay?'

We headed to the famous Tsukiji Market. The actual market, I later found out, was only open between 3a.m. - 6a.m. for industrial buyers, so we visited a local one nearby. The markets were different to the ones in Malaysia, less hectic, cleaner and I didn't feel like I was pressured to buy everything I passed; the floor also wasn't covered in fish spray which was a bonus. We passed stalls of pickled veg, wasabi plants that looked vaguely like premature pineapples, chopsticks, Japanese porcelain, sweet omelet blocks and bean paste cakes. In Borneo, I would have bought several items just out of curiosity, but here, things were much more expensive; a look was all a traveller could afford.

Lunch

I just tried authentic sushi!

The sushi restaurant was hidden in a side alley adjacent to the market. The chefs and waiters cheered, 'Irasshaimase' as we entered and were ushered to our seats. Each place was equipped with some chopsticks, a wet towel, ginger box, soy sauce, a little white dish and a mug of green tea. Shortly after seating, a bowl of miso soup was placed in front of us. Feeling a little like I was in a chemistry lab, I turned to Nanami to mirror her actions. When the menu arrived, she proudly exclaimed that she would pay.

'You have whatever you like,' she smiled.

'Oh, please I would like to get you this, for showing me around!' I said enthusiastically.

'Please, you are a guest in my country.'

'Well thank you, that is very generous of you,' I gratefully replied.

Nanami smiled looking content.

Watching the chef craft each piece was amazing, his hands moved so quickly, rolling balls of rice, dashing wasabi and placing the fish so perfectly, all in about thirty seconds. It was sushi sleight of hand. Two charcoal boards were laid in front of us, dotted with perfect clusters of rice, covered with raw tuna, squid, scallop, shrimp, salmon caviar and sea urchin. The thought of eating slimy squid and little liquid fish eggs made me feel a bit nauseous, but I was in Japan, I had to try it. The caviar tasted surprisingly like salmon, but the sensation of biting the small translucent balls which squirted out fishy juices was a bit off-putting. The tuna had a fruity flavour, a little like mango, and the sea urchin had the most peculiar taste, its sponge-like texture melted in your mouth, capturing the flavour of the ocean in such a delicate way. It was strange to be eating something that I was swimming over just a few weeks ago in KK.

Afternoon

We walked around the classy shopping streets of Ginza before heading to Yokohama, the previous home of my grandparents. I wondered if they ever imagined that, thirty years later, their granddaughter would walk in their footsteps here?

Over coffee, I learnt that Nanami loved to travel. She was eager to show me lots of pictures of all the places she had been to and it was quite inspiring that she was still so adventurous at her age.

'Have you always travelled, Nanami?'

'No. I worked a lot then, when I sixty, I retire and then I free,' she said with a wide smile, 'but, you see, five years ago I had breast cancer, then, when I was cured, I said to myself: I will live every day with no regret,' she said proudly.

'I couldn't agree more,' I smiled admiringly.

'I go to Canada, October.'

'Wow that's great, I want to visit there too at some point!'

'Yes, my mother wanted to go, but she died, so I go for her.'

'Oh, I'm so sorry Nanami. I know how you feel.'

'Yes, you lose someone?' she replied.

'My grandma. When she died in August, I wasn't there, because I was here, travelling. I found it very hard leaving home because, I knew that it may be the last time I would see her. Before I departed, I read her a book about Japan, she loved it, said it was beautiful. I promised her I would travel here for her.'

'And that, you must do,' said Nanami.

Despite the language barrier, I felt we really understood each other and for a moment, I felt at peace.

Nanami had been so kind to me during my visit to Tokyo, I was a little sad to say goodbye at the station. We agreed to keep in touch via email for the rest of my trip in Japan.

Evening

On the way back to the hostel, considering it was my last night in Tokyo, I thought I should try and find a ramen shop for dinner. After half an hour of circling the same shopping centre, I eventually found five ramen shops in the basement. With crazy cartoons of chickens' and cows' heads poking out of the bowl, I figured this was not a place for vegetarians. When I tried to communicate that I just wanted vegetables, they looked at me as if I were the plague.

Determined not to give in, I decided to just order something. A chirpy girl pointed to a vending machine outside the restaurant. *Hmm, a slot machine? What is this, match three wasabis and you win?* She repeated the word 'vegetable' and gestured to my purse and then to the machine. *Oh, you insert money, push the button for the dish you want, and the machine takes your order. Wow, I should have researched this beforehand!*

Not long after I'd sat down, a huge bowl of steaming noodles and salty veg arrived, it tasted pretty good. *Success!*

*Oh wait, hang on, what is that...*I dropped my chopsticks as a large purple tentacle emerged from the depths of the bowl. I prodded the coiled thing bobbing in the broth, a little terrified I'd find a whole octopus underneath the pak choi. Fortunately, it was just tentacle soup. I fished around for the rest of the suckers and lined them up on the rim of the bowl, making it look like an octopus was about to engulf the entire thing from beneath. *I don't think the waitress was impressed.*

5th September
5a.m.

I planned to get the early train, so I'd arrive in Sapporo early afternoon, giving me lots of time to relax and make the journey stress free.

The Shinkansen

First bullet train experience! The train was like a first-class airplane, the seats were spacious, leg room was excessive, every centimeter of the carriage was clean and the train ran smoothly. Despite the lack of conversation from the tired looking businessman sitting next to me, it was a pleasant journey.

Arriving into Hakodate, I rushed to make sure I caught my next connection. Getting to the gate, a guard shook his head when I showed him my ticket.

'This train is cancelled, next one 19:00.'

'Oh, seven this evening?'

'Yes seven, typhoon, cause delay,' he replied sternly.

That was nine hours away! My super early start was for nothing, fab. Talk about a bullet train being fast!

Googling the typhoon Nanami had warned me about earlier, I was horrified. Six people had been killed. I kept scrolling, looking at photos of giant waves, broken cars and ships crushed into bridges. It was the worst typhoon in twenty-five years. *This is horrendous, now I feel bad for complaining about the minor delays.*

Feeling very grateful not to be in the thick of the storm, I tried to look at things positively and turn the day into a spontaneous trip to Hakodate. I walked around a few shops and fancy supermarkets, looking at the displays. Chocolate covered crinkle crisps made me smile as I thought of my mum, her two favourite things in one.

Bored of dawdling around the touristy hub, I headed for the hills. After a while navigating side streets, I made it to the foot of the trail up to Mount Hakodate and set my sights for the top. It was a nice route, mostly covered by dense woodland made up of tall elegant trees. I was also relieved not to encounter any pit vipers, which Alex later told me were incredibly deadly. Following a solid uphill stint for fifty minutes, I reached the summit. The view was beautiful, a crowded industrial island, riddled with buildings and factories, backed by mountain silhouettes and a never-ending stretch of ocean.

Evening

Waiting at the train station, I must have looked a sorry state; crumpled on the floor with only my huge rucksack for company. While I was munching on my onigiri (sushi sandwich triangles), a kind old man turned to me and asked in broken English where I was from. We had quite a good little conversation, with the help of my translator app. They were from Yokohama and were going on holiday to Hokkaido. They planned to rent a car and visit the islands. The old man looked adorable trying to form English sentences. He would pause and screw up his face, like he was trying to crack a really difficult crossword puzzle, before saying each word. They reminded me of my grandparents a little, perhaps my grandma sent them to keep me company whilst I was waiting for the train.

'Ha goo trip,' the old man said.

'Thank you, and you too, it was lovely to meet you, sayonara!' I replied.

Late into the night the train sped, onwards to Sapporo.

NINETEEN

Shaking – for all I knew it was a dream.

6ᵗʰ September
Hostel in Sapporo
3:08a.m.

Shaking. Everything was shaking. The sides of the bed, people's bags, the walls and even the floor. Disorientated and exhausted from the twenty-hour journey, I had no idea what was going on. For all I knew it was a dream. I shut my eyes in panic and shuffled to the corner of the bed, making myself as small as possible. *Please stop shaking*.

9a.m.

I woke-up tired and confused from last night's bizarre dream. I attempted a little yoga, cramped between two empty bunk beds, before checking the messages on my phone. The internet was playing up so, instead, I headed downstairs to do some travel planning for the next few days, whilst munching a slice of white bread with the hostel's apricot jam. It was terribly dark considering it was morning. Looking for the light switch, I noticed a big white sign in Japanese with an English translation scrawled hastily beneath, *'Chitose airport closed, JR trains cancelled'*.

'I know, it's bad isn't it?' the hostel manager commented as I stared at the sign, 'I've lived here for twenty-five years, and never experienced an earthquake like this.'

'So, it was an earthquake last night then?' I asked.

'Yes, and a big one, it had a size of almost seven. Power is out pretty much everywhere on the island.'

'When do you think the power will come back on?'

'Who knows, a few hours, a day, a week, no one knows.'

'Oh okay, so what about transport in the city?'

'None, no one can leave or get here.'

'Ah, okay,' I said with a weak smile.

Well, I guess this day is a write-off then Cece, perhaps a 'research and clothes washing day' instead.

'How much to use the washing machine?' I asked.

The manager looked at me blankly.

'To wash my clothes I mean,' I clarified.

'Yes, I got that. It's two hundred yen.'

'Okay can I use it please?'

The manager continued to stare at me, 'Would that be okay?' I added softly.

'It needs electricity. We are in a blackout,' he said dryly.

'Oh my gosh, yes of course, sorry, how stupid of me.'

With no Wi-Fi for travel research, I spent the majority of the day in a little park nearby, not wanting to stray too far from the hostel in case anything else happened. The city was completely dead, shops closed and cafés shut, all apart from the corner supermarkets which were being panic raided by everyone. Each Seven Eleven had a long queue outside and, by midday, completely empty shelves. Luckily, I managed to buy some plantain chips and a punnet of plums, which I rationed throughout the day.

I tried to keep myself busy, walking around a small pond, reading and allowing myself to look at my phone in snippets to conserve the battery. After a while though, I just felt homesick. I felt alone and a little scared. I didn't know how long we'd be without power or for how long I'd be stuck here. *If only Alex was with me, things would be a lot better.*

I headed back to the hostel at five, while there was still natural light. A few other guests were sat at the table in the dark, no one was talking, or making eye contact. The scrape of my chair cut the awkward silence as I joined the table. The solemn atmosphere was lifted slightly when the kind hostel owner brought out a hot cup of miso soup, a little bowl of pasta and a few candles for each person. I tried to make conversation with the Japanese girl in front of me. She was shy but we had a little chat, she worked in a jam shop in the middle of the island and was visiting Sapporo for a work trip. I explained I was a maths teacher but travelling for an extended break; she nodded convincingly but I don't think she really understood. The room returned to silence shortly after dinner, so I headed back to my bunk. I desperately wanted to ring Alex or home, but instead put my phone on ultra-power saving mode just in case I needed it more during the night.

I went to sleep hoping the power would return to Hokkaido the next morning.

TWENTY

It was the best thing I did in Japan.

7th September

I woke to find a green light flashing from my phone charger – the power was back on! I ran downstairs to ask the owner how the city was doing.

'It's a good sign, transport will probably get sorted soon,' he confirmed.

I heard the word *'transport'* and *'soon'* and interpreted that as *'you can leave the city'*. I guessed that, as Japan was known for its efficiency, by the time I had walked to the station, the trains would have started working again. I packed my things and left. I felt very lonely at the hostel and didn't want to stay any longer than I had to. I took some bread and a small pastry from breakfast, wrapped them in tissue and slid them into my rucksack; I wasn't sure when I would get a chance to buy food again. It was a three-kilometer trudge to the station, which would normally be fine, but when you are carrying over half your bodyweight it feels more like thirty kilometres.

The long lines of people outside the station were a promising sign. My body ached from the twenty-five kilos on my back but I kept going, I would soon be on a carriage sailing away from this place. I turned the corner, ticket in hand, to find all the barriers were closed. Strips of tape were spread across every gate and several guards stood ominously blocking the way. *Okay, so maybe the trains aren't ready but the buses must be working!* I walked back towards the huge queue I'd passed earlier, assuming it was for the bus.

'*Bus no work, cancelled*' a hand-made sign read. The bus terminal was desolate, the queue had been for the taxi rank.

I tried to ask for help but I was turned away with shaking heads and dismissive hand gestures. 'No English, no' and 'you no move' were the only replies I received. Eventually, a nice couple tried to help, they spoke to an information officer but the only knowledge we gained was 'no train, no bus, no travel. Power cut earthquake, no leave Sapporo, girl.'

Doubt started to sink in, I'd just walked three kilometres with all my belongings, I'd left the hostel, and I was completely alone. Even if I returned, my place for the night would be taken. I had nowhere to go.

I returned to the station and finally relieved myself of the rucksack, collapsing next to it in a heap. I used my phone to search for hostels, planes or buses but everything was fully booked or unavailable. *Why couldn't Alex have come with me? Everything would be fine if he was here, we could figure it out together.* After an hour of sitting there, trying not to break down in tears, a pair of Japanese girls approached me. I looked up relieved, *they were coming to be my friends, I'll no longer be alone, perhaps they live nearby and will adopt me for the week.* They handed me a piece of cardboard to sit on and walked off.

'Arigato,' I whispered - my only hope of friendship crushed.

I sat on my strip of cardboard and read the latest news: the death toll had risen; the quake had claimed more victims. Aftershocks were also predicted to happen in the next forty-eight hours. Silent tears began to trickle down my cheeks as panic rose inside me. *What if I become one of these victims? I have nowhere to go. I'll be stuck in this train station when the quake happens and be crushed. No one will even know who I am because I'm completely alone.*

One hour later

A taller Italian guy sat down next to me, disheartened. I wasn't sure when I'd get a chance to communicate in English again, so wiped away my tears and tried to steady my voice.

'Are you stuck too?'

'Yeah, trains are fucked, I'm here on business. I'm waiting for a colleague to arrange my transport out of here. You?'

'I'm travelling through Japan but with the typhoon and then the earthquake, it's not going so well. At least we weren't in the epi-center!' I jested weakly.

We chatted for a while and planned to walk back through town to see if anything was going on. We'd both been at the station for several hours and there are only so many times a person can hear the tannoy declare 'we are sorry to announce; all transport is cancelled in Hokkaido.'

Not far from the station we were stopped by a perky Japanese lady,

'You okay? You hungry?' she asked. I explained our situation and she replied with a smile, 'Okay, you come wi me. I have friend who gi food.'

We gratefully accepted and turned the corner to find a neat little BBQ on the back of a van and several locals serving plates of rice, pickles, omelets and meats.

'All free food, for earthquake,' she exclaimed.

'Wow thank you,' I replied as I was handed a huge plate of rice and seaweed, 'you are so kind.'

'We all volunteers, and hotel next us, help by washing,' she smiled.

I sat watching these amazing people for a while and suddenly thought instead of searching for a hostel that doesn't exist, why don't I help them and actually use my time for good? So, I left my bags in the hotel lobby and offered my hands. It was hard at first, trying to work out what they wanted me to do with the language barrier, but I soon got the hang of it, tidying away plates, clearing chopsticks and plating-up meals. Never before have I said the word 'sausage' so many times in an hour! People came up to me speaking in Japanese, assuming I was a local and asking how long I had lived in Sapporo. When I explained I was just travelling they seemed so surprised that I'd given up my time to help. The only way I could reply was by asking 'why should I not? I have nothing to do so I might as well help out!'

I served Aaron, from Switzerland, about an hour into my shift. He was also travelling and currently staying in an earthquake shelter. He offered to take me there after I had finished serving. I accepted, feeling so much better knowing I would have a friend and a place to stay for the night.

It was amazing, having a purpose, joining a team, helping people and returning the kindness they had showed me. Despite the earthquake, people still worked together and selflessly gave up their time to help others, even if it meant they went hungry themselves. It was inspiring and I wanted to be a part of it. It was the best thing I had done all trip. When Aaron returned to take me back to the shelter, everyone stood up and clapped as I walked away with my big rucksack. I cheered back as enthusiastically as I could. They were all amazing people and I was so thankful to have been a part of their team. The food shelter had saved hundreds from going hungry, saved me mentally, and proved that whatever mother nature throws at our world, we can survive it together.

The shelter

I laid out my yoga mat next to Aaron's and ate one of my ration rice balls. We started chatting about our travel plans for Japan.

'Well, I've come here to hike,' he said

'Me too!' I jumped in.

'Really? Well I'm planning to get to Asahidake tomorrow, then head to Daisetsuzan National Park the day after, you can join if you like?'

'Wow, I'd join you but I have no sleeping bag or any camping gear.'

He got out a large map of the area, pointing to a few places.

'Here there are shelters. They say emergency shelter, but I guess we could use them. Do you have a bear bell?' he asked.

'Um no.'

'Cooking gear?'

'Erm, no.'

'Okay, what about food or gas?'

'Sorry, I'm not prepared at all, I didn't intend to do any overnight hiking.'

'No worries, okay well I have these,' he said pulling out various items from his rucksack, 'a canister of gas, cooking equipment, one kilogram of rice, tinned food and various other power bars. That might be enough for us.'

'Oh, wait I have some oats we could use for breakfast!' I said as I proudly pulled out six sachets, 'Enough for one each.'

'Okay great, if we pick up a few bits I think we could do this. Tomorrow we'll see what the trains are like and go from there. Are you in?'

This question threw me into two minds. One part of me desperately wanted to go, it was an adventure, a chance to leave Sapporo and explore the beautiful national parks. The other half screamed at me not to go. *There will be bears, you'll probably get ill and freeze to death because you haven't got the right gear. Oh, and what if another aftershock happens when you are halfway up a mountain? There will be no one to help you up there!* But I didn't want to face the earthquake alone, this was my chance to escape with a friend. My only chance, so I took it; despite ninety-nine percent of me feeling like it was the wrong decision.

'Okay, I'm in,' I said as we shook hands.

TWENTY-ONE

Orange jelly.

9ᵗʰ September *(Flashforward)*

Travelling with a chronic illness is hard but travelling alone with a chronic illness is brutally tough.

If you make a friend, they aren't going to stick around until you recover and you certainly can't make friends if you are bed-bound. You become a deadweight. I guess many of you reading this are expecting me to overcome my body's shortfalls and just soldier on. Well this is the reality when you have a chronic illness: you miss out. End of. The moment you try and forget your illness, your body reminds you that you can't keep up with everyone else. No matter how strong your mind is, your body will always let you down.

I'm writing this chapter from the bottom bunk of a deserted hostel room in Asahikawa *(a two-hour bus ride north-east of Sapporo)*, tummy swollen from cramps, eyes sore from crying and morale at zero.

7ᵗʰ September
10:30p.m.

It didn't take long to fall asleep after helping at the food shelter, so I was alarmed when I woke up only an hour later. The whole building was shaking. Delirious with tiredness, I thought I was still at the train station. It was like I was lying on the yellow line in the London Underground, the one that you're not meant to cross to avoid being sucked under and flattened by the next passing tube. I closed my eyes and prayed the building wouldn't fall down, I longed to be back home where the ground was still.

8th September
6:50a.m.

I woke, stirred by the sound of Aaron packing his things away. I peeled back the Buff covering my eyes to see very few people left in the shelter.

'Good morning, did you feel the earthquake again last night?' Aaron asked.

'Yes it was huge, I felt like we were lying on the train tracks!'

'I know, it was crazy, the whole building was shaking.'

'This is really scary. They say quakes can happen up to a week afterwards, do you think we'll be okay going to the mountains?' I asked tentatively.

'We're basically treading on eggshells if we don't get out of Sapporo today. As long as we move further away from the epi-centre, we should be okay. You're still good for the hike, right?'

Yes, I'm up for sharing a sleeping bag with a guy I don't really know, risk being eaten by bears, snakes and hornets and experience the whole mountain shaking as the earthquake strikes again.

'Yes, for sure, I'm in.'

We packed our things, filled up our water bottles with the remaining ration water and headed off to the station. I felt a little strange but put it down to the fatigue and general earthquake experience. At the station, few trains were running so we took a bus to Asahikawa, and from there discussed our game plan.

'So you don't have a sleeping bag?' Aaron asked.

'Only a yoga mat.'

'Warm clothes?'

'Well, I have leggings and long-sleeved items I can double up.'

'A thick jacket?' he inquired, dubiously rubbing his fingers over my paper-thin North Face.

136

'I have a fleece?'

His eyes looked me up from top to bottom as if he were interviewing me.

'But I can just wear all the clothes I own if need be,' I quickly added.

'Okay, a blanket?'

'I have a towel,' I said while rummaging around trying to find it.

'A towel, okay I guess that will have to do. Is it in there?' he asked.

'Urgh, where is it?' I muttered to myself. Emptying my whole rucksack to find no towel, it suddenly dawned on me that I must have left it in Sapporo after the rush to leave, 'Fudge.'

'Okay,' Aaron said trying not to judge, 'I have a silver foil blanket, they can be pretty warm to sleep in.'

I laughed, 'Survival blanket? If you say so, I guess I have nothing else!'

What an earth are you doing Cece? You've known this guy for less than twelve hours! Yes, he looks prepared with his bear bell and camping gear but he suggests you stay in an emergency hut halfway up the mountain - you'll freeze!

As I clipped my rucksack around my waist, the pain in my stomach became stronger. *It can't be CVS, I literally had it less than a week ago.* Despite the danger, I desperately wanted to go on this adventure, so ignored my body and carried on. *Perhaps if I don't think about the pain, it'll go away.*

Expedition prep

We toured the supermarkets at the station, trying to find some substantial mountain snacks to bulk up our food supply. We spent half the time picking up packages, weighing them with our hands to feel which ones had more energy.

'No wonder Japanese people are so slim; all their biscuits are as light as air!' Aaron joked.

'Haha, true, it's mad, how can a packet of biscuits be so light? The main ingredient must be air!'

Just after we purchased the densest crackers we could find, Aaron darted off and returned with rye bread and Swiss chocolate in hand.

'Western food! And that is why Europeans are so fat,' he said handing me the goodies, 'feel the weight of this!'

'Ah that's perfect, I can't believe we missed this shop before, this is exactly what we need! I'll get these,' I said, eager to pull my weight considering Aaron had contributed everything else and I was tagging along to *his* trip.

Our bus was at 12:40p.m. so we used the time to re-pack our rucksacks and distribute the food. We must have looked very suspicious, covering the pristine bus terminal floor with all our belongings. An old lady even came over to check if we were okay.

'Hewo, where you froms, you okay. Need hel?'

'Arigato,' I said bowing my head, 'we're going to the National Park, we're okay.'

'Ah, okay, you be carful,' she said sincerely.

Half an hour before the bus

I'm not feeling good. I haven't had breakfast or lunch but am still not hungry, I feel weak and tired and my stomach pain is getting worse. I was almost certain a full-blown CVS attack was coming, for the fourth time this trip. Aaron noticed me looking pensive.

'You're still up for this, Cece?'

Charlotte – you should say no, explain you're ill and quit before you're on a mountain unable to move from cramps and being eaten by a bear!

'Of course, I'm so excited.'

Why did you just say that? In a few hours you won't be able to carry a rucksack let alone hike up a fricking mountain! I didn't want to say no, I was anxious about being alone again, I didn't want to lose my friend. I still believed I could oppose my body, so stubbornly boarded the bus.

Midway through the journey I suddenly realised that if we started to hike that night, we'd be on the mountain on the 10th September, Grandma's funeral. I wouldn't be able to contact my family; I wouldn't be able to attend the service with them. I felt selfish and ashamed that the date had slipped my mind. I missed my grandma so much and had thought of her every day; *how had I overlooked this detail?*

Entrance to Daisetsuzan National Park
One and a half hours later

Aaron looked back and watched as I dragged my heels, struggling to keep up with him. The cramps were bad, I needed more paracetamol. I shoved my hands between my tummy and waist band, trying to relieve some of the pressure.

'Cece, you're not okay, are you?' Aaron asked quietly.

'No, I think I'm ill, it's one of my CVS attacks I was telling you about. Oh, this is the worst timing, I'm so sorry.'

'It's okay, do you need to rest for a bit?'

'Well yes, but in a few hours I won't be able to walk, I need to lie down for the rest of the night until it stops. It will wipe me out completely.'

'Oh okay.'

'I'm sorry, this is so shit, you've come out here with me and now I've become a burden.'

'It's okay, we'll get to the hostel and then decide what we'll do, okay?'

Thirty minutes later

To our dismay, all hostels and hotels were closed. The earthquake had halted the whole of Hokkaido. Nothing was open, the park was desolate. *Cece! What have you done you silly girl? You should have backed out before you left Sapporo, you knew then deep down you'd never make it, you just didn't want to admit it to yourself.*

'Wait, tourist information, let's try there,' Aaron said hopefully.

By the time we reached the building I was doubled over in pain, the cramps were coming in sharp waves. I felt sick and my mind had gone blank. I sat on the steps, head between my knees.

'Well, as nothing is open, we could camp here for the night, you can share my tent, then we'll see how you are in the morning?' Aaron asked softly.

I felt so bad, he was being so nice about it but the last thing I wanted to do was be squished in a one-man tent, throwing up and writhing in pain while bears patrolled the outside. If this had happened at the start of the trip, I might have felt differently, but I knew my body was running on empty, I would need a week to recover before I could get back on the mountain and keep up with him. In complete honesty, I wanted to go home. Tapping my phone, I noticed Mum was online, made up some excuse and hobbled to the other side of the room to talk in private.

'Hi Charlotte, how are you?'

'I'm fine thanks, how are you?' I choked out.

'Charlotte, are you okay?'

I managed a small 'no' before bursting into tears as all my pent-up emotion was released.

'Charlotte, Charlotte, what's wrong darling?'

'I have CVS.'

'Oh Charlotte, are you in pain?'

'Yes, it really hurts.'

'You need to lie down in a dark room, take your medicine.'

'I can't, I'm with this guy in a National Park, we left Sapporo this morning to escape the aftershocks. But now we are stuck in this National Park with bears and only a single tent. I don't want to die on a mountainside, I don't want the earth to shake, I want to be home,' I cried hysterically.

'Charlotte, Charlotte, listen. It's okay. You need to get yourself somewhere so you can get through this attack. Can you get back to a town or a hostel?'

'I don't know, there may be a bus back, but I've come all this way with the Swiss guy, I don't want to make him get the bus all the way back again with me.'

'If he's your friend,' Mum replied, 'he won't want to leave you when you're ill. Take the bus back to the town and get somewhere safe.'

'I just feel really bad.'

'I know, but you will be in a worse state in a few hours, better be in a town with a hospital instead of a National Park.'

'Mum, I want to come home.'

'You can Charlotte, yes come home, it's nothing to be ashamed of, we would love you back here. Get through this attack and then come home.'

In that moment, I was set on coming home, I wanted to escape everything.

'You can book a flight as soon as you are better. Come home darling, come home. Get the bus back with him, don't let him leave you, not while you are ill and then tomorrow you can just explain how you feel and go to the airport.'

'Okay,' I whimpered.

'Okay, go and explain to him now. I love you.'

'Love you too.'

With a tear stained face, I returned to Aaron, 'I'm sorry I'm like this. It's just that I have been ill so much recently, I'm so fed up.'

'I can imagine, it sounds horrible.'

'Yes, it sucks.'

I agreed with my mum; I didn't want to lose the friend I had just made but I didn't want the pressure of having to hike if I wasn't well enough. So I came up with a new plan.

'Okay so I'll get the bus back and you camp here,' I stated.

'Cece I really don't mind...I'd like the company for the hike.'

'I really want to, Aaron, but I know I won't be well enough. I'll take the bus back and you stay here. Then if I'm better, I can come back again.

'Okay that sounds logical. But are you sure?'

'Yes it makes sense, I know you say you don't mind but I really don't want to drag you down.'

'Okay.'

'Okay I'll book a hostel in Asahikawa, to rest and recover for the night.'

'Yes, then the day after next, you can come back again for the hike,' Aaron said hopefully.

'Yes, I hope so.'

'Um excuse me miss,' a slender Japanese man, Tadasu, peered around the corner, 'I work in the information office, I was just about to leave when I heard you. If you want, I can give you a lift back to town? The five o'clock bus is cancelled. You look very sick.'

I looked at the gentleman in front of me, he couldn't have come at a better time.

'Yes please, arigato, thank you, I need your help, yes please.'

5p.m.

By the time the sun was setting, I was so grateful for the lift into town. The cramps were excruciating and I could barely stand. Aaron carried my rucksack and loaded it into the car before we parted. I was too exhausted for a proper goodbye but waved at him as I collapsed into the front seat of the car.

'I put music on, please you go to sleep if you need,' Tadasu comforted.

'Thank you.'

I instantly closed my eyes, trying to block out the pain and prevent myself from vomiting.

Thankfully, hostels were less busy in Asahikawa than in Sapporo, so he dropped me right at the door of the first one we encountered. I gave him my two bars of chocolate that should have been for the hike. He protested but I insisted, in a sleepy mumble, that he should take them as a thank you. Tadasu and the hostel owner helped me inside, carrying my bags, and supporting me up the stairs and into bed. Despite taking all of my medication and lying down, the pain just intensified - I felt dreadful. I spent the next few hours, hunched over a plastic bag, trying to get through each wave of cramps. I felt like I was dying, I wanted to die. At least if I died the pain would end and I would be with my grandma again.

Sometime during the night

I woke to a Japanese lady placing an orange jelly and some kind of vitamin drink on my bedside. I gave her a weak smile before passing out again.

9th September
Morning

I woke properly and realised the attack had stopped. Relief hit me and I lay back down, exhausted. I turned to the side to see the orange jelly still by my bedside. Orange jelly had been the only thing that Grandma could manage in her last few weeks, funny a stranger had given it to me without even knowing my name. A selfless act of kindness. I pulled back the curtain to say thank you, but the lady in the next bunk had left.

TWENTY-TWO

Acts of kindness.

9th September

I eased myself out of bed and sat on the side for a while. I'd only moved a few centimetres but already felt dizzy. There was a short knock at the door before the enthusiastic hostel owner bounced in.

'Ah Charlotte! You okay? You very bad las nigh!'

'Um yes, thank you, I'm a little better this morning,' I winced as I tried to sit up straight.

'Really? Okay, tae easy. Ah, thi for you.'

He produced a small white envelope from his hand which he thrust in my direction. I stared at the paper.

'Oh, arigato, I dropped it last night?'

'No, no, from man. Man who drop you off las night,' he said with a grin.

'Ah, thank you,' I replied with a weak smile.

I unfolded the paper to find a ten thousand yen note. I looked up in astonishment.

'The man say for you to eat,' he nodded and turned, 'I leave you now Charlotte, rest.'

Tadasu, who had already been so kind by driving me back, had now given me eighty pounds worth of yen. I couldn't believe it. I was humbled.

I searched for his business card, hoping there would be a way to contact him to say thank you. I found an address and sent him an email:

Hello Tadasu,

I just wanted to thank you very much for kindly giving me a lift back to the hostel and leaving me some money for food when I am better. It was so kind of you and I cannot repay your generosity.

I am feeling better today but will stay in Asahikawa to rest.

If you or your family ever come to England, please let me know and I will return the favour by showing you my country.

Thank you once again,
Cece (Charlotte Ruth Clark)

Shortly after, I received a reply:

Cece,

Glad to know that you're feeling better today.

I worried that you looked exhausted after having a hard time with the earthquake and when I knew that you were my daughter's age, and a teacher as my daughter is, I felt more anxious about you.

Rest well and eat something good.

Don't push yourself too hard, but I hope you are able to keep going with your special journey.

Take care,
Tadasu

My first week in Japan had consisted of two CVS attacks, a typhoon, an earthquake with aftershocks and my grandmother's impending funeral. This email, however, restored my faith that there was some goodness in the world, people are kind. I had to keep going, I had to be positive despite everything that was happening.

That morning I lay on my bed, shuffled downstairs and rested on the sofa, but after a while, the small amount of positivity I had built up drained away and I just felt alone and exhausted. I tried to go for a little walk to get some fresh air but hobbling at half a kilometer an hour doesn't exactly get your endorphins going. I turned around after a hundred metres, finding it too painful to be upright anyway. My appetite was dulled, I had a few water crackers and made some traveller's gruel. I tried to read but my mind was numb. I was too tired. Besides a brief encounter with the hostel owner and a few kind messages from Aaron, I didn't talk to anyone, everyone at home was asleep until late afternoon and no one else was staying in the dorm at the time. My day was silent, besides my own thoughts. After a few hours, these thoughts became louder and louder until they consumed the room. I felt grief for my grandmother and apprehension about her funeral, miserable because of my illness and anxious about it returning, exhausted from the constant moving around and fear another natural disaster would happen. I wasn't in a good place mentally or physically, and I couldn't escape.

4p.m.

I made it to UK morning time and was relieved when my mum called.

'Hello,' I tried to say excitedly, but it came out like a flat tyre.

'Hello, how are you?'

'I'm okay, just exhausted. How was your holiday with Jemima?'

'Aw it was lovely, we had a really nice time, just what we needed.'

'Yes, I can imagine.'

'But coming back has been difficult, I was in a bubble and now I have come back to be reminded of it all, everything that needs to be done, all of Grandmas thin...'

I could tell she was fighting back the tears, being strong as usual.

'Anyway, you're safe so I'm happy! Are you really okay Charlotte?'

'No,' I started to shake and my lips quivered, 'I just feel so sad. I can't stop feeling so sad.'

'Oh darling.'

'I forget about everything that's happened until I remember Grandma has gone. Then the grief hits me again and again, it never gets any better. I feel like I have been broken a thousand times. I just can't believe that when I come home, she will no longer be there. No one will be there peeping through the window as we drive up the hill, no little wave when I come through the old wooden door, no one standing in the garden to greet us.'

'Oh Charlotte.'

'I want to tell her so much but I can't. I will never be able to talk to her again.'

'I know.'

'It's just so hard. I feel so alone, so al...'

I broke down, and for once, I didn't suppress my tears, didn't cover my face, didn't muffle my cries. I cried out in pain. Grief had consumed me and I let it.

'Darling, you have been so brave, it's normal to feel like this. This is grieving. It is harder for you, you are alone, no one to talk to, we have each other, we can talk about it, but you can't. So you can let it out darling. You can cry.'

The cries got quicker and closer together until I lost the ability to breathe, or the desire to.

'Charlotte, it's okay.'

'I'm sorry, I'm okay,' I managed to say when I calmed myself back down.

'So you're going to come home, can you get to an airport?'

I paused, 'Well I don't think there are airports in Hokkaido that go straight to London, I'd have to get to Tokyo first.'

'Okay, well you could do that. What do you think? It would do you good to come back for a few weeks, to recover and be with us, and then return to China well.'

The offer was so tempting, I wanted to be home, to relax, feel safe and be on the same soil as my family. But I didn't want to quit, I didn't want to give up.

'I know I shouldn't, but I will feel like I have failed if I come back.'

'Charlotte, you have been through an earthquake, any normal person would have flown back home already! This is not a normal travelling experience. I was worried about your illness before you left, I never imagined an earthquake! Come home darling.'

I was so close to giving in. 'I need to rest first, I can't carry my backpack at the moment, it's too painful.'

'Of course, stay where you are for a few days and think about it.'

'Yes, I'll rest here and think about it.'

We talked for a long time afterwards. About their holiday, the nice food, the jobs Mum had to do over the next week. It was nice to talk. Talk all evening like I was back at home.

As I grew up, I respected my parents more and more. A child can love a parent, but respect is the one thing you can only build over time. Both my parents worked hard, my father incessantly building, designing and creating in his room and my mother a talented teacher. They had both dedicated their lives to making sure my sister and I had the best life we could, rich not with money, but with love and experience. When

Grandma was close to the end, my mother had been a saint, spending every hour and doing everything she could to make sure her mother was loved to the very end. I was proud to have them as my parents, and felt I owed it to them to keep going.

I went to sleep not unhappy, but the burden of grief had been lifted slightly through sharing it.

10th September

Felt a little better today, although a bit apprehensive about the funeral tonight. Mum had sent the eulogy she'd written on WhatsApp, but I wasn't to open it until tonight at the point when she was to read it.

I needed to keep myself pre-occupied so, still feeling weak, made a slow trip to a park in the morning. It was a small but pretty park, just like my grandparents' garden. The flower beds were filled with violets, rubies and sunny yellows. I stood in the middle, smelt the sweet perfumes, lifted my face to the sky and imagined I was back in their garden in the summer. I walked across the small arched Japanese bridge, watched the large ducks dipping their heads under the water, sprinkled cracker crumbs to the koi carp and watched cranes elegantly strut through the water. On a bench sat an elderly couple, side-by-side, hand in hand, smiling sincerely as one listened to what the other had to say. I went to a shrine, bowed at the torii gate and washed my hands and lips like Nanami had instructed. It was a dark but elegant temple, the grand roof spread out proudly at the corners and golden Kanji characters were engraved into the charcoal walls. Before leaving, I thought of Grandma and sent her my love.

Afternoon

I walked slowly down the streets of Asahikawa. It was a strange town, laid out like a grid as if a child had drawn buildings in the square spaces of their maths book. The streets were immaculate, they went on for miles. A regular pattern of zebra crossings, lights, cars and parallel buildings repeated far into the distance. Life was slow paced and quiet in the north, people took their time. They'd wait for the green man, even if the road was clear, before crossing. It was nice. I never did anything slowly. My recovery forced me to lead their pace of life. Walk down the street gazing, sit down for a few minutes to rest and walk again.

For the remainder of the afternoon I clock watched, counting down the hours then minutes until seven-thirty.

7:30p.m.
Grandma's funeral

I walked in the cold Hokkaido air to the riverside, a peaceful place I'd sought out earlier in the day. The moonlight reflected off the ripples and only the quiet sound of running water could be heard. The eulogy was beautiful, describing Grandma's entire life, I read it several times. I cannot describe what it was like to be at such a poignant event in one's life alone. Alone and without the people you care about most.

I was not there in person, but I was there in spirit Grandma – as you had wished.

TWENTY-THREE

Recovery, again.

10ᵗʰ September

I cried myself to sleep the night of my grandma's funeral, she would hate to see me cry but I couldn't stop. Most people say they are relieved when the funeral is over, it acts as closure. For me, however, nothing had changed. I felt relief for my family, Mum in particular - reading the eulogy must have been a weight off her shoulders. But I felt that until I returned home and visited the house, I wouldn't be at peace with what had happened.

As I made my way back to the hostel, a line from the eulogy replayed in my mind.

'...you never knew your mum and all you ever wanted was a family of your own, and here we are...'[6]

Grandma had had a tragic childhood. With both parents dying at a young age, she was fostered by her aunt who lived on a farm where she spent her childhood working instead of playing. Her kind older sister, Joan, sent her little envelopes of pocket money each month to buy necessities. But after she passed away, Grandma had no one left, no one who really loved or cared for her. She didn't give up though. Succeeding in boarding school, she escaped and carved out a life of her own as a fashionable, young nursery teacher. There, she met a handsome police officer, my grandfather, and before long they were married with my mum on the way. She finally had a family of her own, the one she deserved as a girl. I always listened in awe at the tales of her childhood, from walking miles each day to get to school to meeting my grandfather for

---

[6] *My mother. "Grandma's Eulogy". 2018.*

the first time on her night shift. What I took from it, was that she had never stopped hoping. She had endured, kept fighting, until she achieved what she deserved in life. I was proud to be her eldest granddaughter. I was proud to have been part of her little family. I was proud to be one of the last people to show her kindness on this earth.

11ᵗʰ September

After being emotionally overwhelmed yesterday, I wasn't surprised to wake early in the morning with cramps. The emotional pain was so great it had started to break down my body too. Deflated, I lay on my back and looked upwards.

'I can't take another CVS attack, I can't!' I whispered as I began to cry.

I can't go through a whole day of lying in a bed, alone in pain with only my thoughts about Grandma's funeral circling my head. It will destroy me. I felt as if I'd sunk to the bottom of the earth's core and been buried alive, left to suffer in pain alone. I wanted to give up.

After a while, my mind became numb as the cramps got worse. I came to terms with the fact I was ill again and turned to CVS survival mode. I collected all the things that I would need later on in the attack, when I'd be too ill to move: plastic bags, wet wipes, tissues, meds, water and other bits. There was always the fear of the unknown when an attack started, I never knew what the timespan or severity of an attack would be. How long would I have to lie in the dark? How many times would I throw-up? Would I end up in a hospital? I swallowed as many pills as I could and tried to drift off into oblivion.

Afternoon

Waking at one, the pain had stopped. Afraid it would come back again, I lay there for another hour until I was confident it had gone. I was about to ring my grandma to tell her the attack had finished until I realised I couldn't; I would never be able to call her again.

I had little energy so just lay in bed for hours and hours, I couldn't face reading because I associated it with Grandma. She loved stories and had a gift for describing moments and writing cards.

'…getting those everlasting messages just right…'[7]

Whatever I thought of brought me back to her. I couldn't control my mind, it was emotionally suicidal, making me trawl through childhood memories that left me in so much pain I could barely breathe. I pictured cards Grandma had written, her visits on Christmas day, running up the hill as a child and knocking on the old wooden door of Donnington House before being welcomed in by her soft jade eyes. There was no one who loved me more dearly than my grandma had.

By the evening, I had nothing left. My eyes were tired, my body ached and my mind was numb. I had nothing left at all.

---

[7] *My mother. "Grandma's Eulogy". 2018.*

TWENTY-FOUR

The return of resilience.

12th September

I woke for the first time without cramps, relief washed over me. *Today I will not give up, today I will see something in Japan, see it for my grandma.*

I took it slow, not wanting to push myself too hard in case it brought on another attack. The pace of my day was slower than a care-home trip to the garden centre. How have I come to this conclusion? Because I was overtaken by several pensioners on the way to the bus stop, which was only one hundred metres away from the hostel.

After completing my geriatric sprint, I caught the bus at stop number nine. I sat across from an old man, who watched sympathetically as I hobbled to my seat. I smiled to him and he returned a weak smile, his face was aged but his eyes were alive with a youthful sparkle.

'Were you from?' he asked in a hoarse whisper.

'England,' I replied.

'Aowh Engwand!'

'Yes, are you from here?'

'Hiere heire,' he said enthusiastically.

Ten minutes later he pointed to a passing field, 'Onon.'

'Onon, are you from Onon?'

He shook his head and thrust his finger towards the window.

'Onon, onion.'

'Onion, oh onion?'

'Hei, onion.'

I studied the field we were passing; he wasn't wrong. The field was dotted with hundreds of bronzed globes, baking in the sun. I smiled, my grandparents used to grow onions at the top of their garden, along with sweet peas. Before I had time to dwell, the old man spoke again.

'Corr.'

I looked back to the old man as he motioned to the field once again.

'Corn, oh yes, aha.'

The next field was asparagus followed by carrots and then turnips. I must hand it to him, his knowledge of English veg was pretty impressive; it seemed like I'd jumped on the 'get your five-a-day tour of Hokkaido'! When we got to my stop, the old man motioned for me to get off.

'Blu Pon, Blu Pon.'

'Thank you, Blue Pond yes, I'll go now,' I said, giving him one last fond smile.

I turned to wave goodbye, just in case he was looking back, and there he was, waving his hand slowly like he was watching his granddaughter go to school. I felt uplifted by this encounter, as if my grandparents were watching, so with a smile I carried on towards the Blue Pond.

The Blue Pond

Several Japanese families were already exploring the area when I arrived, they seemed so happy. The mother of one looked lovingly at her husband as he held their baby, its plump little hands gripping tightly around its father's.

'…and then Daddy swept you off your feet and, as I like to put it, scooped you up and took care of you from then on. Then in 1962 came me…'[8]

I pictured my grandparents with Mum, and for the first time I accepted the simple pleasure of having your own family. The older I became, the more I understood the value and importance of family. It was a privilege, not a right.

---

[8] *My mother. "Grandma's Eulogy". 2018.*

'...all you ever wanted was a family and here we are...'[9]

The pond was completely hidden by trees. It wasn't until I'd crept through the crisscross of roots and leaves that I saw my first glimpse of the magical blue water. I'd expected the colour to be an average powdery grey, guessing the tourist boards had just turned up the saturation of their photos, but no, it was real. The bright icy-blue water was guarded by a circle of thin silver tree trunks, standing motionless, like gods of the water. I stood mesmerized, it was beautiful, like something out of a fairytale Grandma would have read to me.

From the Blue Pond I took a gentle walk through the forest, following the river until I reached the Shirahige waterfall. A huge body of water streamed off the rock, splitting into six mini cascades, giving the mountain face a long white beard. In the distance, the elegant mountain ranges of Daisetsuzan National Park lined the sky, it was a peaceful place besides the active volcanoes. White puffy clouds spilled from mountain tops like a great steam engine pumping out smoke. I couldn't help but pray for the volcanoes to contain their eruptions; *not sure if I can deal with a third natural disaster this week!*

Onsen

I'd heard stories from my grandfather about onsens, Japan's natural hot spring, 'a blessing in their icy winters' he'd say. Aaron had suggested we visit one as a reward after our huge hike, but sadly that plan never happened, so it was up to me alone to find one. I approached the Shirahige hotel, hoping they'd let me enter the baths as a day guest, without charging me an entire week's budget. To my relief, I paid 850 yen for a day pass, *bargain*. I was handed a towel and a locker key. Unsure if this was a no-clothes spring, I drew a bikini in the air with my fingers, gesturing if I needed one or not.

---

[9] *My mother. "Grandma's Eulogy". 2018.*

'No, no clothe,' the receptionist smiled.

No clothes, well this will be interesting. Okay maybe it's a good thing our post-hike onsen plan didn't work out!

A red cloth barrier with a white outline of a woman in a kimono, guarded the female baths. Dipping my head under the curtain, I was faced with a wooden sliding door followed by several bamboo shades, eventually revealing a small space with wicker baskets, dressing tables and mirrors. Elegant Japanese women walked freely like peacocks, their thick black manes brushing the bottoms of their spines as they prepared to bathe, washing their bodies with mountain water and natural potions. I liked the routine, each step was gracefully acknowledged and completed, reflecting their respect for the mountain and its natural resources.

There were several pools of varying temperature and size, uncertain if there was a special order to enter, I waited pensively to copy one of the more onsen-experienced women. The outdoor pool was my favourite: an irregularly shaped basin, formed by large sedimentary rocks and filled with murky mineral enriched spring water; steam rose as the hot bath met the cool mountain air. Little trees, recently reddened from autumn's early touch, flittered in the light breeze as silhouettes of dragon flies, on their evening commute, darted across the sky's blank canvas. Easing myself down the rock steps, my muscles relaxed and, despite everything that had happened recently, I finally felt calm.

To finish the day off I visited a little farm in Kano, the majority of trains had started to work again so I made the most of my rail pass. Fields were rainbowed with red, lavender, bright yellow and orange flowers. Alex rang so I put him on video chat to give him a twirl of the flower field.

'Can you see, do you like it?'

'Wow it's really pretty, you'll get some great photos!'

'Yes for sure, I'll send you some.'

'Cece also, I wanted to tell you, you know the job I applied for in Cambridge a few weeks ago? Well, I got it!'

'What, you got it? Oh Alex that is so amazing. Congratulations! I am so proud of you!'

'Yes, it's such a relief to have something and they seem like a really cool firm to work for, they even have a pool table in the entrance.'

'Now, that's the jazziest law firm I've ever heard of!'

The firm was based in Cambridge, only an hour from London by train. We'd be so close next year, as opposed to the five-hour commute from Bath to Hastings we were used to. Slowly fate was bringing us closer to each other again.

13th September

Stomach cramps. I can't take it anymore. *As soon as I get back on my feet, I'm knocked back down again.* Spent the day in pain, in bed and in darkness.

14th September

Life is trying to kill me. My stomach is so weak, and the dull ache remains. I haven't seen anyone in over forty-eight hours. Feeling low.

15th September

I have little energy to write. My mind and body are weak. I feel hollow. I'm fading away.

TWENTY-FIVE

The Sushi Translator.

16ᵗʰ September

During the past week, I'd lost count of the number of times I'd been ill, the number of times I'd cried and the number of times I'd thought of Grandma's death. Asahikawa was a good place for recovery, quiet, not much going on and very few people passing through the doors. But it was lonely, not a place to make new friends; I needed to move on.

This morning I woke without pain, so seized the opportunity and finally left this small city, the home of my recovery. I said a fond farewell to the crazy owner, leaving him a note and a little something to say thank you for taking me in. For the majority of days, it had only been him and I, and so I felt a little sad to leave the only familiar face I knew. I'd miss our awkward conversations in the evening, the tourist flyers he'd present to me every morning and his insistence to wear a specific pair of slippers for each room in the house.

I boarded the train for Sapporo and then from Sapporo I'd travel to Hakodate where I would spend the night. The corner of my lips curved upwards ever so slightly as the train left Asahikawa. *I was moving on.* I felt more stable; I was okay. The promise of a new place had given me energy, but I'd be lying if I said returning home wasn't on my mind. Never in my life have I felt so low as I have this past week.

Despite the length of the journey, it went by in a blur as the train raced through Hokkaido. Huge grey concrete factories sprawled over the land whilst fishing stations and docks lined the coast. Everything was grey except the small coloured buoys that, from far away, seemed like a pile of fairy lights waiting to be strung on the Christmas tree. Leaving the industrial areas, charcoal granite cliffs stacked the shoreline, seas became bluer, large peaks rose through the salty mist and stretches of land appeared as faint silhouettes. Whenever I'd been on trains before, I'd had reading, essay writing or marking to do, but now I had nothing. It was strange having no task to complete, no purpose, so instead I simply watched the world go by. But at points it was hard to stop my mind from wondering beyond the view out of the window.

Arriving in Hakodate was a welcome relief. I smiled when I saw the two red figures bridging outside the station, the first statue you see when entering the city. I'd always taken for granted the sense of familiarity, returning to a place you've been before, but now I appreciated it.

After riding the tram for forty minutes, I made it to the hostel. My next mission was to find something for dinner. Hoping for a simple meal like veggie ramen, I wondered down the street seeking a restaurant. Around the corner was a little building with traditional Japanese sliding wooden doors. Drawn to its quaintness, I peeped through the window and before I knew it, the owner had caught my eye and had ushered me into a seat. Ginger, chopsticks, a wet towel and a little blue enamel dish for soy sauce; it was a sushi place. *Oh no, I'm still recovering, the last thing I want is raw fish!* They were keen to have me as their guest and awaiting eagerly for my order, I couldn't walk out now. I looked around for a menu, *perhaps they could just do me something simple like veggie nori rolls?* The waitress observed me and gestured to the menu. *Ooh, all in Japanese*, I turned to the lady pulling a slightly uncomfortable expression.

'Um is there an English menu, please?'

She gave me a sassy look back, shaking her head, which I interpreted as, '*This is Japan, tourist, you should know how to speak our language.*'

Okay, how am I going to do this? It would be okay if I had no diet issues, but with my condition, I had to be pretty careful what I fed my body. Using a photo translation app on my phone, I took a picture of the menu and looked for a word

I recognised. *Nigiri, okay well you know what that is, just rice with fish on top, you can eat that Cece.*

I watched as the little old man set to work, moulding the rice and slicing fish. His hands moved quickly, like he was performing a kind of dance with effortless expertise. After ten minutes of watching the artist at work, he proudly presented the result on an ornate platter with painted cranes on either side. I held my breath, praying that there wouldn't be any slimy slugs or tentacles. To my relief, only salmon, tuna, and another grey fish made an appearance. *Okay Cece, you can handle this.*

Being the only one in the small restaurant, all eyes were on me as I began to tackle the sushi. I sensed my every move was being analysed, from picking up the chopsticks to placing the piece in my mouth. *Eugh, wasabi, I forgot how much I hate this flavour.* Trying not to draw too much attention to myself, I began to subtly scrape it off. Obviously not subtle enough - the waitress waved her hands and gestured for me to pass the platter back. *Oh no, I hope I haven't offended them, maybe there are sushi rules that I've just broken and now they're going to kick me out of their sushi kingdom!*

To my surprise, the platter was passed back to the sushi master as he smiled and began scraping it off. *Oh bless him, that is so sweet.*

'Arigato,' I whispered graciously.

I hope he's not too frustrated with the silly tourist who can't handle a bit of wasabi.

When the platter was returned, the waitress came around to my side of the counter with a piece of sushi for herself. *Oh lord what have I done wrong now?* She motioned dipping the sushi and popping it into her mouth with her hands.

'Ohh, it's okay, thank you, I am learning to use the chopsticks, I like practising,' I said.

But every time I picked them back up, she repeated the motion with her hands. In the end, defeated and fed up with her staring at me, I used my hands. Only then did she smile and leave me in peace to enjoy the rest of my wasabi-free nigiri.

By the end of the evening I think they liked me. The chef struck up a conversation but, with my minimal knowledge of Japanese, I found it difficult to determine the topic. I think my smiles and nods were so convincing, however, that he thought I understood him so continued to chatter on, becoming more enthusiastic with his expressions and hand gestures. I kept smiling but was wary that at some point he would ask me a question and expect a reply. I decided it was time to leave before it got to that point. I was accompanied to the door by several bows and smiles from the couple, *what an evening!*

17th September

Today was another travel day: a tram followed by a train from Hakodate to Shin-Hakodate-Hokuto, then the Shinkansen (bullet train) to Tokyo and finally another Shinkansen to Kyoto. For the train ride I bought some pickled plum onigiri and orange cantaloupe melon, which everyone seemed to be crazy for. I was excited for Kyoto. I hoped this city would be a fresh start to my travels in Japan.

TWENTY-SIX

Beauty was free to those who were there to see it.

17th September
Evening

I held my breath as I arrived into the station. I was nervous, Kyoto was the place I had most wanted to visit, I wanted to love it, for nothing to go wrong and for my illness to remain in the north.

I boarded a bus packed full of locals and was sandwiched between my blue rucksack and the door, meaning I couldn't move or turn in any direction without taking somebody out. Every time the bus came to a halt, I had to brace myself to avoid knocking down the other passengers like dominoes. After forty minutes of a moving 'legs, bums and tums' work-out to remain upright, the bus dropped me off at a darkly lit street with little yellow side lights glowing like toadstools. When my eyes adjusted to the darkness, I recognised the shadows of curved tiled rooves and silhouettes of pagodas and temples - the traditional old quarter of town. I'd made it, I was in Gion.

The ornate guesthouse gate revealed a grey pebbled garden with little bonsai trees. Entering through several sliding doors and tiptoeing down plain corridors to my room, I imagined myself as a geisha, returning after a night's work to her okiya, just as the novel I had read to my grandma had described. I went to sleep excited for tomorrow's adventures in this wonderful new city.

18th September

I woke excited and ready for the day until the all too familiar pain in my stomach returned as I rolled onto my side. *It can't be! I literally had CVS two days ago. It just can't be, all I've done is travel and sit on a train. I can't have an attack today; I have to move to the other hostel. Oh damn, CVS, you're going to kill me.*

I have little more to say, my sixth attack in two weeks, ridiculous.

One hour later

I hobbled to the next hostel with my rucksack strapped to my back, the weight and tightness of the waistband squeezing my cramped-up tummy. By the time I arrived at reception I was in a lot of pain.

'Ah hello, Charlot, sorry check in at tree. You come back then. But, can leav your bag now.'

'Please, I am, er not feeling very well.'

'Ah okay, sit down and wait till tree or maybe park bench.'

'I'm in a lot of pain, please is there a spare bed?'

Tears started to well in my eyes. *I can't go through this again. I want to be at home! I want to be looked after, to go to my own bed and not have to beg for a place to suffer in.* He didn't understand.

'You come a tree.'

'Please,' I paused, tears started to spill down my cheeks and stole my words.

The owner looked uncomfortable and got the hint that I was in no state to sit on a park bench for six hours.

'Ah okay, I see, you come with me, hei, le me take your bags, yes you go, I take them.'

I was so grateful at the time but with the pain and exhaustion, 'arigato' was all I managed to choke out as I collapsed onto the bunk. *My first day in Kyoto and I am ill again, my positive energy has run out, I'm burnt out.*

I spent the rest of the day and night there. It was a painful attack and despite the meds it was very difficult to manage. At one point I woke in the night to a hand placed over my forehead.

'Charlotte, I owner's wife, you okay? We no see you all day. You sick?'

With all the medication I was delirious, so can't remember what happened after that. I probably passed out from the pain.

19th September

I woke and the cramps had thankfully stopped, I was just left with the fatigue. All the energy had drained out of me and I felt faint every time I tried to stand. I had to get the taste of stale saliva and medicine out of my mouth, so crawled to the bathroom and clung to the basin for support as I scrubbed my teeth.

After a few hours of feeling okay, I knew I had to eat something to get my energy back so tried to make it down to breakfast, hoping there'd be something I could eat within my diet. To my delight I was greeted by a table filled with slices of melon, huge purple and green grapes, kiwi halves and peeled pears, a vat of miso soup, rice, yoghurt, an abundance of rolls, fruit bread and the ring layered cake Baumkuchen.[10] Feeling my last strands of energy evaporating after using them on the stairs, I quickly sat down and started to nibble on some fruit bread and melon, hoping my body would tolerate it.

By the afternoon I felt revitalised and, although I should have stayed in bed resting, I felt another day inside would mentally suffocate me, so I made my way outside. The cobbled streets were alive with street vendors selling mochi on sticks, fried fish cake balls, pickled cucumbers and floral Japanese sweets. Young girls dressed in pastel kimonos shuffled coyly on their way to school, avoiding temptation from Kanzashi shops and sweet ice stalls. Old fashioned rickshaws wheeled through the streets, carrying travellers

---

[10] *Baumkuchen originates from Germany, however, this cake is also a popular Japanese snack or dessert. It's created by cooking over twenty layers of cake batter on a spit to form several rings, giving it the name 'tree cake'.*

from place to place and tourists dawdled along the pavements viewing the sights. Between the crowds, I noticed two women in grander kimonos, they were different to the other girls, their fabric was brighter, more ornate and red obi belts were wrapped tightly around each of their waists. Their black hair was immaculately looped into large bows and their skin was painted white, save two arrows running down the napes of their necks, revealing the only patches of naked skin. I froze, not quite believing my luck, they were real geisha. I had told my grandma I would see a geisha for her and now I had fulfilled that promise. They were beautiful to watch, floating elegantly over the cobbled streets, their dark eyes occasionally flickering upwards, gracing the public with a single glance. These were the women of Kyoto, living art forms that have mesmerized the world with their mystery for centuries; they are at the heart of Japanese culture. Asahikawa was grey and bleak, but in Gion, beauty was free to those who were there to see it.

Evening

The rest of the day was spent happily wandering the streets, gazing at shop windows, kimonos and taking in Kyoto's sights. I tried gyoza for the first time, a Japanese dumpling filled with a gingered cabbage and mushroom stuffing. Later, I treated myself to a slice of Kyoto fig layer cake from a boutique patisserie near the station; feather light sponge filled with vanilla cream and glazed baby pink figs. I took it back to my capsule bunk to savour as I read my book, happy to be well and no longer in so much pain. My positivity was returning.

TWENTY-SEVEN

The orange path to the mountain.

20ᵗʰ September

Today was the day, I was determined to visit Fushimi Inari-taisha. Arriving by train and negotiating the crowds, I arrived at the entrance to the shrines. Hundreds of large torii stood proudly one after another, the orange pillars gleaming in the morning sun, lined up like soldiers in the ancient forest. The scene was meant to be beautiful, but it was spoiled by the mass of people. It's hypocritical of me to say, because I was one of those people contributing to the crowd, but at least I was being respectful. Tourists were everywhere, screeching, shouting, flashing cameras, pushing and running their greasy hands all over the torii. This was not how I had imagined it. I had dreamed of visiting this place ever since I was twelve. I wanted to take my time, look around, absorb, appreciate and live in the moment but I was being pushed and blocked by people deciding to stop every thirty centimetres to get another selfie.

Getting to the end of the first section, I noticed there was a parallel torii corridor used as an exit that was practically empty. From this side, you could see each individual inscription, I couldn't begin to imagine the number of hands that had spent hours etching into the brilliant orange coated wood. *This is what I had imagined! I'll walk down the exit for a moment of calm, then loop back again to continue through the crowds, bingo.* And I did. I ran down the corridor with my arms spread like a bird, face tilted upwards, just like the little girl in the novel; just as I had described to Grandma.

The torii continued all the way up the mountain, some were large, grand with wider gaps, others small, more compact, the vivid orange a stark contrast to the dark wet green of the forest. The higher I walked, the number of tourists decreased, snap-happy sightseers gave up lower down, satisfied with their photo against the first torii they encountered. The mountain became quieter, more private, as it should be. I felt at peace with the world inside the orange gateway, it was like the path to heaven, the path to see Grandma again.

Reaching the top, I took out a silver fifty-yen piece, the one with the hole in the middle. I held it close to my heart, kissed it then threw it gently into the slots in front of the shrine, clasped my hands together and whispered what I would have said if I had been at Grandma's funeral. My words were carried by the wind to her ears in heaven, never to be heard by anyone else. I clapped twice, bowed three times and turned to descend back down the mountain.

'That was for you Grandma,' I whispered.

Afternoon

I headed to Arashiyama bamboo grove. A narrow pathway that ran inside a hollow within the green shady forest. Tall shoots of bamboo stood proudly, rising like knights into the woody blue mist, it was like I was entering a new world. Looking further into the grove, it was clear where the typhoon had ripped through the forest, gigantic shreds of bamboo leant on one another like they had lost the ability to stand, a sad reflection on nature's relentless ability to build but yet destroy.

From the grove, I meandered through the forest until I came to a giant gorge which overlooked a light green river snaking between the mountains. Heading down to the water I spotted two elderly men, dressed smartly in shirts, trousers and ties, but with plastic bags and metal cooking tongs in hand. Their movements were slow and careful, but their faces were relaxed with resting smiles. *It's a beautiful Sunday afternoon and they're litter picking, oh bless them. They must love this area, that is so good of them.* I sat and watched for a while, admiring their goodwill until I realised instead of sitting and watching, *I should just go and help them. Plastic pollution is a growing problem, one that has already taken over the coasts of Malaysia, it can't invade Japan too!*

After a moment of deliberation, I plucked up the courage and began to help them, collecting the pieces that were too low down for them to reach. I litter picked with the two golden oldies for several hours. I didn't have tongs so just used my bare hands, but I didn't care, I was using my time for good. We couldn't say much to each other but, communicating through smiles and 'arigatos', we got along like old friends. I don't think they could quite believe an English girl had randomly given up her time to litter pick as they told the story to every local we passed, pointing and smiling at me. Old in movement but young at heart, giving up their retired hours of relaxation to do good - complete babes and retirement goals. People can be so inspiring. I need to do more. I have experienced so much kindness on this trip, I must do more to help others.

Evening

Arriving back at the hostel, I saw two Romanian girls in the opposite dorm dressed in kimonos, they looked stunning. I think the owner's wife saw me ogling in the stairway as she called me over after they had left.

'Charlotte san, I dress you, enkata.'

'Sorry, kata?'

'Yes I dress you enkata, one moment.'

Kata, kata, what does that mean? I smiled and nodded, unsure what I had just signed up for. *It cost up to three thousand yen to hire a kimono, surely she's not going to dress me this late in the evening?*

'Okay you sit,' she ordered, returning to the room with a big box of fabric, hair pins and wooden sandals (also known as geta).

Oh wow, she really is dressing me in a kimono! I was so excited I could barely sit still. I was amazed how she tamed my curly hair; in a matter of minutes she had flattened, twirled and pinned the mass of twirls into a neat low bun. Next, I was told to stand and raise my arms as several layers of fabric were wrapped tightly around my body: an under sash, a floral white and navy kimono and a decorative obi belt pulled tight to form an elaborate bow at the back. The outfit was completed with a little clutch and geta.

'Now, you go for a walk, you beautiful,' she exclaimed proudly, looking at her work.

I stared at the woman in the mirror, finding it difficult to believe it was my own reflection. Over the past two weeks I'd looked sickly and frail, but she had transformed me, made me look alive.

'Arigato, thank you so much, I can't believe you have done this for me, I can't thank you enough!'

'Pleasure beauty, now go, go for walk!'

Recruiting two boys from the hostel who had watched the kimono dressing, we descended as a trio into the centre of Kyoto. We sat at a riverside bar drinking saké as the moon danced upon the ripples of the water. I couldn't help but notice the heads that turned as people tried to steal a secret glance at my outfit. For once, I wasn't being stared at because of my ridiculous rucksack!

Back at the hostel

We arrived just in time for the late-night tea ceremony. Sweet red bean mochi and cups of matcha green tea were laid on a pristine tablecloth by the owner.

'Pick up the cup with your left hand, clasp it with your right, turn the cup three times and then sip,' he explained.

So there I sat, taking part in a tea ceremony in Kyoto, dressed in a Kimono. Childhood dreams come true.

21st September

I spent the morning seeing the Golden Temple with one of the guys I went for a drink with the night before, Bram.

We then looked around Nishiki market in the afternoon – a never-ending line of stalls under a colourful stained glass roof. Bright Japanese pickles, black sesame seed fudge, green matcha soft serve, fish balls, small red octopi on sticks and many other weird and wonderful items were on display. I bought my only souvenir from Kyoto: a metal hair pin decorated by a black bead with tiny dangling pearls; a way to remember my night in the Kimono. It was an interesting trip but the hour with Bram started to grate on me. At first, I thought he was nice, but after spending the day with him, I realised he was both condescending and self-righteous.

'I'm twenty-two, I have two cars and my family are high up in the country. I think I have it pretty good. I mean, they have connections. I could get anyone in the Netherlands fired if I wanted to, aha.'

Oh brilliant what a useful skill to have. He was opinionated, weird and I felt uncomfortable in his presence. I made up an excuse to leave him shortly after the market.

At a bit of a loss, and trying not to bump into Bram again, I dawdled around the shops - something Mum would have enjoyed. I missed her. Giving her a quick call, I told her about the orange torii, the river cleaning with the old men, how I had fulfilled my promise to Grandma and about all the shops she would love to see here in Kyoto. I could tell she was happy but also sad, shopping was something Grandma loved too. We both missed her.

Evening

Tired and with little energy to find a restaurant that wasn't serving surprise octopus, I copped out and had a stack of tiramisu pancakes for dinner. *I guess that's one perk of solo travelling – you can go wherever you want.*

9p.m.

The hostel owner also owned an onsen and offered free trips to his guests twice a week. I went along with two

German sisters. This one was certainly more homely, more of a local bath than a mountain onsen. The place was packed with old women scrubbing their bodies with white bars of soap and flannels. Women were shaving, brushing their teeth and chatting away, all completely naked. Sharing an awkward smile between the three of us, we followed an old lady into the washing area where we sheepishly showered and then tried to squeeze into the first bath. The water was hot, too hot. After a few minutes I felt lightheaded and a bit nauseous. I got into the cold one to cool down but when I tried to get out, I felt very faint and had to cling to the side not to fall over.

'Sauna - we go, you come as well?' the sisters asked.

'Ah thanks, but I feel a bit dizzy.'

'Oh, are you okay?'

'Yes, I'll be fine, I'll just stay here for a bit!' I said, crouching on the floor and lowering my head.

This is the last thing I want to do, pass out naked on a dirty floor with a load of strangers. Luckily, with some deep breathing, I managed to remain conscious until the owner returned to take us back to the hostel.

22nd September

I had planned to visit Nara, famous for its free roaming deer, but waking up I knew CVS had returned. *Fuck.* I went back to sleep after taking a load of Japanese painkillers. *At this point in the trip I think my blood was half paracetamol.* Waking up a few hours later, the cramps had dispersed and I was just left with the usual fatigue. I was fed up of bed days, so made my way stubbornly, and very slowly, to Nara.

Deer were everywhere, I am not really an animal person but I admit they were pretty with their soft brown coats and white dots like Bambi. You could feed them biscuits, but I didn't want to chance having my fingers bitten off by a hungry buck. Within the first ten minutes of arriving at the deer park, I had already witnessed two tourists having their coats torn and fingers nibbled. I liked seeing the deer in packs, grazing on the grass in their natural environment, as opposed to galloping through tourists.

By the afternoon I could just about handle some food, so I tried ochazuke - a rice bowl with pickled veg, over which hot tea was poured to make a kind of soup. *A different way to take Earl Grey!*

23rd September

I was sad to leave Kyoto, I loved this place, the place where I had discovered the true Japan. The hostel owners couldn't have been more generous, providing breakfast, the kimono dressing, the tea ceremony and the public bath visit all for free; not to mention taking me in when I was ill and just being kind and cheery people to stay with. They really cared about each traveller's stay. I gave the owners a fancy box of biscuits to say thank you, but the hostess refused at first.

'No, no, our pleasure,' she said waving her hand.

So the male owner gratefully took them instead, 'Arigato Charlotte-san.'

'Thank you, I've had an amazing time, the best experience in Japan, you showed me true Japanese culture and much kindness when I was ill. Arigato.'

The owner gave me a warm-hearted smile and took my hand to shake it sincerely. The lady gave me a little tight hug. Descending the hill to the train station, I turned to have one last look to find them both standing outside, waving me away until I was out of sight. I felt like I had found my own family in Kyoto. They reminded me of my grandma, how she would always stand at the door, waving as we drove away. I took a deep breath, swallowed the lump in my throat and smiled.

'Onward to the station. Bye bye Kyoto, land of the geisha, I'll be back some day.'

TWENTY-EIGHT

The bell was heard throughout the city.

23rd September

The bullet train sped angrily alongside the platform. A sleek, white coated metal frame stretched over the train's front, dipping below the driver's window to create angular cheekbones; making it look like a face that had been stretched back from the years of racing across the tracks.

I sat down and removed my rucksack to relieve my shoulders and waist. Thick red marks and indents from the tight straps crisscrossed my skin. *Owh, no wonder my insides keep cramping up.* I enjoyed the journey, it was a nice length, one and a half hours. I ate my sultana bread and butter I had taken from breakfast, put on some Vance Joy and gazed out the window. It was raining. The sky was a blanket of greyish white so I couldn't see much besides a few houses and tree covered hills. My mind drifted to different memories as the train coasted along the tracks. I thought of Alex, my family and inevitably my grandma. I was getting better at controlling my thoughts, I'd stop before tears had a chance to form; *sometimes it worked.*

Taking a single tram to my hostel, I was glad I'd booked something by the sea. I was tired of big cities, I liked walking to places without the need to take a bus or a tube. Because of the cloud, I couldn't see much apart from a few silhouettes of boats and stalks searching for fish. Reigning in my temptation to explore, I followed my dad's advice to take it easy. *I'll find somewhere cool for dinner, then chill for the rest of the evening.* After a bit of research, I found a place that wasn't far from the hostel - an Okonomiyaki restaurant. It was a local delicacy that had been around for decades, I tried the veggie version: a thin pancake layer, shreds of cabbage, noodles, beansprouts, tempura crumbs, scrambled egg layer, sesame seeds, seaweed sprinkles, salt and pepper, topped with a heavy garnish of spring onions and a suspicious brown sauce (that looked a little like BBQ sauce but had a stronger flavour). I sat at the bar, watching as the chef worked at the metal hot plate that stretched the entire length of the countertop. She cooked everything on this one strip of metal, it was the entire kitchen. In a matter of minutes, with her two metal spatulas, she had chopped, flipped, swirled, flipped again and topped to create a mega portion of fried Okonomiyaki that was served for only five hundred yen.

Evening

I walked back in the drizzle, content with my cultural food experience and ready for an evening of writing, reading and munching chocolate coated pretzel sticks – also known in Japan as Pocky.

TWENTY-NINE

What a world we live in.

24ᵗʰ September

Hiroshima was smothered in a blanket of cloud, the continual drizzle reminded me of home. Don't get me wrong, I'd much prefer sunshine, but the familiarity of it was nice. I headed to the Atomic Bomb Peace Memorial Park. The rain was plummeting down by the time I got there, so I took refuge in the museum. I spent hours reading about the victims' stories, they were harrowing. I've never been brought to tears in a museum before but listening to video clips of the victims made me understand their horror. They had seen pain, suffering and death. People had had friends die in their arms, seen bodies blasted to pieces, felt the radioactive heat wave tear off their bare skin and lose everything and everyone in their lives. It didn't stop there, even after the blast, victims saw the destruction bleed into their futures with the long-term effects of radiation. Hiroshima was haunted by cancer, hair loss, internal bleeding and many other nasty side effects for decades to come. Moving further down the museum, mutated and burnt artefacts were laid out like a graveyard. Toys never to be played with again, a watch which stopped when its owner's heart did, battered cooking scales left as the only reminder of someone's mother. Each item had a story, one that deserved to be heard. The disaster and years of aftermath were horrific. But the worse thing? This was a man-made disaster.

The story that touched me most was a girl who had developed cancer almost a decade after the bombing. In a hope to recover, she believed that if she made one thousand origami cranes, she would be cured. Sadly, she died nine months later. Miniature cranes made from medicine wrappers were presented in the museum, I imagined the poorly little girl, desperately folding them as she became sicker each day. My heart went out to her, I could empathise with her story. *I have spent hundreds of days with nothing but drug wrappers by my bedside and will probably spend many more.* Now the city is scattered with origami cranes, a national symbol of health and happiness. School children from all over the country make paper cranes and send them to the monument. In the peace park, a metal girl stands proudly, her arms raised above her head holding a giant golden crane, proclaiming to the city that hope lives on. Next to it stands a large brass bell, I clasped the rope with both hands and shook it as hard as I could so the sound resonated throughout the city. *I have heard your story Hiroshima, and I have listened.*

Evening

I headed to a ramen joint for dinner, listed as a good option for veggies. You were given a tick-box list to decide what kind of ramen you would like, from firmness of the noodles to the amount of spice, oil and fat in the broth. It was not as simple as it sounded and once again, I was faced with the vending machine. I got chatting to some surgeons from New Zealand standing behind me in the queue, who were equally as puzzled. When we finally figured out how to order, they invited me to join them. We were seated in a little private booth, separated from the staff by a bamboo curtain, so anytime you had a request you just had to push a buzzer – a little odd! When the guys' food arrived it looked delicious, however I was presented with a plate of congealed noodles topped with some dry seaweed and rubbery mushroom shreds. Apparently, this wasn't the spot for non-meat eaters after all. So, trying to embrace the situation, I poured some of my cold drinking water into the bowl to make it more edible and attempted to swallow the dried noodles and seaweed. Not the best meal I have had in Japan, but at least the company was good to laugh about it with!

THIRTY

Miyajima - land of the floating shrine.

25th September

Kari was from Norway, I met her the night before last when we got chatting in the female dorm room, comparing travel notes on 'Jay-pan' as she pronounced it. She was nice, twenty-five, very friendly, open and keen to make friends; she was also obsessed with Instagram. I must admit, her account was pretty impressive, she had some beautiful photos of flowers and landscapes in Norway, clearly very talented with the camera.

This morning we both headed to Miyajima, making use of our free ferry tickets from the JR rail pass. We saw the impressive floating orange torii and multiple shrines on the seafront. It was only then, that I realised just *how* much she liked photography. Out came the tripod, three different lenses, and forty-five minutes of photo-taking. It was cool at first, I asked loads of questions, trying to learn how she got the pictures so perfect and offered to hold things like an assistant. Yet after walking for five minutes, out came the tripod and lenses and another forty-five-minute photo shoot. Then we walked a further ten minutes and the whole process started again.

Trying to mix up the day, I convinced her to walk up the small mountain, Mount Misen.

'Can't we take the cable car?'

'Well, we could, but I think it will be so much more rewarding if we get up there ourselves!' I replied eagerly.

We encountered a small waterfall eight minutes in, *I know because I was clock watching*, and out came the tripod and lenses. *Oh lord, if this is what it is going to be like the whole way, we'll never make it to the top!* This time she suggested I model in a few of the pictures. I called it statue modelling, because I had to remain completely still for an entire minute so she could get the blurry water effect with a super low shutter speed.

Eventually we made it to the top of the mountain, I don't think she was accustomed to much walking as we had to stop every few minutes. I kept saying to myself, *you could do this so much quicker by yourself.* But then I heard my mum's voice in reply, *make the most of having a friend, you are meant to be relaxing for your health, this is not a race, enjoy the gentle walk.* So I did, encouraging her often and allowing myself to enjoy both the slower pace and good company.

The view from the top was beautiful, light blue sea circled the coast of the mainland and small tree-covered islands peeped out of the floating blue mist. The ocean seemed to go on forever. I scrambled onto some larger rocks and raised my arms in the air so Kari could take a picture. Although, I immediately regretted it when she made me stand there for ten minutes with my hands raised, *people must think I'm creating a distress call! Just take the bloody photo!* I've never been more relieved for a thumbs up to come down from a rock!

Having only eaten a local momiji manju all morning, we headed back into town in search of some lunch.[11] Over bowls of spring onion soba noodles and shrimp tempura, we looked through the photos she had taken. I felt bad for being impatient along the walk because the pictures were incredible, crystal clear with such vivid colours; the ones of me were beautifully composed. I was grateful for her friendship. She was a lovely girl and we had had a fun day...I just couldn't put up travelling with her tripod all the time!

---

[11] *A croissant pressed into the shape of a maple leaf and filled with red bean paste.*

THIRTY-ONE

Danger is coming.

26th September

Fuck you stomach cramps.

They kept coming back. I had no choice but to swallow all the pills I could, heave my huge rucksack onto my back and head to catch my train out of Hiroshima. My energy levels were low, I felt drained of life and fed up with everything. Getting to the station I swallowed a few more pills. The attack started to dull on the train, but I was completely dead by the time I made it to Kokura. Feeling faint from the lack of food, I was resigned to an afternoon of resting. I sat on the balcony that overlooked the spacious café attached to the hostel; at least it was a nice atmosphere to relax and people watch.

'Hey, are you travelling alone?' I turned to see a round-faced girl in her mid-twenties with wispy blonde hair. Before I'd had a chance to respond she added, 'Because I am, and I'm fed up of being here solo. So, when I saw you were European, I thought I'd come and ask.'

I was exhausted but she sounded lonely and I had done exactly the same thing when I first landed in Singapore; it took guts to approach someone and I appreciated her coming over.

'Yes I am, I arrived a few hours ago. You just arrived too?'

'Yeah I've been here a few days, but it's for study, I'm getting questionnaire responses for my master's thesis. Do you want to grab some dinner later on?'

I could barely move I was so tired, but I felt bad turning her down, so agreed. It would be nice to have some company this evening, as opposed to the slightly odd Korean man in the dorm room who kept talking to me.

'Sure, I'd love to!'

I met Sophie an hour later, as planned, at a Japanese curry house a few metres from the hostel. It was nice to chat. I learnt all about her life and how she felt she was outgrowing her family, being the only one who had travelled while the rest stayed at home judging her for not settling down with a job.

'It sounds bad but I just feel I've become superior to them, outgrown my position as the little sister of the family. They judge me for not settling down but I see more opportunities in life than living in the Netherlands.'

I could understand where she was coming from. She continued to tell me about her long-term relationship for six and a half years, which broke when she moved to Japan to study.

'I cheated on him with my current boyfriend who's from the States. I recently visited him in America for three months but am now struggling with the distance. I hope one day we'll live together, have a long engagement perhaps. I'll apply for a fiancée visa and then green card, work permit etc...' she paused scooping another spoonful of rice and katsu into her mouth. I'd finished my meal a while ago, since all I really seemed to be doing was head nodding and the occasional, 'mm yes, sure, of course!'

That said, it was nice to have a catch-up as if I was with an old friend. It was easier to be a listener, rather than making continual small talk which is often the case when you meet someone for the first time.

27th September

Sophie had a spare ticket for the hostel breakfast, so kindly invited me to join her. An array of miso soup, salad, Japanese pickles, curry, rice and some tinned fruit were laid out in the hostel café, quite a breakfast! In return for her kindness, I upgraded her train ticket so she could take the fifteen-minute Shinkansen as opposed to the one-and-a-half-hour local train. We would then meet each other again for ramen in the evening, after she'd completed more questionnaires for her thesis.

I spent the afternoon walking around the city at a leisurely pace. I visited Kokura Castle and a Japanese garden, filled with brightly coloured koi carp, small wooden arched bridges and raked pebble patches. Well, it was leisurely until I had to run away from an intrusive male tourist.

'Hey, lady, come, you English?'

'Hi, yes that's right,' I said hesitantly.

'Well English girl, you look'in aroun? Yeah, so we look around together, yeah?'

'I'm actually just going, thank you though.'

'Come on pretty girl.'

'I'm actually meeting a friend, sorry.'

'Ah really, where is she now? Not with you?'

'She studies here, she's in class but I'm meeting her soon.'

'But now you are free, come on!'

Ergh, I'm fed up of encounters with strange men!

'Sorry, I have to go,' I said pointing to the pond.

As he looked to the pond, I started a fake conversation on my phone and darted away.

'Oh really, haha yes, I'm just coming. You're there already, fab I'm on my way.'

Little did he know I was having a conversation with the koi carp.

Back at the hostel

I had been admiring the paintings on the walls of the hostel café for some time. They portrayed the same cartoon character in various poses: in an onsen, eating onigiri, drinking saké and running errands. I was unaware anyone was watching me until a sweet Japanese lady approached and placed a yellow sticker of the same character on my table. Chatting to her for a while, I learnt she was in fact the artist, and was doing a tour, exhibiting her work around local cafés and hostels. They were very sweet, and I wanted to support her work, so bought a packet of six postcards. She drew me a little thank you note for buying the cards, writing my name in Japanese. *It's these small encounters that I love about solo travelling.*

After dinner I received a phone call from my dad. He was in Shanghai for work and it had been a Chinese public holiday for Mid-Autumn Festival. Making the most of the day off, he had gone sightseeing with another colleague and ended up in the shopping district, not exactly the highlight for two middle-aged men! I must admit, it was nice to be in the same time zone as one of my family members.

28th September

I planned to leave Kitakyushu late morning, just in case the stomach cramps returned. Waking up feeling okay, I enjoyed a simple breakfast of sliced nashi pear and icy grapefruit water, whilst watching the comings and goings of the café from the balcony. A pair of glamourous Japanese city girls in their early-twenties gossiped over a fancy curry, a group of middle-aged locals laughed loudly as they fed each other forkfuls of berry pancakes, a mother and daughter chatted over some miso soup and a few hostel guests enjoyed the rest of their pickles and rice from breakfast. It's funny how even though these people were speaking a different language, you could tell from their facial expressions and hand gestures exactly what they were talking about. I was so distracted people watching that I only noticed Sophie arrive when she plonked herself down next to me.

'I had a fall out with Dayn,' she huffed, pouting and folding her arms.

I didn't even need to ask before she started to explain, recounting the entire story up until we arrived at the train station. Essentially, her boyfriend was being lazy and making her do everything. *The poor gal* – I did feel for her. By the time she had finished her story it had reached midday. We wished each other well, with a quick parting hug, before heading to our platforms. Another friendship had come and gone.

Waiting to board the Shinkansen, I couldn't help but notice that a Nozomi was on the other track. Nozomi was the fastest bullet train on the Tokaido line, taking only a fifth of the time of local trains. A spark of adrenaline rippled through my body. *I could take that train instead.* It was prohibited with the rail pass and I'd get into trouble if I was caught; but it was only a fifteen-minute journey. *When else would I get the chance to ride it again?* The station board flashed and speakers bleeped in countdown as the train prepared to leave. *This was my chance, should I risk it?* I knew Alex would hate this if he were here; breaking the rules. I jumped through the doors just as they began to close. *Well Cece, there's no going back now.* I hastily found a free row in the non-reserved carriage and pushed my rucksack below my seat. *I'm guessing not many backpackers can afford to ride this bad boy.* The train began to move and within a few seconds we had left the city. We were whizzing through tunnels and mountains so quickly I could barely recognise the shapes outside.

In just under fifteen-minutes we had arrived, I hopped off the platform with a huge smile. *And nobody even checked my ticket.* I knew it was cheeky, but sometimes you have to be a little cheeky to get through life and all its challenges. I proudly messaged my dad and he was thrilled I'd tried it. *'Wow, that's fast,'* he replied on WhatsApp, *'Good for you for doing it.'* I knew he would have done the same. I didn't plan on telling Alex.

Fukuoka

Arriving at Fukuoka Backpackers, it was clear I had chosen location over ratings. Rundown and smelling of old slippers, I was glad this was only a one-night stop. Tomorrow I would be on a sunny beach in one of the many islands of Okinawa.

I headed to Ohori park in the middle of the city. It encompassed a large lake and island that you could access via two bridges from either side. Feeling the need for some veg, I picked up a simple salad with grated radish, seaweed and lettuce and sat by the lake in the intermittent sunshine. A terrapin floated by, sticking his red spotted head out of the water like a periscope, observing the passersby. He hung around for a while, so I tried to offer him bits of my lunch which just ended up floating to the bottom; turns out he wasn't such a big fan of salad after all. *So, it's really come to this Cece, spending lunchtime with a terrapin.*

Filling time, I ambled around the lake and castle ruins. On the way back, I was stopped by an old Japanese man.

'Hello, hello there.'

'Oh, hello, good afternoon,' I replied.

'Beautiful accent English, I like English,' he slurred, 'beautiful.'

I felt uneasy, he had caught me at a point when I was hidden to the public, the old castle wall blocked my sight to any nearby roads or paths.

'Oh yes, England is really pretty, have you been?'

'No, but I want to go.'

'Great, well nice to meet you!' I said, starting to edge away to a more visible space.

As I turned, he took my wrist with force, bringing my body back round to face him.

'Be careful, young layee,' he said severely, pausing as he tried to articulate his point.

Frozen and in shock by the physical contact, all I could do was question him, 'What do you mean?'

'Danger, there is danger here, be careful. Yes, be careful.'

'Um, I'm sorry what do you mean, I don't understand?'

He released my wrist and started to walk in the other direction. I turned around to see if anyone else was around. It was just me.

'Was a pleasure to meet you, English girl,' he said bowing his head as he disappeared round the corner.

I ran in the opposite direction. *Danger? What did he mean? I thought Japan was meant to be one of the safest countries in the world.* It was getting dark by this point and the sky had turned an ominous greyish purple. *Did he mean the weather?* I ran until I was back in view of the public and rang Alex, I needed to feel like someone else was with me on the way back to the hostel. We chatted about the usual stuff, work, home in the UK, the number of days until he was flying out to meet me in China and finally the plan that he would bring my medication with him.

'Oh and Cece, that box of meds your mum sent to my house,' he paused, 'I, I don't think I can bring it all to you.'

My stomach sank.

'But Alex I need those meds. You know how ill I have been; I've used more than I could have predicted.'

'I know but it's just so much, it weighs several kilograms; I won't be able to fit it in my rucksack. I can try to bring the vitamins and buy non-prescription anti-histamines but the prescription stuff, well, I don't feel comfortable doing it.'

I took a deep breath before speaking to make sure my frustration didn't transfer over the phone.

'I know Alex, but I wouldn't ask you if I wasn't desperate. I've been really ill and I need these meds. Right now, this is my only option.'

Technically what I was asking him to do was forbidden, it wasn't fair of me to ask.

'I don't think I can do it Cece.'

'But I don't know what else to do, I don't want to get more ill Alex,' I said, trying to stop my voice from wailing.

His voice became a little harsher, 'You're putting me in a difficult position.'

I knew what I was asking him to do was wrong, but if it had been Alex who was sick, I wouldn't have questioned helping him.

'I know, Alex, it is not fair of me to ask, but I am desperate. I don't know what else to do.'

'Cece, I can't.'

'Please Alex, I need the med...' I trailed off, trying not to cry. I was frustrated with myself for asking him to do something like this, it was unfair. But I didn't know what else to do. I was alone and scared of becoming more ill.

'Cece, if it was legal, I would do it but I'm not getting caught. I can't do it.'

My one lifeline had disappeared. I knew Alex would do his very best to get as much of it to me as he could, but the medication I really needed would remain at home. I couldn't help but feel a little empty. We cut the call shortly after as he left for work.

Back at the hostel

Lying on the top bunk I checked my emails, trying to think of a new 'drug action plan'. I smiled when I saw I had an email from Nanami. The smile was quickly wiped from my face after reading the first line.

'Charlotte,
I hate to break this to you, but you must not go to Okinawa. There is a very powerful and dangerous storm coming, you will be caught in it.
Please do not go.
Nanami.'

I immediately checked the weather to see what I would be faced with. My mouth fell open when I saw the satellite image of Typhoon Trami. An immense mass of cloud had formed a spiral around a perfect black circle - the eye of the storm. It was like the earth had pulled the plug. Four hundred miles south of Okinawa, fluctuating between a category four and five, this monster was heading towards the islands within the next few days. *Fuck.* I rang my mum. Breaking the news about the typhoon and the drugs was probably the worst combination I could have chosen.

'You need to come home Charlotte. Just buy a flight home, get your meds, wash your clothes and fly back out again when it's all over.'

'Um Mum.'

'Charlotte, I mean it, just do it, look up flights now,' her voice became assertive, 'Charlotte, do it now.'

Trying to keep calm, I reassured her I would check as soon as I put the phone down. But as I hung up, I burst into tears. She had made me feel so scared and stressed. I couldn't handle two twenty-four-hour journeys in a week, it would drain me. However, I would get more ill without my medication and I didn't want to die in a typhoon. But I did not want to give up on my journey either, I had come this far. Composing myself, I rang Dad; he had a cool head and was good in stressful situations. We made a plan to research doctors in Hong Kong and look for flights that would leave Japan earlier. I had a few days to escape, otherwise I'd be stranded in Japan until the storm passed.

I was scared but I wasn't going to give up. I wasn't going home just yet.

THIRTY-TWO

Hakata: The canal city.

29th September

I felt tired and achy as I hauled my rucksack onto my back in preparation to move hostels. I had been kept up late by a sweet, but very chatty, guy from the Philippines who had arrived just as I was going to sleep. Keen to make friends, he gave me a little bag of dried Philippine mango and nattered on relentlessly about his travels. He had just come back from Okinawa and was singing its praises, making me even sadder not to visit the place. But as much as I wanted to see the islands, it would be stupid to visit a beach while a typhoon was raging.

Hakata City Centre

The sea bled into the land forming several canals, the veins of Hakata. My new hostel was in the middle of a lively shopping street, sandwiched between two canals; the city had a fun vibe. When I asked the hostel owner for sightseeing suggestions, she gave a simple response.

'Eat. The food is amazing wherever you go.'

She wasn't wrong, the streets were filled with stalls and cafés selling green onigiri, fried fish balls, sugar dusted mochi, big bowls of ramen and sweet custard. I thought I would try udon noodles for lunch, a national delicacy I had yet to sample. Waiting in line at the noodle bar, a pair of Japanese and Thai women were seated before me, even though they were behind me in the queue. I ushered them along, trying to show that I didn't mind them going before me. In return, they invited me to join them for lunch!

Despite feeling like I was in a speaking and listening exam, it was nice to lunch with the locals. I learnt that the older, broad faced lady was teaching the petite Thai woman to speak Japanese. With a brisk manner, enthusiastic hand gestures and a tone of voice that was slightly authoritarian, I could tell she was a teacher without understanding a word she said. As soon as she had slurped her broth, she flew off to the tourist information centre, returning with a handful of maps, leaflets and gimmicky plastic fans; and before I'd even had the chance to pick up my second slippery noodle, she had paid the bill for everyone's meal. I had known her for thirty minutes and she had already bought my lunch, given me help and made my day a whole lot better. Such kindness.

Afternoon

Fukuoka Tower was my next destination, I waited behind a line of eager school children with their teacher on a day trip. We took a lift up through the centre of the tower, whizzing past the metal brackets and interior scaffolding that were invisible from the outside. The view was nice but the vast mass of buildings from the expanding city had started to invade the mountains and sea, so the whole area was covered in shades of brown and grey. I spent most of the time on my phone, trying to get an appointment with a doctor in Hong Kong for medication.

Heading back to the hostel

On the way back I bumped into a man playing with a cup and ball. He was old, very slim and was so focused on the child's toy. It was quite adorable.

I smiled, 'You're good at that.'

When he noticed his observer, he chimed 'Cup and bawl, cup and bawl.'

'Ah yes, very good, tricky though!'

'Ah, practice, much practice.'

We got chatting and it turned out he was a sixty-six-year-old student.

'I love study,' he smiled. He had taken 330 exams and was aiming to get to five hundred before he was seventy.

'I wan get into Guinness Book of World Records,' he proudly exclaimed, 'I love knowledge, love learning.'

When he learnt I was a maths teacher, he started scrawling differential and integral signs along with several complex summation formulae on a scrap of paper. I raised my eyebrows to show him I was impressed.

Leaving him at the bus stop, I called back.

'I'll look out for you!'

He gave a huge smile and waved, 'Thank you, you watch for me in record book!'

Evening

I knew I had to decide tonight. I wasn't ready to leave this country, but I needed to get out of Japan before the typhoon hit and my medication ran out. If I didn't leave tomorrow, I risked airport closures, missing my trip to China and getting more ill.

So, that was it. I booked a flight, making this my last night in Japan.

PART THREE

China

THIRTY-THREE

Culture shock.

30th September
Hong Kong (HK)

The bus was noisy, streets were dirty, and people were grumpy and unwilling to help. Hong Kong seemed like a different world and I didn't know how to adjust. I had taken Japan's calm, ordered way of life for granted over the past few weeks; now I longed for it. I regretted booking a hostel so far away from the city centre. The bus from the airport was long and the driver shouted at me when I didn't have the correct change. I spent the whole journey praying Google Maps wouldn't crash so I'd know when to get off. Several hours later I made it to Aberdeen. The area was rugged, rougher than anything we'd driven through; the glamourous skyscrapers and glitzy shopping malls were a long way away from this district. Life was different on this side of the island.

Thankfully, my hostel was clean and modern with a beautiful view. It overlooked the floating fishing village and harbour which didn't seem to stop moving. Sea traffic floated in and out all day and all night, bringing trade from far and wide. In my mixed dorm I met a Chinese guy in his mid-twenties. He'd been travelling in South America for the past few years and was on the final leg of his journey home. He took me to his favourite ice-cream place where we both had large scoops of tofu ice-cream.

'It's so good, I've been here almost every night!' he said smiling eagerly.

'Okay, I'll try some, if you recommend!' I said taking the cone, 'Mmm, tastes a little like I could put it on my cereal but kind of nice, I like it!'

We spent the rest of the evening trying to navigate back to the hostel, after touring the shopping centre for tabasco sauce.

'I know it's an odd request, but my girlfriend loves it and they don't sell it back home.'

So, first night in Hong Kong consisted of tofu ice cream and a hunt for tabasco sauce. *I'd say that's a pretty good start.*

1ˢᵗ October

Feeling tired but not wanting to waste the day, I forced myself to have a little walk around town in the morning sun. I needed to get a SIM card so I would have data for the next few days, *I wasn't chancing anymore dodgy bus rides alone.* After five minutes of walking, exhaustion hit me, I felt dizzy and it became difficult to keep my eyes open. I found myself crouching on the shop floor, trying to regain my balance. I managed to buy a SIM Card but feeling nauseous and even more dizzy, I decided it was time to return to the hostel. I clutched the railings along the pavement as I walked back down the road. It was only fifty metres to the hostel but it felt like five hundred, with every step I took, the hostel moved back a further three. I could barely keep my eyes open and I felt like I was about to throw up. Within a few metres of the hostel, my vision went black.

Unknown time

'Ca va, ca va? Que s'est-il passé?'
'Pouvez-vous m'entendre?'
'I don't know, she just collapsed.'
'D'accord.'
'She's not waking up.'
'Allez, call 999.'

Unknown time

A door shut. I was lying down but was somehow shaking from side to side. I was too tired to open my eyes.

Unknown time

I forced myself to open my eyes. There was a cannula in my arm and I was on a hospital bed. I closed my eyes again.

Unknown time

I opened my eyes. I tried to sit up but collapsed back down from the exertion. There was no one beside me except an elderly lady moaning in the bed next to me. The smell was foul, she was clearly unwell. *Where am I? In a hospital? What happened? Oh, I'm completely alone.* I lay very still, trying not to cry. I was scared, alone and very scared. A doctor came in after ten minutes. She spoke little English but I learnt that I had passed out and been brought here by an ambulance.

'We do test and you okay,' she said, handing me a slip of paper, 'you can go when you ready, I gi you pill for dizziness, you take tree time a day.'

'Um okay, thank you.'

'If you feel bad, you come again and we do more test, okay?'

'Okay.'

'You wait here while we dischar.'

'Okay thank you,' I whispered as she rushed behind the white curtain that separated me from the rest of the hectic emergency ward.

I looked down at the paper, *'$500 for day'*.

Oh shit. Now what do I do?

I felt my phone vibrate on the bed. *Thank goodness, the SIM card, I'm not completely alone!*

I messaged my mum to explain what I thought had happened. Luckily Mum had a friend of a friend, Iris, who lived in Hong Kong. Iris would come after work and pick me up from the hospital to make sure I didn't pass out again on the way back to the hostel.

[01/10, 15:59] Mum: Everything is going to be okay Charlotte, she will look after you. Can you make it out by yourself, maybe they could give you a wheelchair?

[01/10, 16:04] Me: Yes, but I have no one with me to push it and I don't think they'd understand. I can't speak Cantonese. I think I'll be okay. I can sit up now without feeling too faint.

[01/10, 16:05] Mum: Okay good, just take it really slowly, sit down on the floor if you need to, just make your way to reception where Iris will pick you up.

Still feeling extremely lightheaded, I made my way to reception, clutching the railings for support. I sank into the nearest chair, *I'd made it, just about.* An older lady approached, tutting and giving me dirty looks, ushering me to give up the seat for herself. With no energy to protest I used my hands to lower myself onto the floor, shuffled slowly to the wall and sat with my head between my legs. I think the old lady tried to give me the chair back by this point, but I didn't look up in case I passed out. I waited alone, trying to remain conscious until Iris arrived.

THIRTY-FOUR

The Healing Room: On the seventh day, God took a break. So loss,
pain and loneliness evolved.

1st October
5:32p.m.

Iris was a devout Christian and a primary school teacher. She dressed elegantly like a Hobbs model and her face was lightly coated in foundation giving her a pearly angelic glow. She kindly dropped me off at the hostel with a little M&S picnic, so I wouldn't have to worry about food for tonight.[12] Before leaving, she said a little prayer and suggested I go to The Healing Room if I was feeling better tomorrow.

'I volunteer there on Saturday mornings, it's an incredible experience. I think it will really help you, with your CVS. I believe this is your time Charlotte.'

'So, is it like a hospital?'

'No no, it's in a church, the healers come every Saturday. They will try and help you with the pain, everyone deserves to be well in the Lord's eyes,' she smiled. 'There have been so many testimonies. People have been cured from all sorts of things, even cancer, after attending The Healing Room.'

'Oh wow, that's incredible. Well I'll certainly think about it if I am feeling well enough tomorrow,' I replied, knowing inside that I would never go to something like this. 'Thank you so much Iris, you've been so kind to me.'

20 minutes later

I successfully made it upstairs and into bed without passing out. *Victory.*

---

[12] *Yes, they really do have M&S food in Hong Kong.*

As the evening went on, I thought more about The Healing Room. *Perhaps I should go, it wouldn't hurt, what was the harm in trying? No, it's ridiculous Cece. There's no science behind the idea, illnesses don't disappear overnight with a few prayers and waves of the hand.* I rang my mum and she confirmed it wasn't just I who thought it was a strange concept.

2ⁿᵈ October

I woke to a simple message.

[02/10, 08:23] Mum: I think you should go, Mxx

Maybe I had been too closed-minded. It wouldn't hurt to try. I've tried pretty much every drug, treatment and diet on the planet, what harm would one more attempt do?

I decided to go, if not for myself, for my mum. She had sacrificed so much of her time looking after me when I was ill, the least I could do in return was try and fix myself. *You never know Cece, if your CVS is cured, it could be a miracle.*

Sitting upright made me feel dizzy, so it took me a while to get ready. I edged onto the bus, taking deep breaths to remain upright and conscious. Dropped off in the centre of town, I struggled to find the church Iris had described. I walked around in circles searching for any form of holy building in between the tower blocks. I tried asking for help but passersby carried on, dismissing me with their hands, annoyed that I'd interrupted them. I leant against a metal fence, it was hot and I had started to feel dizzy again. Luckily a smiling couple approached me and gave me some pointers in the right direction. *No wonder I couldn't find the church, it was inside a flipping tower block!*

Walking up the stairs, I entered a narrow corridor, crammed with a desk and a row of chairs. It looked more like a GP surgery than anything else.

'Hello, are you here for prayer or call of healing?' a woman asked.

'Umm, I'm not sure, Iris invited me.'

'Iris who?'

'Iris Idell. I have an illness, so she suggested I come here.'

'Oh, Iris Idell!'

'Yes that's her.'

'Okay perfect, fill in one of these,' she said handing me a form on a clipboard.

'Thank you.'

I flew through the registration form, age, birth, address, next of kin, illness, medication etc... I'd filled out so many forms in the past decade I could do them with my eyes closed. The last question, however, made me pause, '*Are you suffering from anything else not listed already?*'

I hesitated before writing 'bereavement', but a few moments later scribbled it out again. I wasn't sure why, I guess I knew I wouldn't be able to contain myself if they brought up Grandma.

Returning the form, I was taken to a darkened room, with candles and spiritual music playing '*Let Jesus find a place in your heart...*' There were two others waiting, one of them dabbing her tears while the other prayed silently with his eyes closed.

'You are put in here to soak up the Lord's presence and holiness,' the woman whispered as she rested her hand on my shoulder before closing the door.

I didn't quite know what to feel or how to react. It was so stereotypically Christian it was almost funny, but on the other hand it forced me to think about the last month, how ill I'd become and how grief had invaded everything. The room became oppressive and I felt terribly alone.

'Number twenty-two, twenty-two?' a woman called as light flooded into the room from the corridor. I checked my paper and twenty-two was printed on my ticket, *the Lord's very own game of bingo.*

'That's me,' I said, raising my hand cautiously.

'Come here dear, I'll take you to the room with God's healers and victims,' she said quietly.

What was this, the Hunger games?

I entered a bright, and surprisingly noisy room filled with healers and victims chanting, praying and crying out. Being pushed through the crowd of people I was introduced to my healer, Bonnie, accompanied by her entourage of two young Cantonese women who stood behind me on either side, enclosing me in a holy triangle.

'So today is the last day you feel pain, okay?' Bonnie boldly pronounced. 'God created us to feel joy, not misery. You know where you are? This is the world, the home of God's children. Do you know who you are, apart from Charlotte and your parent's daughter?'

'Um, a sister?' I replied quietly, taken aback by the cult-like nature of the room.

'God's daughter, you are *his* daughter and he will take care of you. Now close your eyes, yes close them. Hands out and palms open, facing upwards. Repeat after me. Dear Lord.'

'Dear Lord,' I repeated.

'I come here today to be healed.'

'I come here today to be healed.'

'I praise you Lord.'

'I praise you Lord.'

'I open my heart to yo...'

We were stopped by a petite lady wearing jazzy black and white chequered trousers and thick black-rimmed glasses. She bounced onto the stage like a karaoke host.

'Soooo it's time for the testimonies!' she rallied.

Everyone cheered and clapped as a man with his healer walked on stage.

Bonnie whispered. 'These are the people who have come today and already been healed, they are testimonies to God's work.'

Confused, I listened. *How could anyone be healed instantly?*

The man's healer began preaching to the crowd, 'When Jan arrived, he had pain all down his left side, a pain level seven out of ten. So we prayed, and what happened Jan?'

'The pain went down to five.'

'So we prayed again. And the pain went down to what Jan? Tell us what happened to your pain.'

'It went down to three.'

'And I said, three is not acceptable, not in the Lord's house! So we prayed again.'

The healer was almost shouting by this point, waving his arms up to the sky like he was a conductor at a grand hall.

'And tell them Jan, what happened next?'

'It went to nought point five,' said Jan smiling.

'Nought point five, well would you look at that. Nought point five ladies and gentleman, nought point five. Nought point five from a seven. Well, praise the Lord!'

'Thanks Jan and healer,' congratulated the host as she jumped back on stage, 'so, all you out there who suffer from pain, step forward, step into God's light, God's Healing Room. And let's heal!'

The crowd cheered wildly.

'Now, all those who feel pain, put your hands in the centre.'

Bonnie gestured for me to follow the instruction.

'Now, Jan, share God's power with all our sufferers,' jeered the host.

So, Jan hovered his palm over the pile of hands, including mine.

'Jan, share the love,' the host continued, 'share the joy, share the peace. Everyone repeat after me. My pain is cured, from now on my pain will go.'

'My pain is cured, from now on my pain will go,' chanted the crowd of victims.

It was empowering; to see so much hope in a room filled with so much sorrow. I tried to open my heart, to feel the hope that everyone else did, but fury and pain filled its place.

I closed my eyes to fight the tears but they still fell out of my tightly closed lids, dropping from my eyelashes, staining my cheeks. My body convulsed from the effort of containing my cries. I wanted to feel the hope, but all I could feel was anger, because none of it was true. Pain couldn't just disappear. And even if it could, it wouldn't happen to me because it hadn't happened to my grandma, nor her sister, nor my Grandfather. Cancer had claimed them all. *Where was the Lord when my grandma was in so much pain? Where has he been for the past twelve years as CVS has tried to take over my life? If he is so benevolent and omnipresent, then why did I have to travel to a foreign land and repeat the words of a stranger to be cured? How is that just when half the world's population could never afford the plane fare? In God's eyes, do you have to pay in order to live without pain?*

Jan was shortly followed by two other victims who had miraculously recovered. *Were these people ever really ill?* Seeing my anguish, Bonnie led me out of the crowd. It was too much. I thought The Healing Room would have been one councillor in a quiet place, not a room filled with fifty wailing people, film cameras, stages and microphones. I burst into tears. My world was collapsing.

'Okay Charlotte, God loves you, dry your eyes,' Bonnie's voice commanded. Her entourage echoing 'Amen' and 'oh yeah' after every word she spoke.

They placed a tiara on my head to symbolise my place in God's kingdom.

'Smile Charlotte, smile to show God you love him,' Bonnie encouraged as she took my photo.

What is this? The last thing I want to do is wear a fricking tiara when I'm crying my eyes out!

'Here,' she said handing back my phone, 'now you can remember you are always God's daughter and princess.'

I tried to focus my teary eyes on the image. I was far from a princess. My curls were flattened from last night's heavy sleep, deep shadows hung under my eyes, my nose was red from crying and my smile was fake. I looked lifeless. If anything, it was a reminder of the loss, pain and isolation I felt.

'Right, I have another client, so I must go,' Bonnie announced. Giving me a limp hug, she whispered, 'Remember, God is with you, the pain stops now, finished. No more pain, okay?'

'Okay, thank you Bonnie, for your time.' A fake smile plastered my face to hold back the tears.

It was very kind of them to give up their Saturday to help innocent people and I really was grateful. I desperately wanted it to work, I wanted to be healed. But as much as I tried, I could not believe it. As soon as I got to the bathroom, I collapsed onto the floor.[13]

---

[13] *My opinions are my own, I do not mean to offend or challenge anyone's beliefs. I believe these organisations do a lot of good work and help many people, but it just wasn't my time.*

THIRTY-FIVE

Family is a sacrifice, but it is the only thing worth sacrificing for.

2nd October

When she learnt I wasn't feeling well, Iris took me back to her flat after The Healing Room closed. I tagged along with her weekend routine, picking up a late lunch for her husband and doing a few chores in town, before taking a taxi to a forty-seven-story block of flats. Her flat was simple and neat, filled with well-worn furnishings and cabinets lined with photos of her only son, Noah (who coincidentally attended the same university as me in the UK). I slid onto the sofa, hoping it would inhibit the dizziness.

Hearing our arrival, Iris' husband burst into the room, throwing his hands out in a rather intimidating welcome. He seized the bag of sushi and rushed to the kitchen, evidently hungry. He spoke little English, so Iris had to do the translating. I knew he was welcoming me into his home, but the Cantonese style of speaking made it seem more like he was telling me off. He spoke gruffly as he shoveled huge pieces of sushi into his mouth, chewing loudly like a bear devouring a fish. He didn't match Iris' calm and refined character. He was rougher, his skin was darker and his face creased from age and experience. Aberdeen born and bred; he had experienced a different kind of life.

'There's a big contrast on the island, the rich and the poor, separated only by the short peak of Victoria,' Iris explained.

She quietly told me how her husband works with a lot of tough families in which drugs and alcohol are more common on a shopping list than rice. 'He loves helping these people because he grew up in a similar environment. Our two worlds were close but very different,' Iris said looking admirably into her husband's eyes, 'he's a tough man, but caring. He says that until your boyfriend arrives, we'll look after you,' Iris smiled.

'You stay with my family, we look after you,' grunted her husband, 'I worry bout you, a young gurl. You stay here, okay?'

I was touched. It had been two months since I had been in someone's home, a place of memories, a place with meaning, a place where people cared for you. I felt at ease; at least if I fainted again, they would look after me.

Afternoon

Iris and her husband had a long-standing tradition that every Saturday afternoon they would go and see a movie. This Saturday, I joined as a third wheel. After the film, and knowing I liked the food in Japan, they took me to a Japanese restaurant. Iris had her usual ramen and her husband ordered eel with rice for him and I. I was apprehensive at first, but the soy marinade and light frying made it taste tender and, actually, rather good. We chatted about lots of things, including the challenges Iris faced at her primary school.

'You see, there are only two words to express emotion in Cantonese, happy and sad. So the only way to express degrees of emotion is by adding "really", and "really really". For this reason, it's difficult for Chinese children to express how they feel to their families. So I have to encourage them to use different words in English, but it's a challenge!'

After dinner they popped me on a minibus back home. It was nice, being in their world, being a part of their family. For the first time in a while, I felt at ease again.

3rd October

Woke up not feeling too bad today, the dizziness was not as strong as it had been. I joined Iris and her extended family at a traditional local restaurant in the centre of the high-end part of town, Causeway Bay. Circular tables filled a huge room which took up an entire floor in the shopping centre. The place was packed, I heard the restaurant before I'd even left the lift. Hundreds of conversations in Cantonese took place as families caught up over Sunday lunch. I think it was meant to be nice, but to me it seemed like noisy table fights with chopsticks. I felt nervous approaching the table, every pair of eyes fell on me. *What is this British girl doing here? She doesn't belong here.* To my relief I was met with welcoming smiles and was introduced as 'Charlotte, the English girl'. *Nice, but I felt a bit like a cucumber sandwich on a plate of steamed dumplings.*

Within five minutes of sitting down, a multitude of wooden circular baskets were placed on the lazy Susan, a spinning table that allowed everyone to access the different dishes. I watched the seamless dance of spinning, picking up an item, placing the food into your mouth and repeating. Trying to blend in, I negotiated a small cube of fried tofu onto my plate with chopsticks. *Success, I'm in.* Even when the table was full, waiters continued to come, ferrying away empty baskets and replacing them with steaming pork dumplings, rice paper parcels, chicken feet, pork in black bean sauce, prawn wontons, rice rolls, fried vegetable folds, marinated fish heads and countless other dim sum dishes. This feast was all washed down with steaming jugs of green tea.

'It helps to cleanse the body of the oil,' Iris explained.

I enjoyed blending into the vibrant atmosphere, families laughing and shouting. I didn't know exactly what they were saying but I smiled anyway, content at just soaking up the ambiance and being part of the large family. Watching me observe the scene, Iris commented,

'I know it looks like an argument is going on from the way conversations sound, but if they are smiling, it's normally a happy conversation.'

'Ah okay ahah, so I'll keep smiling then to join in!' I chuckled.

Opposite me, sat Iris' father. He was a generous, sage and very successful old man. Throughout the meal, he made sure I always had enough to eat, spinning the table around so

I could take from the veggie plates, and respectfully smiled when we made eye contact. He paid for the entire meal, graciously handing his cheque to the waiter with a grin that expressed his pride at providing for his family. When everyone got up to leave, I thanked him personally, bowing my head to show how grateful I was. His generosity reminded me of my grandfather.

Church

Iris took me to church in the afternoon. It was mad, like a concert with religious songs where people were proclaiming their love for God rather than Ed Sheeran. They were swaying, fist pumping, dancing eccentrically and even crying. It was quite entertaining, probably the most engaging service I'd ever been to, but not what I had expected. Iris and her friend prayed for me at the end of the service, placing their hands on my shoulders and speaking as if they were doing a dramatic reading from the Bible.

'Oh Father God, we thank you for bringing Charlotte to life. From deep within her mother's womb you have brought her here, to guide her, to show her, her true potential. Oh Father God...'

The way they spoke about God was almost orgasmic, sighing 'Amen' every thirty seconds. It was a unique experience, to say the least.

Post-church bubble waffles

On the way to the bus station, we stopped at a small slot in the wall to buy a famous HK bubble waffle. We watched as the sweet batter crisped-up in the bubble grill until it was a golden brown. In exchange for fifteen Hong Kong dollars, we were handed a steaming buttery waffle wrapped in paper to share. Iris invited me to her flat for dinner, but I was tired and had started to feel dizzy from fatigue so made my excuses and left for a quiet evening.

Evening

I'd had a lovely day, but finally being alone with myself, I allowed my thoughts to get the better of me. I felt exhausted and just flat. There was so much I wanted to tell my grandma, about Hong Kong and Iris' family and parents, but I would never get the chance again. No matter how many things I filled my day with, the grief of my grandma always consumed me in the end. Each day it stole another piece of me; it was personifying itself into a thief. This evening, I didn't feel like it would be long until there was nothing left, until Grief had taken everything.

4ᵗʰ October
Evening

After a quiet day to myself, I joined Iris for a family dinner at her parents' house. I felt like I should take something so picked out some pretty white flowers earlier in the day. Getting into the taxi, Iris' eyes widened as she stared at the bouquet in my hand.

'Oh,' she exclaimed.

'Sorry, are you allergic?'

'No no, it's just in Hong Kong, we have certain flowers that we only use for certain occasions.'

'Okay, did I choose the wrong ones?'

'Yes, these ones are only used to commemorate the dead.'

'Oh my gosh I'm so sorry! I can't believe I've bought flowers for the dead, I'm so sorry Iris!'

'Yes you did. It's okay, I like them, give them to me, I'll put them up in my house, but my parents are traditional, they will be very offended if you present them.'

'Okay, I'm so sorry.'

'It's okay Charlotte, just don't let them see the flowers!'

Despite the floral fiasco, the evening was lovely. The flat was huge and in a very affluent part of town. The mother cooked a banquet for her family with the help of a Filipino woman who I'd met at lunch yesterday. I learnt from Iris that she was paid very well for a domestic helper, but even that wasn't enough to afford a flight back to see her family in the Philippines more than once every two years.

'It is a tough life, but the best chance she could give to her family,' Iris whispered.

For the rest of the evening I chatted to Iris' son, Noah, about times at university. We reminisced about the different bars, streets and places we had frequented as undergraduates at Exeter. Close to midnight we watched the fireworks from the balcony, it was National Day Fireworks.

I was sad to say goodbye to Iris, it was an incredible experience and a privilege to have been welcomed into her family for the week. I was so very grateful for her kindness; she had given me the strength to recover after hospital and continue with my travels.

THIRTY-SIX

The Dragon Trip begins.

5th October

I packed up and left Aberdeen, my recovery home for the past week. My doctor's appointment was at 1p.m. at a private practice on the other side of the island - I was lucky to get the slot with only a week's notice. It was my last hope of getting the medication I needed for the rest of the trip. I explained everything to the doctor, the multitude of CVS attacks, the sickness, the fainting and the fatigue. To my relief, she prescribed all the medication I needed. After twenty minutes of unboxing and re-packaging, I managed to fit every sachet and pill into my rucksack, but I was left with a bill of 562 dollars for medication that would have been free at home. *Oh well, you can't put a price on health.*

My rucksack was now backbreakingly heavy. Walking through town, with the weight and heat, I was feeling increasingly dizzy. Feeling close to fainting by the time I arrived at The Dragon Trip's first hostel, I slid down the wall and sat with my head between my knees waiting for the lift.[14] *Shit, I can't pass out again.*

'Cece? Cece! I've been trying to ring you!'

I looked up hearing the familiar voice.

'Alex! Hey!'

'Why didn't you pick up your phone? Your mum has been ringing me like crazy because you haven't answered any messages all day!' he exclaimed.

'I'm sorry my data ran out so I couldn't contact anyone.'

---

[14] *The Dragon Trip was an organised tour booked prior to leaving. I wanted to see many provinces in China, so considering the country's size, a tour seemed like the best option taking into account my timespan and health.*

'Are you okay?'

'Yeah, I just feel really faint again.'

'Oh no,' he said sitting down beside me.

'I'm okay I just need to rest for a bit.'

He put his arm around me, 'I've missed you so much!'

'I've missed you too Alex.'

It was such a relief to be with someone I knew again, but I won't deny it felt strange. A lot had happened in the month we'd been apart, I'd been through so much alone.

6th October

After a night spent in bunk beds, The Dragon Trip group united in the common room where we met our guide, Alfred. An eccentric sixty-year-old man with wiry grey eyebrows that spilled out over his glasses and moved every time he spoke. He had a passion for spouting Hong Kong history and waving a little red flag like he was in the military. Introduced in one go, everyone's names were a blur to me, but I knew there was a Welsh, Southern and Scottish couple, two Northern pairs, a thirty-year-old Essex lad, two chatty nurses and us.

We left at 7a.m. for Victoria Peak, where we had breakfast and were informed about the rest of the day's agenda. From there, we boarded a coach, tube, train, another tube and finally a bullet train that would take us to Yangshuo. The train station was huge and it was a slog to heave the rucksacks on and off the X-ray belts at every gate we entered. *It was worse than an airport.* After the long journey, we arrived in Yangshuo and headed straight to a restaurant for a group meal. Plates of steamed rice, chilli broad beans, oily tofu, baked aubergine, fresh fried carrots and lemon chicken were repeatedly passed around the table until we could eat no more. Paying forty yuan each (less than five pounds) for the plentiful meal, we retired back to the hostel ready for the trip to officially begin tomorrow.

THIRTY-SEVEN

People sea. People mountain.

7ᵗʰ October

By the second day, the group had started to divide, the alkies and non-alkies. Those who'd rather sightsee under the glow of neon light and stumble between bars, and those who'd rather fill their days with sunlit adventures. With the pressure to bond, drinking in the evening had become an unofficial part of the agenda, something Alex and I weren't interested in when there were so many opportunities during the day. When our dorm mates crawled in, unsteady from beer consumption, we'd be waking up. Luckily today, however, a few people were still keen to head to the river, *even after several beers.* The first activity was kayaking on the Li River; exposing us to the true beauty of Yangshuo. The water was bright green and so clear you could see every reed and fishing net at the bottom. Chinese men and women, waist high in the water, were dotted along the banks, plunging their hands down to collect large snails to sell to restaurants. I became the group's photographer with my waterproof camera as we paddled down the river, exploring small caves and wildlife. We posed with paddles in the air, couples smiled and individuals raced on the river as the sun warmed our bodies. It was a happy morning.

Evening

We headed into the city centre, pushing through the crowds of people. Standing on the bridge that looked down the main promenade, I was stunned. Never before had I seen a collection of human bodies on such a scale. I can only describe it as our tour guide, Jia, did:

'People sea, people mountain.'

There were thousands of bodies. It was impossible to move through the masses. Jia and I were the smallest so we could scurry between the crowds but the rest of the group were left standing, waiting for the wave of people to ripple further down the street. Wherever you looked there was something, a smell, a sound, a show. Brightly coloured lanterns covered arched bridges and fairy lights illuminated little trees. Sweet coconut pastries and buttery tart samples were handed out on cocktail sticks. A man pummeled spices to the rhythm of house music, glow in the dark head wreathes were catapulted into the air and passionfruit pipped ice-lollies melted in children's hands, as vendors sold juicy chunks of dragon fruit, persimmon, melon, mango, guava and pineapple. There was nothing but smiles, as people enjoyed the wonders of Yangshuo during Golden Week.

8th October
10a.m.

Alex and I enjoyed cool mango smoothies for breakfast, sweet cubes of fresh mango were whizzed with ice, creating a light, sweet and energising morning drink.

Being super keen, I'd convinced a few couples to sign up to rock climbing in Yangshuo valley. We were driven into the heart of the countryside, where top ropes were set up by friendly local climbers.[15] It had been so long since I'd been on a rope, I was itching to get back on the wall. *If only we'd brought our quickdraws to lead.* The rock was elegant, dotted with smoothly carved out pockets that had sharp enough edges to create a sea of crimps; great for technical climbing. After a few easier routes, the guides set up some more challenging climbs for Alex and I. By the end of the session, I had managed to work my way up a route called 'Little Homie', graded 6c+. It

---

[15] *Top rope climbing means the climber is securely attached to a rope which then passes up, through an anchor system at the top of the climb. While lead climbing is the more adventurous version where the climber takes the rope up with them as they climb, periodically clipping into rockface as they ascend.*

was sustained, a crimpy route that continued for thirty metres. I was determined to climb it. Despite my forearms burning and my hands threatening to release, I made it to the top, tapping the metal rings in victory. Before being lowered back down, I turned to look at the view - limestone casts protruded out of the ground like natural skyscrapers. As far as the eye could see there were hundreds of moss-covered mountains; titans of the earth. It was breathtaking. I felt alive.

Afternoon

Visited a strange cave and mud bath. It was horribly touristy, neon lights flashed continuously, vendors slouched against walls selling souvenirs and people bulldozed through the narrow passageways running their greasy fingers all over the formations. The mud bath was a strange experience, moving through cold brown clay and feeling the silt between your toes isn't the most reassuring feeling, but floating on the surface was pretty cool. After a cold hose-pipe shower to wash away the thick coat of dirt, we all plunged into the steaming hollows of the cave to warm up in the hot springs.

9ᵗʰ October

The alarm chimed. My weary eyes reluctantly opened. We'd done so much recently a well needed lie-in was due, but bamboo rafting wouldn't wait. Sitting on the steps of the hostel lobby, Alex and I halved a brilliant pink and green dragon fruit and, holding the skin as a natural cup, scooped out the subtly sweet flesh for breakfast.

Each group member was given a rusty, slightly dented bicycle, along with a helmet that didn't quite fit. Making a mishmash of a line, we commenced our journey to the Li River. Scooters nipped in and out, fruit carts appeared out of nowhere, buses honked, battered cars swerved around corners and locals dodged with expertise. While the traffic lights counted down, bikes revved and cyclists prepared their pedals, ready to dart off at the first flash of green like a game of Mario Kart. It certainly was an art, negotiating the streets of rural China. Parking our bikes, we queued on the edge of the waterfront, ready to board the small bamboo rafts. They were lightweight with two wooden deckchairs strapped precariously to the base. A punter, wearing a conical straw hat, controlled the boat with a long bamboo stick that he gently pushed into the riverbed. Jia approached the two loud nurses, Alex and I, her face looking a little guilty.

'Caa I ask yu guys a fayvour?'

'Yes of course,' I replied. She was such a sweet guide, I'd do anything for her.

'Becauose the rarft is so liii-ght,' she said over annunciating each word from nerves, 'I woill hav to spli yu two uap for one hour. An pair you wi the girls.'

'So you're saying we're too fat to sit together?' accused Geena sarcastically.

The four of us looked at each other and tried to suppress the awkward laughter.

'Oh no surely not?' reassured the rest of the group.

'Surely,' Darren commented, 'Rachel and I are the largest, look at us.'

Being the eldest couple of the group aged around fifty, he probably wasn't wrong.

'Ah okay,' Jia murmured, looking distressed.

'It's fine,' Mia said, waving her hand down, brushing off the unintentional insult.

'Tank yuu,' Jia whispered gratefully.

So, Alex went on a date with Geena, and Mia and I became a couple. It would have been a nice activity for couples, a smooth ride along beautiful mountainous countryside, a personal punter and only the water around you, but it was nice to have a different partner. Mia worked as a surgical nurse, she often had to work twenty-four-hour shifts and sometimes multiple days and nights in a row.

'Wow, I can't imagine it! How does your body function with so little sleep?'

'The shift lasts as long as the operation takes, so we do some crazy hours! But when you're focused the time just goes. It's intense but I love it,' she confessed.

I had a lot of respect for her.

The ride climaxed at the bottom of a gentle waterfall; in front we could hear Geena shouting in relief to be reaching dry land again.

'Oh my Lord Cece, I squeezed Alex's hand so tight as we went down that last bit, the photos will be hilarious, we'll look like a couple!'

Alex winked at me whilst shaking his, almost crushed, hand out.

With time to spare before lunch, and not wanting to waste an hour of our last day in Yangshuo, Alex and I climbed up to a little hill-top pagoda that overlooked the city. Reaching the top, I leaned over the edge and felt two arms wrap around my waist, holding me tightly. We were alone for the first time since arriving in China, it was just us.

We caught up with the rest of the group for a quick bowl of Guilin rice noodles for lunch. It was a very basic café, with tables and chairs spilling out into the streets and only a single kitchen counter for preparation. All meals were served in deep metal dishes, not dissimilar to a dog's water bowl. The noodles were mixed with chilli oil, pickled cucumber, chopped chives, spring onion and coriander, making a colourful midday feast.

An afternoon of deep-water soloing

While the girls went for an afternoon of cocktails and cake, the boys and I rammed into a minibus and headed to the river for deep-water solo climbing. We picked up our guide along the way, a small, tanned but very toned Chinese man in his early twenties. After dumping the life jackets and dry bag full of climbing shoes, he sat solemnly next to me, avoiding eye contact. I tried to make conversation but he was shy and reluctant to speak; I got as far as learning that we would swim across the river before starting to climb. I saw Alex's face turn a little paler when he learnt we'd have to start by swimming, he hated cold water, even more than I did.

All kitted up, we walked as a line of blue life jackets to the water's edge. The river was surprisingly cold and there was a strong current. I stayed close to Callum who, announced loudly by his girlfriend this morning, had only just learnt to swim. He seemed confident enough, but I knew if I were in the same position, heading into a strong current with little experience, I would have appreciated someone close for reassurance.

Halfway across the river, Jim leered in his Welsh accent, 'Hey how come Callum is the worst swimmer but he's ahead of all of us?'

'Nah mate, I just want to get to the other side before I drown,' Callum responded breathlessly.

Successfully reaching the rock on the opposite bank, our guide gestured where to climb. Being the one who had convinced everyone to join, I felt obliged to go first. I stripped off the life jacket and pulled myself out of the water, gripping onto a large slippery jug. The route traversed just above the water for a few metres before leading up to the top-out. After several sketchy moves I was standing on top of the seven metre stack. The water was far below me and an unnerving silhouette of a deep green rock extended out from the riverbed underneath.

'Just jump out, careful not straight down, otherwise you hit rock, not good,' cautioned our guide.

'Ah aha, yes noted,' I replied.

'Okay Cece you first,' the guide shouted.

'Um, from here? Perhaps you should show us first?'

The guide clambered up and timidly peered over the edge, before bottling it and tiptoeing back. 'Urgh it's quite scary!' he whispered with a girlish giggle.

'Well, how am I meant to do it, you're the guide!' I joked.

217

'Lady first?'

'No, you go first! I'll follow,' I replied.

'Ahi, okay, I just go here,' he squeaked.

He jumped off into the expanse of air between the rocks before hitting the water with a huge splash. We held our breaths until he burst back through the surface, whistling loudly in triumph.

'Cece! You follow me!'

I shuffled to the rock's edge. *Shit, this was my turn, you just have to do it Cece.* I scanned everyone's faces looking for Alex. I widened my eyes, hoping for the reassurance he would have given me if we had been trad climbing. He was shivering on a rock further away, he looked very cold but continued to watch me. Everyone counted down.

'Three, two...'

Come on Cece, in you go.

'One!'

I leapt off the edge, as far from the rock as I could. Seconds passed slowly as I plummeted through the air, my stomach turned and a panic rippled through me, *had I jumped far enough to miss the rock?* I shot like a missile, deep into the water towards the riverbed. The impact crushed my body and the weight of the water bore down on me. I pushed my arms downward to send my body back up to air, but I'd fallen so far I had to kick with my feet. With a gasp, I emerged amongst a bubbling spray of white. *I could still feel my feet; I hadn't hit the bottom.* I opened my eyes to see the grand tower of rock that I had just jumped off. Cheers and jeers resounded from the riverside. *I did it. My first deep-water solo.*

The cold got to Alex, turning him white and sapping his confidence; I could feel the fear as our fingers shakily touched. He bailed twice from the top, so on the third go I followed up behind for some encouragement.

'Come on, you can do it, it's scary but I know you can do it, we've done far crazier trad climbs!'

'Okay, I'll give it one last shot,' he shivered.

'I'm right behind you, I know you can do this.'

I watched hopefully as he approached the edge of the rock. *Come on Alex, you can do it, jump!* After a moment's hesitation, he disappeared out of sight. A few seconds later a crash exploded as he hit the water beneath him. I took a run-up and jumped in to join him.

'Yeaaaah, you did it!' I screamed as I fell through the air.

'Haha, thanks, that was fricking terrifying, but pretty awesome!'

After the nerve racking first jump, the rest of the afternoon was filled with adventure, unhindered by fear. We tried shorter traverse routes, with steep shards of rock that stuck out from the riverbed. The rock was sharp, solid and pocketed - beautiful to grip.

I grasped two flakes, my fingers folded over the sides, cementing into the creases. I pulled up, lifting my torso out of the cool water and placed my feet below. The lower rocks were covered in green slime, built up over years of lying beneath the river's surface. My left foot slipped and I crashed back into the water, splashing the others. Determined, I pulled myself back to the base. *I am going to do it this time.* I grasped the rock again, this time carefully positioning my feet. I locked off, holding my body out of the water and pulled my foot up higher so I could reach the next placement. The holds were gritty, tree roots and small dried plants had covered and weakened the rock. It felt like the holds could break off at any point and I'd come crashing back into the water and risk hitting the bottom; the river was shallower here than beneath the last route. I persisted, not wanting to give up and grabbed a small hidden handle of rock which pulled me up higher until I reached the top. I gave one quick look around smiling, before jumping back down to join the boys. The others became equally as addicted, repeating the same routes again and again, perfecting their technique and changing the way they bombed into the water. The sun started to set and the evening engulfed the river in shade. We swam back, weary and tired from the long but blissful afternoon.

Evening

Before heading to a nighttime cormorant fishing show, Alex and I tried a special Chinese vegetarian restaurant where we treated ourselves to stir-fried tofu, fresh veggies and a selection of purple vegetable dumplings. We were both relieved to be eating something that definitely did not contain cow intestine, which was unfortunately what last night's local dinner had entailed - *dumpling surprise indeed*.

Cormorant fishing

The show modelled ancient fishing techniques to visitors. We were all keen to go except our guide, Jia, who appeared on edge as she watched us squeeze onto the minibus. As soon as we arrived, I understood why. The performance was led by a short businessman twirling a toothpick in his mouth. He stood at the end of the river platform ushering us onto a small raft, his face wide with the smile of a toad. Onboard, we watched the vessel opposite glide ahead; a light was suspended at the front of the boat like an angler fish. Flies and moths buzzed in circles around the harsh glow as cormorants, with strings around their necks, prepared to dive. It was exciting at first, the birds dipped and dived like dolphins in the Cornish sea, scooping fish into their gullets before emptying them into the fisherman's bucket. But after a while, they started to tire. They wearily heaved their wet bodies back onto the raft before the fisherman quickly beat them back into the water with a bamboo stick. Even in the water, if their heads weren't submerged for more than five seconds, they were pushed back under the surface. It was cruel and hard to watch; the authenticity was debatable. The only laugh during the whole excursion was when Veronica's seat collapsed beneath her. The leg slipped through the raft leaving her crumpled on the floor.

10th October

Long day travelling. Bus, then train to Chengdu for seven hours. Big Tommy joined Alex and I's row and we became hysterically silly - hyper on pot noodles and dried sweet potato, that we'd mistaken for mango during a sleepy visit to the supermarket. Tommy was the only member of the group who had joined the trip alone, meaning he had no one to reign in his mischief! Following his cheeky ways, we made up games to entertain ourselves: seeing how many carriages we could run to between stops, tracking down the driver for a selfie *(we only got as far as the trolley staff - who were surprisingly keen),* chatting up old Chinese ladies with Google Translate and telling stories that brought us all to fits of hysterical giggles. It certainly beat the lonely train rides in Japan.

THIRTY-EIGHT

He never left my side.

10ᵗʰ October

'Okay guys, you've arrived in Chengdu, my name's Bo, I'll be your next tour guide. Now I could do a long introduction but listen, you've all had a long train ride and I'm sure you just want to get rid of your rucksack and grab a beer. So, let's cut the bullshit and get going.'

We caught the metro: a pristine version of the London Underground but with luggage scanners at every gate - turning the simple journey into a rucksack lifting workout. By the time we got to the hostel, energy levels were running low and I felt like my rucksack was driving me into the ground.

The guest house was panda themed, with soft toys and panda murals covering the entire building. Each block of rooms was connected by rickety bridges to the central area which featured a small bar, restaurant and pool table. We gathered in the lobby to be briefed on the next few days. Bo was a cool guide, he wore black rimmed hipster glasses and baggy trousers, his arms were pricked with tattoos and he rocked a wiry goatee beard that made him look slightly monkish. He was a freelance photographer who guided to bump up his salary. His English was impressively good considering he'd learnt from films alone, but this also explained why 'fuck' and 'shit' featured so frequently in his vocabulary. He seemed a lot more experienced than Jia.

We had a simple supper of noodles and veg in chilli oil, before heading up to our first private room of the trip; upgrades only cost three fifty yuan (around 40p), so it was a no-brainer. The others followed shortly, despite the cheap beer, because according to Bo, 'no one is allowed to get fucked tonight as tomorrow, we see the pandas.'

11ᵗʰ October

The alarm went off at 6:30a.m. I was so tired. I shuffled towards Alex, pressed my head into his chest and held him tight, not wanting to leave the bedcovers. It had been almost five weeks since we had woken up next to each other, I wanted to stay in the moment forever.

I fell asleep again on the coach to the pandas. After forty minutes we arrived at the sanctuary, it was cold and wet so I pulled my black waterproof hood right over my face making me look a little like a panda myself. I felt super groggy, but more than usual, perhaps even a little drugged.

'Cece, you look so unhappy!' Ned called.

'Aha,' was all I could mutter.

My eyes kept closing and all I could focus on was the floor in front of me. It felt like I had taken a double dosage of my night meds by mistake. Others in the group noticed my lack of engagement and started asking questions, but I could barely answer; I couldn't even smile. All my energy was being used trying to stay awake. Alex held my hand tightly and led me round, realising I wasn't well. I remembered seeing the pandas, huge balls of black and white fur rolling around, but I couldn't take it in. I lulled against the fence post, trying to remain upright.

The rest was a blur, I think I sat down at one point and must have collapsed. I woke to Alex trying to pour a sugary drink between my lips, with the rest of the group crowded around behind him. I was taken back to the bus where I must have passed out again until everyone else had finished the tour. Back at the hostel I slept until the evening. I didn't realise it then, but throughout the whole day, even when I was asleep, Alex never left my side.

'Cece, oh my God, are you okay?' Alex whispered as my eyes opened.

'Aha yeah a little groggy but awake now.'

'What happened to you? I've never seen you like that before!'

'I don't know, I think I accidently took my night meds this morning, because I felt really drugged.'

'Yeah you were like a zombie, sleep walking with your eyes closed. Whenever someone said something to you, you just looked blank, it was really scary. We even thought about taking you to hospital. So...it was your meds?'

When I checked my pill purse, the seal on the new pack of amitriptyline was unbroken. I looked up at Alex in alarm.

'I can't have done, this is a full pack and I haven't taken any since the train last night.'

'Oh, but you looked so drugged.'

'I know, maybe it was just severe fatigue?'

'Perhaps, we have been busy the past few days, but this was on another level, it's quite worrying.'

'Yea, I know.'

'I'm worried about you Cece.'

'Yes, me too. I don't know what's wrong with my body.'

'It's okay, I'll look after you, we'll just take it easy tonight, chill here while the others go to the Sichuan Opera.'

'Oh, gosh Alex, I'm sorry, you should go, you already missed the pandas because of me, I'll be fine.'

'No, it's no fun without you, I'd rather stay with you.'

'Are you sure?'

He wrapped his arms around me and whispered, 'It's okay, I have everything I could ever want in my arms.'

I looked up at him, half smiling.

'Okay that sounded incredibly cheesy out loud, but I meant it,' he blushed.

'Alex, I love you,' I said, squeezing him tightly.

12th October

This morning I felt alive again, so we joined the rest of the group at a Western style coffee shop along the riverside. A cheer rippled across the table when everyone saw I appeared to be functioning like a normal human being again. We were both starving, so ordered waffles with sweet blueberry jam, while hearing all about the mask changing performance at the opera we missed last night.

Midday

I liked Buddhism, or the idea of it. While at the Wenshu Monastery, Bo explained that the aim was to escape this life and move into a higher state of enlightenment, otherwise you remain in the circle of life, being reborn as a different creature or object each time. To leave this life, you have to do three things: forget desires, wishes and the trickiest part, forget yourself. A difficult concept considering human beings are built selfishly in order to survive.

'So basically the idea people apply today, is to live in the present,' Bo concluded.

2p.m.

After sampling some spicy Sichuan cuisine, we visited the People's Park: a park dedicated to the millions who died during World War Two. According to Bo, only ten percent of soldiers returned, so this park was built to honour those who never returned. With this in mind, I didn't expect to see so much happiness and energy inside. There was music, dancing, games and singing. Several group members joined in with a game of hacky sack while Ben and I joined the group dancing, which was like an outdoor Chinese Zumba class. We were in hysterics trying to keep up with the old Chinese women who knew all the moves by heart.

There was even a 'dating garden' where people pinned their CVs to a fence in the hope of being chosen by another, a little like a formal version of Tinder.

'Yeah, it's quite a weird concept,' explained Bo, 'often it's the parents who put up a poster of their son or daughter because they are worried they'll never get married. Quite often the kid has no idea they're on the wall. It's tough because in

China, you are meant to have a family and then focus on your career, so it doesn't give you much time to sort out your love life after school!'

'Wow, that's intense,' commented Geena.

'Yeah. Now guys, I want you to find your own date, take a picture of one of the posters and bring it back to me to translate. I'll let you know if you've scored or not,' Bo said sarcastically.

Tommy was quick to pick one, standing smugly as Bo read out the description.

'Aged forties. No bad habits, good money, car, curvy and good cook. Not bad Tommy, although perhaps a little old for you?' Bo laughed.

'You know what mate, I like a woman with ample mass, a frumpy Filipino is my type, so she'll do,' he said trying to keep a straight face. *Classic Tommy.*

Late afternoon

We popped to the local food market to buy some steamed tofu and green veggie buns before boarding the train to Xi'an, our next destination.

The group had been together for eight days and people's true characters had started to emerge. During the longer journeys, I enjoyed taking a step back and observing each couple's mannerisms and quirks. The way Amy leaned into Ned with subtle affection, how Melanie wide eyed her husband Ben when he wouldn't stop eating or walked in the wrong direction, Rachel softly tapping her husband's arm on the train to stop him from snoring, Veronica eye-rolling as Callum wrapped his arms tightly around her neck in protest to her bickering, the two nurses unconsciously sleeping on each other's shoulders with their mouths open and the way Jim power walked ahead, only to stop five strides later remembering his wife Lauren and checking everyone okay, 'Ye'll right guys?' he'd say in a thick Welsh accent. Then there was Big Tommy, who had enough personality and bravado for two people and a huge chest that spilled out of his wife beater. He walked around like he was a weightlifting security guard and talked loudly about women and alcohol. That said, he had a big heart and was in fact, very sweet. When he smiled, the deep-set wrinkles on his face seemed to be pulled up by puppet strings, turning his resting grimace into a childlike smile. Considering he was the only solo traveller of the group, he'd sort of become our third musketeer.

THIRTY-NINE

It was a different life, one of discipline, strength and beauty.

12th October
10:30p.m.

We arrived at the hostel, exhausted from carrying our heavy bags. Alex bought us both a slice of cheesecake for a cheeky late-night treat, but before we could take our first bite, a small hyper Chinese man in his early twenties, Bibi, took centre stage. He spoke like a bullet train, words fired out like steam, a continual stream of statements and questions with no stop for breath.

'Early start late night long days you guys be very tired oh yes very tired...' he rattled on.

I went to bed feeling stressed, which was silly because this was meant to be a fun tour. I like being busy and cramming my time with as many activities as I can, but this was on a different level. I was anxious about my health and how much more my body could take before another CVS attack was triggered.

13th October

Despite the lie-in, I woke up feeling exhausted. My shoulders were killing and I felt like I was still wearing my rucksack. Alex went to breakfast while I took my morning meds and scanned through my contract for my new job in January. It had conveniently been sent to me in the only country I was visiting in which you needed a VPN to access the internet.

While everyone else went to the fake goods market, I stayed at the hostel. I had zero energy and knew I wouldn't make the cycling that afternoon if I joined in the morning activity.

'I'll try not to pass out again,' I jested to Alex.

I think he felt a little guilty leaving me alone, but I explained that I'd gotten this far by myself so he needn't worry. I enjoyed my chilled time alone, reading and looking for a place to eat. The guide last night made out that we *had* to eat at the hostel's Western café downstairs, as this was the *last* opportunity we'd have to eat Western food. *Because apparently English people self-combust if they can't eat fish and chips for more than a week.* Due to my health, Asian food, as long as it had no chemicals in it, was actually better for me. So, passing the overpriced hostel food, I ventured into a little noodle shop across the road. Turns out I'd struck foodie gold. The café was one of the best noodle places in Xi'an, serving the local specialty, spinach noodles for just nine yuan *(a little over a pound)*. Waiting in line, I watched an old chef rolling, pulling, slicing and stringing the green dough into tagliatelle-like strips. I wrapped my hands around the large steaming bowl filled with a rich chilli broth, thick green noodles and steamed cubes of potato and carrot. *Chopsticks down, it was the best dish I'd tried in China.*

I headed to the hostel's rooftop garden until the others returned. I found a little spot amongst the potted plants and sat on a white swinging chair in the sun. I spoke to one of my best friends from home and then to my mum. She was heading to Grandma's garden, sounding distant as her mind multi-tasked. I worried about her. I was still dealing with grief, it would follow me like a shadow and catch me unannounced, but it was a distant grief. Mum, however, was living in the wake of her grief; it was inescapable.

Midday
Cycling on Xi'an's City Walls

Alex and I shared a tandem bike. *Need I go on?*

We'd been advised against it, but with my stubborn determined mind I said we had to give it a go. I immediately regretted my sassy mouth when we mounted the bike. Our balance was completely thrown and just taking our feet off the

229

ground was a challenge. We wobbled from side to side, almost hitting the floor, and to make things worse, I couldn't see a thing with Alex's huge rucksack in front of me. We figured pedaling faster made it a lot easier to balance, so after a bit of practising, *and an exercise in trust*, we were sailing across the ancient walls, watching the city from above. The sunset dyed the sky a beautiful orangey purple, turning the grey stone battlements into dark silhouettes. As the sun disappeared, hundreds of streetlamps awoke to illuminate the city, it was beautiful, *even on a tandem.*

Evening

Bikes returned and all limbs intact, we were taken to a busy night market. Vendors called out and waved their hands at their displays of fake t-shirts, jade buddhas and rip-off designer bags. Heated discussions echoed along the crammed street as numbers were bashed into calculators, tourists and locals alike bartering for the best price. Most of it was tat, but it was nice to watch other group members, who had the luxury of rucksack space, try their hands at bartering.

From there, we were taken to a Turkish-Chinese restaurant hidden in the Muslim Quarter of Xi'an. We squeezed around a circular table as hot green tea was poured into little porcelain cups and spun to each person. We watched the waiters flow back and forth, bringing an array of sixteen dishes. Bowls full of sweet sticky fried aubergine, steamed garlic broccoli, stir-fried tofu, chilli glass noodles, potato and chive omelet slaw, blanched mangetout, spiced dry naan and bowls of fragrant rice amongst many other flavourful dishes. Soon the laughter and chatter dispersed as hungry travellers negotiated their chopsticks to sample the array of food.

14th October
9a.m.

After a quick breakfast of banana bread and persimmons, we boarded a bus bound for the Terracotta

Warriors. The journey took us through busy roads that led us out of the city and into countryside; past barren fields, clusters of villages and pomegranate orchards in which each pomegranate wore a plastic bag like a little raincoat. *Now that's caring for your crops.*

Bibi, our guide, machine-gunned us with information before entering the site. He enjoyed the sound of his own voice and seemed to find pleasure in rattling through the highest number of facts in the lowest amount of time. Of the few phrases I could comprehend and retain, we learnt that the slaves involved with the sculptures' creation, were in fact thrown into the furnace along with the clay, ready to rest with the emperor in his tomb. The idea being that the slave's soul would be incased in the warrior, so the selfish emperor would have thousands of soldiers to serve him in the afterlife. *Talk about self-indulgence.*

The first exhibition we entered was underwhelming. A space as wide as an aircraft shelter covered the excavation site. A few remnants of the terracotta bodies lay feebly on the ground while the rest of the space was filled with tunnels and marks from the dig. I felt uncultured saying it, but in the words of Mia and Geena, 'it was just a big sandpit'. Alex on the other hand seemed to be fascinated by the sandpit and followed Ben around the site, discussing and analysing every mark in the dirt until they were qualified to write a paper on it. I became frustrated and restless at their slow progress, so walked off ahead with the girls.

The second chamber was a little more impressive and I felt ashamed at letting my first impression get the better of me. Deep trenches ran like a maze between the towers of muddy rock, leading to the individual burial grounds of the Terracotta Warriors. Lines of innocent souls rested side by side, their expressions glaring ahead, frozen in time, waiting to be released. Alex had caught up with me by this point and he gently held my hand as we both stood in a terrible awe at the result of such nefarious craftmanship. It was magnificent, but the number of lives that had been sacrificed to make the Warriors made it seem like a celebration of all that is evil in human nature.

Evening

We spent the evening on the rooftop garden with Norman, an adorably sweet Chinese guy. He likened himself to a big panda, which was funny as he was actually from Chengdu, land of the pandas! We played several rounds of ping pong and he taught us how to hold the bat properly: two fingers behind and the thumb curled around the handle. It was safe to say, Norman the panda and ping-pong champ, thrashed us both.

15th October
6:30a.m.

Arriving in Shaolin after a seven-hour bus ride, a lot of us were grumpy, hungry and wondering why we couldn't have just got the bullet train straight to Beijing.

'We'll be in Shaolin for less than twenty-four hours, what's the point in that?' Lauren complained.

'Yeah, I'm famished, my throat feels dryer than Gandhi's flip-flop,' Tommy protested.

The group's expectations weren't helped after Bibi had convinced us all that we'd be going back in time to a rural farmyard.

'The food be horrible, no shower, no Wi-Fi, and toilet are for pigs, just slit in ground,' he said with an evil grin spread across his face, 'then after sweaty walk, you go straight onto night train.'

Looks of horror spread around the room.

'Well, it's a farm in rural China, what you expect? It's experience guys,' Bibi responded.

'I can't stay there!' exclaimed Veronica.

'No, me neither,' sulked Mia.

I winked at Alex and whispered excitedly, 'I've always wanted to stay on a farm!'

Just before others could protest, Bibi burst into laughter.

'Ha ha! Guys, I joke. I play good joke with you!'

'That's not funny Bibi!' shouted Geena, looking like she was going to faint from relief.

To be fair to Bibi, it was a good practical joke to play on Westerners.

Shaolin – The birth of kung fu

After being shown our rooms, we were taken to the outhouse for dinner. Women squatted to pick up green beans out of the soil, corn husks lay in a big pile next to a pig pen and chickens ran freely over the dusty makeshift roads. After a generous portion of chow mein, we took a short walk to the local kung fu school. There were sixty schools in the area, housing students aged three to twenty-one. The smallest school, which we visited had thirty students, but the largest extended to forty thousand. Students were taught the martial art for six hours a day, in addition to the core subjects: maths, Chinese and English.

'So, what happens to them after they finish, they can't all be in films?' questioned Tommy.

'Ah yes, this is a good question,' replied our new guide, 'once they graduate, the most popular career is the military, some become teachers like our master here, while a lucky few either get cast as stunt doubles or get to compete in competitions. But here in Shaolin, it is the highest honour to represent your country in the Olympics.'

Shortly after, a group of twenty boys dressed in grey uniforms walked into the courtyard. They stood solemnly, palms pressed together, heads bowed as we took our seats. One at a time, they ran onto the stage somersaulting, back flipping and cartwheeling. Their hands sliced through the air like invisible swords, followed in swift succession by rapid turns and high kicks. The way they moved reflected the rigorous training they completed six days a week. They were working towards controlling, retaining and utilising *qi*, the energy that flows through your body, in order to take down an opponent, imitate an animal, obliterate boards or break glass with the mere throw of a needle. It was a different life, one of discipline, strength and beauty.

At the end of the show, roles were reversed as it was the young artists' turn to teach us. Half our group took to the stage, trying to imitate the fine routine we had just observed. The remaining members sat comfortably in their seats, giggling and videoing the clumsy jumble of arm and leg movements that formed our attempt. I enjoyed the balancing moves, squatting low, swift changes of feet and spinning like a praying mantis, but fighting with our opponents was more difficult. We had to smash our forearms together, kick each other's knees and pull one another's shoulder down. Hands down, my nine-year-old teacher was far stronger, but after being conditioned to never touch a child in my teacher training, it was difficult to suddenly have to hit him! After ten failed attempts, I finally mastered the move; a smile appeared on my partner's face followed by a sharp 'yessss': the sign of a satisfied young teacher. The session finished with a bow to our partner and a gift presentation; we were presented with an engraved wooden bracelet to remember the school. It was a window into the life of a kung fu master, and despite complaints at the start, everyone was glad they came.

16ᵗʰ October

Breakfast was a feast of garlic naan slices, fried bread filled with hot honey, tangy satsumas and sesame cookies, which we stashed away to snack on during the Dharma Cave hike. The cave was named after Bodhidharma, who lived there for nine years; he was known as the transmitter of Chan Buddhism to China.

Bibi had put many people off the hike, claiming it was an epic feat for only the fittest.

'It four time the size of Moon Hill in Yangshuo, FOUR time!' he said, waving his four fingers to everyone as if he was announcing the number of people who had died attempting to summit the Dharma Cave.

It was a complete exaggeration, we got to the top in forty-five minutes. Yes, there were a lot of stairs and it was quite sustained, but it was doable. I was annoyed Bibi had put-off some of the less confident hikers.

Big Tommy joined us for the hike, as we started to separate from the group, he chased our heels, eager to be part of our speedy team. Tommy was a funny guy who swore frequently and waffled on about a lot of things, but he had a kind heart. He kept asking us if we wanted a couple photo or if I had enough vegetarian food to keep me going.

'We need to find something for Cece to eat though mate,' he repeated to Alex.

In his life prior to The Dragon Trip, he'd worked as a security guard and mental healthcare assistant, looking after people who were a risk to themselves. He went to the gym a lot, sometimes for five hours a day and ate as much as a buffalo, *a buffalo obsessed with protein and gains*. He'd recently broken up with his girlfriend, who was meant to be on the trip, and was clearly a little lonely. He had spent his life around people; people mattered to him. He'd tagged along with the boys, then with the nurses, but now in his words, 'I'm just fed up of hearing their complaining, yous two actually are keen and like travelling en that, and I like that too, history and culture en that,' he smiled.

I was flattered by his indirect comment, but felt a little sorry for him, I knew what it was like to travel alone, let alone solo in a group of couples. He was a little slower than us, panting as he hauled his gigantic torso up the mountain, but we waited at every corner. Halfway up the mountain, we all bought incense and I prayed for the health and happiness of those around me and sent my love to my grandma; something I had started to do at every sacred place I visited. It was a way of showing her that no matter what I was doing, I thought of her every day.

At a point it was just Alex and I, I wasn't feeling great and my energy levels were running low. Despite the many options at breakfast, I hadn't eaten much because my stomach was cramping after taking laxatives (I had to take these regularly whilst travelling due to the side effects of amitriptyline). Nearing the top, a Chinese woman held her camera in my face and pushed my shoulder back to shove me into her photo.

This was not the first time in Asia I'd been the star oddity in people's pictures. Normally, I would have obliged and laughed it off, but today, feeling pretty rough, I was fed up with being treated like an animal in a zoo, this time, I couldn't let it pass.

I forced out a 'No,' giving them daggers and shoved my way through the rest of the ogling group. Enough was enough. *Yes, you can have a photo, but you need to actually ask politely! I will not put up with being pushed or touched without permission.*

It happened again when we reached the top of the mountain. Everyone gathered for a group photo when a random Chinese guy ran into shot.

'Ah for God's sake, can't we just have a normal photo of us for once,' Callum complained.

'Eurrghh,' shouted Jim.

Judging from the group's reaction, we all felt the same - it was rude and intrusive. So, I stood up to him and, in Tommy's words, 'unleashed the sassitude'.

'Búyào,' I shouted, shaking my head and pointing my finger, 'one minute, let us have a photo first, then you can join.'[16]

---

[16] *A Mandarin phrase, roughly meaning 'I don't want'.*

He turned red-faced and scuttled back to his friends.

'Cece that was amazing!' Jim cheered.

'Haha, Veronica, did you hear what Cece just did?' Callum exclaimed.

'That was brilliant, I wasn't expecting that!' Tommy laughed.

'Haha I love it, I just go aggressive,' Geena said, 'when Cece goes sassy, she still does it with some decorum!'

Veronica's camera had even caught me in action. I looked like a teacher who was telling a child off for not having their homework. The boy looked so embarrassed as I stood, hand on hip, scowling and waving a finger at him.

Early evening

We headed back to the hostel to get ready to board the night train. The carriages were small with three layers of bunk beds. Basic, tightly fitted and fairly clean.

I switched with Tommy for the top bunk as he complained, 'I'll never fit in that rat hole.'

It was the smallest space but had the best aircon and was tucked away from the bustling carriage below. While everyone else remained chatting and drinking, I let my meds kick in and fell into a deep sleep.

FORTY

His blood will be forever smeared across The Great Wall.

17th October
Beijing
5:30a.m.

Bright lights stream through the window invading my eyes. Someone has opened the cabin curtains just behind my head. *It's too early.* The carriage rocks from side to side, a sickening motion, as it chugs along the tracks. The bunks below rustle as passengers pack and pass through the cabin with toothbrushes and washbags in hand.

'Cece?' Alex poked his head around the corner. 'Are you up?'

'Mmm,' I moaned.

'You should start to get ready; I think we'll arrive soon.'

'Mmm, okay.'

The amitriptyline was still in my system, I felt groggy, sleep deprived and nauseous from a night on the train. The early arrival had cheated us out of sleep. *Here we go again rucksack.* Our group trudged wearily through the station, looking for our next guide.

A petite elfish history master's student with a grey bob, waved enthusiastically from platform nine and three quarters, (she was halfway between nine and ten). Due to her fascination with Harry Potter, she'd chosen her English name to be Luna, her favourite character. After dropping our large bags at a hostel in the city, we were ferried off on a two-hour coach to a smaller hostel in the outskirts of the city, close to The Great Wall.

The Great Wall

A thick mist coated everything. The wall snaked through the fog, only raising its head at the lookout towers. It was immense in size and age. Slippery wooden steps ran up and down the mountainous terrain, supported by a foundation of crumbling stone and rusty nails.

We were given three hours to explore the section of the wall. Tommy tagged along with us for the first part as we took a few photos and awed at the landscape.

'Wouldn't it be incredible to hike the entire length of the wall?' I said.

'Yes, but it would take forever,' replied Alex.

'I know but, if you did fifty kilometres a day and the wall is roughly 21,200km, it would only take...424 days.' The boys stared at me. 'Okay it would be a project, but what an epic project. To know you had walked the entire length of the wall, that would be incredible!'

'Yes, that's true, it would be epic, would you do it alone?' Alex asked quietly.

'Well, it would be nice to have a partner,' I winked at him, 'someone to help carry all my meds!'

'Ha, you'll be lucky missy, only if you carry the tent and all the camping gear!' he replied.

When Alex walked off the wall to relieve himself, Tommy decided it was time to cause some mischief.

'Oi, mate, put it away, the guards are coming. I don't think you're allowed to urinate within a hundred feet of the wall.'

'What! Are you sure they are guards?' shouted a flustered Alex.

'Yeah, they look pissed, quick come back up.'

'Okay okay, I'm coming,' he shouted running back up the steps.

'Hahaha, mate we got you there,' shouted Tommy in hysterics. Alex's frown lasted three seconds before he burst into laughter, you could never be mad at Tommy for long.

'Right guys and girls, I think that's enough cardio for me, you two enjoy the rest.'

'Are you sure? We can come back with you?' Alex asked, 'Cece?'

I knew we should have gone back with Tommy, but this was our chance to see the wall, I wanted to get as far as we could in the time we had.

'Maybe we could go a little further?'

'Stay with your bird mate, I'll catch you back at the bus,' Tommy shouted as he turned to go.

Alex looked at his watch, we had an hour and thirty left.

'We've been walking pretty slow, I think if we speed up a little, we could get a bit further?' I suggested.

'Hmm, I just don't want to be late back.'

'Come on, we're on The Great Wall, we have to try and get as far as we can!'

'We don't *have* to Cece, not everything is a competition.'

'It's not, but you only get one chance to be on The Great Wall, I just want to make the most of it, what happened to your fun side?'

'Fine, we'll get to the fifth watch tower, then we turn back, okay?'

'Yes, we'll make it back in loads of time, I'm sure,' I grinned.

I liked exploring just the two of us, it seemed like a proper adventure, like we were back in Borneo, but all Alex seemed to do was watch the clock as if it were a time bomb. As soon as we reached the tower he started to run back down.

'Hey, it's fine, we still have an hour twenty, loads of time, I don't think we need to run.'

'I don't want to keep everyone waiting Cece,' he called back.

'But it's slippy,' I shouted.

'Oh, come on, what did you say to me? Where is your fun side?' he replied mockingly.

He continued to run down the steps until his leg slipped beneath him and his body lurched forward. His arms flung to the side, trying to save himself from smacking the wet stone, but he missed. The momentum of reaching out flipped his body, causing him to roll steeply down the hill until he reached the base of the wall. *Alex!*

I followed him cautiously, taking care not to slip. I found him lolling at the bottom like a piece of roadkill, his legs were limp and bloody, his arms were spread across the ground and his face was screwed up in pain. A million questions and outcomes ran through my mind. *What had he broken? How quick could I run to get help? What was the distress signal? Did he have a silver blanket? When would it get dark? Did I have any pain meds? What was the recovery position? Why did I push us to go further?*

'Aomm,' he moaned.

'Alex, Alex are you okay?'

I cradled my arms beneath his head, the mist had become heavier, collecting around us; small drops of rain chilled our skin. His trousers were ripped, revealing two deep red cuts on his knees. He lay there for a few minutes in silence, just breathing and grimacing.

'Alex, Alex just nod, are you okay?'

'Yeah, it just really hurts,' he exhaled.

'Okay, it's going to be okay, I promise,' I whispered.

'Do you think you've broken anything?'

'I don't know, I, it just really hurts.'

'Okay, it's going to be okay. Here, put your arm around my shoulder, let's see if you can stand.'

Thankfully, he hadn't broken anything, he was just badly cut, bruised and in shock. We hobbled back along the wall, taking care over the slippery steps, and made it back to the minibus where the nurses attended to him with Ben's extensive first aid kit.

With his head rested on my shoulder, I whispered into his ear, 'Alex, I'm sorry for making you go further with me, I just got so excited to be here.'

'It's okay Cece, I shouldn't have run.'

'Mate, at least a part of you is now on The Great Wall, what a rad story - Alex's blood will be forever smeared on the ancient stone,' Tommy pronounced.

'Haha, to be fair, that does make a cool story for the scars you're going to have!' I replied.

'It will indeed,' smiled Alex.

Evening

Back at the hostel, everyone got into their pyjamas and sat round the fire in the log cabin. Our cheeks were rosy from the walk and we laughed and shared stories of everyone's experience on The Great Wall. Alex and I were squished into an armchair, our bodies pressed close together, I felt content. *Everyone was okay, we were happy.*

18th October

We boarded a bus back to the city centre, making a short stop at the Olympic park to see the Bird's Nest and Water Cube. The park was impressive but eerily desolate and empty, a ghost town. Roads once walked by athletic heroes were now only used by litter pickers and the odd tourist. From glory to desolation. It seemed such a waste, countless homes ripped apart and families forced to re-locate, all for sixteen days in 2008.

Arriving at the hostel I didn't feel good, my stomach hurt and I was exhausted. I knew it was a delayed CVS attack. By the time we were allowed into our rooms I was in a lot of pain, I burst into tears as Alex helped me lie down in bed. I spent the rest of the day in the dark, alone, until Alex returned from sightseeing in the evening.

19th October

To my relief, when I woke at 8a.m. the attack had stopped. I was tired and had little energy but was determined to join the group on a tour of the Forbidden City, *featuring Mulan's palace – one of my childhood heroines*. I walked slowly and had to sit down when I felt dizzy but, with Alex attentively by my side, I managed to see the whole thing.

20th October

We visited the Palace of Heaven before boarding a fourteen-hour night train. Alex and I managed to get the adjacent top bunks. Like gargoyles of the carriage, we giggled and chatted from above. Occasionally swinging down like orangutans to join the rest of the group in their late-night antics, before retreating to our private little space. As we slept, the train took us eight hundred kilometres south to Moganshan.

FORTY-ONE

He took my hand, and we stared into the limitless expanse beyond.

21st October

      Two peppy Chinese girls picked us up for the next leg of the tour, Sapphire and Yina. We piled into a small minibus and drove for two hours into the countryside. We passed vast lakes, mountainsides spilling with bamboo and fields ribbed with tea bushes. The terrain was coloured many shades of green, like an emerald fan lying over the land. Alex fell asleep on my shoulder; he was struggling to sleep on the night trains and it was catching up with him. He was sweet, with sleepy eyes and slurred words, I loved him in his drowsy state. For once, it was me looking after him, normally I was the one falling asleep.

      Weary from the overnight train and over sixteen hours of travelling, we tumbled off the bus. Looking up, our jaws dropped. In front of us stood a ridiculously steep hill that curved slyly around the corner to the hostel. *Let's just say that if it was slightly wider, it would have been the perfect site for a funicular railway.*

      A few hours later, recovered from the hill climb and settled in one big mixed dorm, we were each given a rusty bike for an afternoon cycle. Along with the 'support vehicle' - *a dodgy looking local on a moped*, the guides sped off on a mission to take us to this supposed 'beautiful location'. The crunch of rusty gears and old chains created an unnerving rhythm, as each of us pedalled to keep up. We cycled through the traffic that ran between the yellow fields carpeting the valley. It was quaint but surprisingly industrial. If you closed one eye and looked through the gap between your fingers, you could block out telephone wires and old vehicles to frame an almost pretty view. Moganshan was meant to be a place of tranquillity and beauty, 'a calm passage through the bamboo groves' was how it was listed in the itinerary. *It was more of a slog through the bamboo commercial transportation link.*

'Ceese, watch out!' Alex shouted.

I turned to my left to see a truck, covered in a mass of green, bulldozing towards us. *Shit.* Bamboo leaves brushed my face and I felt the heat of the engine roar. When I opened my eyes, a cyclone of green leaves was left swirling in the truck's path. *It had just missed me.*

One hour later

The final destination was a building site. A once beautiful lake was now a toxic green colour and partitioned by a dam. Overlooking this wonderful example of humanity destroying nature, was a construction site of a soon to be hotel resort. We all gave each other the look, trying not to burst into laughter.

'Photo, you want a photo?' Sapphire asked.

'Umm, well I think we're okay thank you, though,' replied Callum.

'What does she expect,' whispered Veronica, 'for us to have a selfie with a digger? Swim in a half-filled lake and try not to get swept into the dam?'

'Yea, I think this must be their first time guiding, bless them,' replied Jim.

'Well guys, you never know, this could be a very famous monument in ten years' time,' commented Tommy.

'Yeah Tommy, you're right, I think it could make the eighth wonder of the world,' laughed Ned.

Evening

After a hot shower, we had another group meal at a local restaurant, sharing plates of fried veggie rice noodles, green beans, pak choi, mushroom, sweetened carrot and black pepper bamboo. We ended the night nibbling some corner shop sweet potato crisps while playing a few games of pool and chess.

22nd October

We hiked through the bamboo forest to Mount Mogan. We played around in the bamboo, trying to climb up the ridged green poles but with little success. Alex got the highest, moving both his feet and hands simultaneously to shimmy up the pole. I managed to bridge between a few poles, making me look like Kung Fu Panda, *even if I was only a foot off the ground*. The view from the top was stunning, blue layers of mountains continued into the distance, blending into the cloudy sky above. I sat next to Alex, he took my hand and we stared into the limitless expanse beyond.

FORTY-TWO

I think you should come home earlier.

22nd October

It was dark by the time we exited Shanghai train station. Bright lights from street signs and buildings illuminated the haze that hung above the bustling streets. Late night street vendors offered dried meats, buttery jack fruit pancakes and dubious bubbling drinks.

We entered the hostel through a wooden door, split into semicircles. It revealed a series of corridors stemming off to dorm rooms that were separated, *to our disappointment*, by gender. Above travellers' sleeping heads lay a rooftop bar, which would become our local for the next few nights. The girls were split into two groups; Amy and I were sent to the fifth floor to a girls' dormitory. I waited for her to shower and do her make-up before re-joining the others on the rooftop. By the time we'd grabbed a drink, Alex was a beer down, already merry and keen to explore the city.

'Yo Ceese,' Tommy called, 'we're going out girl, I'm just alive in this city you know, alive. I feel its energy, this is my vibe.'

'Soooo, you want to come out?' Alex asked spritely.

By this point I was tired and jaded. I wanted to be as happy and energetic as them both, but by 11:30p.m. I was drained. They all seemed so hyped up and I just felt like crashing. We'd just arrived in the city and I didn't want to blow all my energy in one night. I quietly declined. I'd learnt throughout this trip how far I could push my body, and sometimes with a chronic illness, you just have to say no.

23rd October

I'd worried the night before that my tiredness was causing a strain on our relationship. I hadn't been in the nicest mood over the past few days because of the side effects of the Hong Kong medication. I'd been curt, selfish, short tempered and perhaps bailing on another night out was the last straw. Waking up to a message on my phone, however, I realised how understanding and accepting Alex really was.

[23/10, 00:09] Alex: Gooood morning for you (still evening for me)! I have some good news for you - Ned and I have managed to upgrade for tomorrow night (for 200 yuan). So we will need to check out of our current dorm rooms tomorrow morning before 12, leave our big bags downstairs and then check into our new room on our return...and then check back into the dorm rooms after (unless another private room becomes available). I know it's a little bit of a faff, but I think it's worth it as we only have a short time left...hope you agree... ;)
[23/10, 00:10] Alex: (You don't need to worry about the mons, it's my treat! ;))
[23/10, 00:10] Alex: Love you!
[23/10, 00:11] Alex: Sleep well! Xxx

A big smile spread across my face as I replied. Bagging a private room on the tour was like finding a real jade Buddha in a fake goods market.

[23/10, 09:03] Me: Yaay, I'm so excited!! I'll pack quick, thank you Alex!
[23/10, 09:05] Alex: Meet me in reception at 10.
[23/10, 09:05] Me: Will do, can't wait see you then!

As we entered the lift, I threw my arms around his shoulders, bounced onto my tiptoes and kissed his cheek.

'We have a private room,' I squealed.

'We do Cece, we do,' he smiled.

Key-card swiped; the door flew open to reveal a bright room with a big white double bed. *Clean, new and private. Perfect.* Slinging our rucksacks to the floor, we fell onto the bed.

Hands in hair, lashes on cheeks, lips on skin; blood rushed to the surface as our bodies became entangled within the sheets.

'I love you Cece,' Alex whispered.

Resting my cheek against his chest, 'I love you too. But we only have a week left before we leave each other again.'

'I know,' he said squeezing me, 'I know, we just have to make the most of now.'

11a.m.

We visited the Yu gardens, a little quarter of the city filled with rock gardens, bonsai trees and nine zigzag bridges (symbolising the nine good fortunes). We sauntered around, Alex never losing contact with my waist, our hands always touching; no one could separate us.

We had a late lunch with Callum and Veronica. Despite being together for almost three weeks, we'd spent little one-on-one time with them. She was sassy but very down to earth, I liked her. As a couple, they were always in each other's pockets and constantly bickering. Veronica, at times, seemed to be more of a matriarch than a girlfriend, looking after the money and making all the decisions. Yet they both seemed happy, *evidently opposites do attract.*

Afternoon

We headed to the People's Square and then to the longest shopping street in the world, filled with fancy boutiques and shopaholics, *basically an Asian Oxford Street.* Unable to even afford a look in the shop windows, we ventured on a quest for ice cream. Navigating the labyrinth of escalators in various shopping malls, we managed to find a place, but at the expense of my embarrassment. I found a security guard, but he didn't speak any English, so decided to act out eating an ice cream, holding a cone and licking an invisible scoop. The guard stood bewildered for a few moments before laughing and pointing to the right.

'Man Cece, that could have gone wrong on so many levels, you could have been arrested for indecent gestures!' Geena giggled.

'What? It was just an ice cream!' I defended.

'Yeah, that's what you think!' laughed Mia.

Alex laughed with his head in his hands, then pulled me close to his chest.

'What am I going to do with you? You cheeky monkey!'

An evening on The Bund

Gigantic buildings lined the riverside as lasers and glittering spotlights illuminated the sky, creating the iconic Shanghai skyline of The Bund. We stood in awe, Alex behind me, his chin rested on the top of my head, arms wrapped around my waist, feeling a light breeze from the water's edge.

9p.m.

We sampled a cocktail, sitting in a hot tub (which was actually quite cold) on a rooftop bar, overlooking the glamourous city below. It was a nice treat after three weeks of basic backpacking. Everyone enjoyed it, except Tommy who seemed to have developed an alcohol addiction as the trip progressed. He ordered numerous drinks, racking up a large bill, and complained to staff that the drinks weren't strong enough. He was loud, rude and embarrassed us all. But at quarter past midnight, he really took things to another level.

'Gee come here. I need you to get a photo of me,' he called.

'Okay, okay, you could say "please,"' Geena responded sassily.

'Everyone move aside! Just take it Gee.'

'Fine, then we need to go Tommy, taxis are here.'

I stood waiting until Alex turned my cheek and started to hastily lead me out. When I turned to see what had happened, I saw a trouser-less Tommy facing the window.

Hands on hips with his two hairy bum cheeks on display, looking down as if he owned the city below.

'What is he doing? He'll get us kicked out!' I gasped.

'I know, he's gone too far this time, let's go, he can find us outside,' muttered Alex.

We all reconvened at the taxi rank, Geena looking incredibly embarrassed, towing a drunken *(now fully clothed)* Tommy behind her.

'You're annoyed at me Cece, aren't you?' Tommy whined. 'You don't like me?'

'No Tommy,' I replied sternly, 'I like you as a person; I just don't like what you did. It was inappropriate and embarrassing. This is a nice place and you might have just got future tour groups banned. You took it too far.'

He looked sad for a moment, scowling in the front of the taxi before choosing to interrogate the poor driver's love life instead. *Thank God he didn't speak English!*

24th October

While everyone else chilled at the hostel, Darren, Rachel, Alex, I and a very hungover Tommy visited the Water Town. A little like a Chinese Venice, the Water Town consisted of a series of red curled roofed houses connected by a network of little canals and ornate bridges. We watched boatmen paddle tourists through the rivers and browsed the shops, but apart from that, there wasn't much else to see. Sapphire was a sweet girl, but an appalling tour guide. She marched through the streets, getting lost every five minutes and huffed impatiently whenever we stopped to look at something.

'I think we could have learnt more about the Water Town from a local speaking Mandarin than Sapphire,' Darren joked.

Eventually given some free time to explore, Alex found a nice puzzle shop, owned by an enthusiastic carpenter. He bought presents for his younger brothers, *which to this day we still haven't solved,* and I purchased some pretty chopsticks, my only souvenir from China.

Late afternoon

Back at the hostel, Tommy had sobered up and was feeling a little guilty about last night, so we had an early supper with him. The restaurant next to the hostel made the most amazing clear soup with pak choi, beansprouts, fungus and thick noodles like tagliatelle; all for fifteen yuan.

Shortly after dinner, I received a message.

[24/10, 17:23] Dad: Hi C, nice to catch up with you earlier, there are two things I wanted to talk to you about in private, hence why I didn't mention it on the phone when you were with Alex. First one is about Christmas: With everything that happened this summer, we are having Christmas in Cornwall. Mum thinks it will be hard to be at home without Grandma.

I breathed a sigh of relief; I'd been dreading Christmas for the exact same reason. For twenty-three Christmases, we'd spent the day at home with my grandma, this year would be hard but easier to deal with if we were in a different place.

[24/10, 17:25] Secondly, I think you should come home earlier. I'm not forcing you, but you're tired and have been getting ill a lot. You need to be fresh starting your new job in January. We want to see you and you need time to deal with Grandma's passing. Think seriously about it. Lots of Love, Dxoxox

I stared at my screen. This was the first time Dad had requested me to do anything, he rarely spoke about emotions or my illness. Yet, in this message, he'd done all three.

[24/10, 17:45] Me: Okay I'll think about it. Cxoxox

252

FORTY-THREE

KTV.

25th October

A big night out had been brewing since the start of the trip. We'd heard KTV was a popular Chinese version of Karaoke, but way more fun. A few of the others had tried it on previous nights, but the nurses wanted everyone to join. So, it was agreed that at 8p.m. everyone would meet on the rooftop for pre's. Both being lightweights, a few drinks were enough to transform Alex and I into KTV rock stars…*or so we thought*. It was so much fun to lose yourself completely in the moment, forget about everything, about what happened in August, about my illness and about the fact that we would be separated in a few days. We chatted, danced around and just had fun, surrendering to the moment.

'Aren't Cece and Alex the cutest couple? I love these two, they're hilarious!' Geena called.

'Yeah, you guys should come out more often!' Veronica called.

After numerous bottles of Tsingtao beer, several rounds of ping pong (followed by let's play *find* the ping pong ball because Cece hit it down the stairs again), the group hit the town. We headed to the plaza in search of a KTV club.

'Shit, everywhere is closed,' replied Callum.

'No, it can't be, we were here last night?' whined Mia.

'I tried but apparently it's closed today,' repeated Callum.

Alex, in his brilliantly drunken state, came running back to the group.

'I know where to go,' he shouted breathlessly, 'a local showed me where to go, follow me, I will take us to KTV!'

Everyone cheered and started to follow. I was happy Alex had taken control, everyone was very drunk by this point and we were in the middle of nowhere.

He led us to the twenty-first floor of a seedy block of flats, which looked suspiciously like a strip club or brothel. We were taken to an individual KTV booth with a wide screen, leather sofas, minibar and two flashy Elvis-style microphones that produced a horrendous echo, making the singer, even if they were good, sound wildly out of tune. Duos took to the stage and sang their hearts out to the likes of Ed Sheeran, George Ezra, The Vaccines and John Denver. As the night went on, people continued to drink making their performance all the more entertaining, wildly swinging their arms and cheering to the crowd of travellers. Alex used his best Mandarin to order six more bottles of beer for the group, which conveniently, was exactly what our Mandarin lessons had taught us: 'Liù Píng píjiǔ duōshǎo qián'.

Miraculously, six bottles of beer appeared. I jumped up to him and wrapped my legs around his waist in celebration. We took to the stage and sung our favourite, *Castle on The Hill*.

As the night drew to a close, I tried to negotiate the bill. It was getting late and I started to feel a mild anxiety rise inside me. I knew I shouldn't stay out too long; very late nights were a CVS trigger. I felt tired but if I could just organise everyone to leave safely, everything would be okay. Using my slightly bossy teacher skills, I herded everyone out and settled the bill. *KTV Success.*

At 3.56a.m. my head touched the pillow, whirling with funny memories.

26ᵗʰ October
5:59a.m.

Shit, CVS.

It hit and it hit hard. The cramps were really bad, and no matter how much paracetamol I took, they would not cease.

I tried to sleep to pass the time, but sleep eluded me. I tried to sit up and lie back down but that made my back hurt. Nothing would make it better. I hated how the one time I had let go and gone out with everyone, my body had taken revenge. I had had two drinks at the hostel and drank water for the rest of the night, I had been so careful. It wasn't fair. It was a harsh reminder that my body was not like everyone else's. It was restricted, cursed. *I hate you CVS. I HATE YOU.*

Alex was badly hungover, he'd drunken some of Tommy's cheap toxic spirit from the corner shop and was feeling the effects. It was a horrendous day. The others slept-in until late, so I lay on my top bunk alone, consumed by pain. At 4p.m. Alex's stomach had finally settled and he eventually made it up the stairs to see me. I was so relieved to see someone that I honestly didn't care if he vomited all over me, I just didn't want to battle the pain alone anymore. It had been ten hours since I'd last seen anyone. He lay down beside me, squeezed my hand when my face crumpled in pain and soothed me when I heaved from the nauseating cramps. I had never loved him more than in that moment. He was there, at my side, even when I was at my worst.

'I'm here Cece, it's okay, I won't leave,' he whispered.

At one point the manager entered in a rage, shouting at Alex for being in the girls' dormitory.

'You need to leave; this is a female dorm!'

Despite the fact I looked like death and was practically throwing up, the manager continued with his rant. After five minutes, Alex had had enough of his protestations and stood up for me.

'Well I'm sorry but she is very ill, if you want to sit with her all afternoon then fine, I'll go. But I'm not leaving my girlfriend. She is unwell and needs someone.'

The manager was taken aback and, clearly feeling guilty, softened his tone.

'Oh, I'm sorry, well when it gets to 9p.m. you have to leave, but for now, stay. Does she need anything? Hot water? Medication?'

'She has a condition and is having a bad attack. She has had all the medication she needs thanks.'

'Is there anything else I can do?'

'Do you have a private room so I can be with her? This is too loud and bright.'

'I'm sorry but nothing is available.'

In my drugged state I couldn't respond, but disappointment sunk inside me. I was on the top bunk and with everyone now awake, it was loud, very bright and impossible to rest. Later on, even Tommy snuck into the dorm to flirt with a girl he had met last night, which was ridiculous because Alex would get into even more trouble if the manager came back.

It was bad, really bad. The pain made me convulse as the cramps twisted and tore my whole abdomen. I took deep breaths but eventually ended up in tears as the pain not only defeated my body but my morale as well. After several rounds of night meds, sleep consumed me. Sleep was the only way to be free of pain. I remember waking up a few times in the night when Alex placed his hand on my forehead, but the rest is a blur.

27th October

I woke, sat up and waited. *It's stopped, yes, freedom. No more pain.* I sunk back into bed; I was exhausted.

Alex came in shortly after, he explained that the others had left to travel to the next destination at 4a.m.

'But it's okay, I knew you would be in no state to travel so I've sorted our transport to the next place.'

So, the previous evening, even in his hungover state, Alex had re-scheduled our whole journey for a day later.

'We'll catch up with everyone, it'll be okay Cece, we can just rest today.'

A few hours later, I managed to shower and as I was rummaging around for a new change of clothes, I found a thin sheet of folded paper balancing on the top of my rucksack. I unfolded and read the mysterious note:

Hi Cece,

Really hope you're feeling better today! Sad to leave a soldier behind but clearly you need the recovery time! You are so brave travelling with this horrid condition, but nothing keeps Cece down! Well…maybe only for a day or two, but then you are back climbing anything possible!

You are such an amazing person and your karaoke singing isn't too bad either, I won't be forgetting that night anytime soon! I hope your journey is okay, but don't worry – Alex has got you! All you need to worry about is recovering – don't think about time.

See you in a few days!
Love you lots Cece,
From GeeGee
x x x x
P.S. expect a wicked hug when you arrive!

Reading this note from Geena, I found strength to continue the journey.

FORTY-FOUR

When the sun sets, and darkness fills its place, all you can see through a train window is the occasional dot of light from a streetlamp, a chain of headlights on a busy road or the blur of a cityscape. On a bullet train, you travel so fast it's hard to differentiate between the source of light and the light itself.

28th October

We navigated the Shanghai Metro and spent nine hours on a bullet train, travelling all the way down to Nanjing. In the final hour of our journey, travel sickness set in. It was bad, and recovering from my attack, my stomach was in knots and felt like a balloon about to explode. I closed my eyes and turned up the music, trying to distract my brain from the sickening jolt of the carriage. To make it even worse, we then had to take a two-hour minibus through the steep twisting mountains.

Fujian
11p.m.

Stepping out into the fresh night air was bliss. Ornate bridges criss-crossed the quiet river, yellow and red lanterns illuminated the dusty paths and huge round buildings towered in the shadows. *I've missed rural China.* Our guesthouse seemed to overflow onto the street, with tables, water bottles and children's toys splayed on the floor outside. We were greeted by a smiley guide, Dao, who had just been sharing a pot of stew with the large family that owned the house. Due to our late arrival, we'd been placed in the family's home for convenience. The bathroom and showers were outdoor wet rooms that also housed several large moths, green bugs and even a frog! The house was messy, but clearly every object was, or had been, a vital part of the family's basic livelihood.

Dropping our things, we went for a short walk to try and settle my stomach before bed. We didn't get far in the darkness as every street seemed to...

'Snake!'

'What?'

Alex skirted out of the way to reveal a thick five-foot brown snake. It sat coiled with its head erect, defensive and ready to strike. I don't have a phobia of snakes, but when you've just arrived somewhere new and you already feel sick, the last thing you want is a snake in your path. Taking a deep breath, I slowly tiptoed past until my nerves buckled and I sprinted back into Alex's arms. That night I made him check under the bed, behind the curtains and everywhere else before we fell asleep.

29th October

Not feeling so good. I'd spent most of the night in the outside bathroom. When I woke in the morning, I felt exhausted and the CVS cramps were back. I fell back down into bed, exhaling loudly.

'Morning,' Alex said spritely, 'Cece, are you okay?'

'Yea, I just feel weird, my stomach feels cramped-up again,' I replied with a tremor.

Alex squeezed my hand and kissed my forehead. 'It'll be okay, we can just lie here for a little bit, and if you can't get up, you can just chill here for the day.'

'But we've travelled so far to get here, and I've only just finished one attack.'

'It's okay, rest here a little bit, breakfast isn't till ten, so you have time.'

After a thirty-minute lie down and a good dose of paracetamol, I felt a little better. *It was just a 'scare' attack.*

We met everyone downstairs tucking into hot steamed buns and salty chive omelettes. I couldn't stomach anything but enjoyed hearing an account of the past few days from Ned and Amy.

11a.m.

I felt like a piece of paper about to fold in half, so was relieved to learn the cycle ride would be mostly downhill and we'd take a minibus to return. *You can do this Cece, you've made it this far so you can go just a little further.*

'Here, I know you're not hungry, but just eat some of this, it will give you a little energy to cycle,' Alex handed me a bit of a cereal bar.

'Thanks,' I said nibbling the mouse sized piece.

'I'll be right behind you, okay, just do as much as you can.'

We cycled on small roads that meandered down through the valley. Rows and rows of tea plantations made the mountains seem like they were covered in giant pieces of corrugated green card. Wind whipped our hair as we sped down the hills, I felt weightless, like a bird finally free of its indoor cage. I was no longer in pain; *this is what being alive feels like.*

'This is what it feels like to be alive Alex!' I shouted.

'Alex?'

The road was empty behind me.

'Alex?'

We stopped to wait for everyone to catch up, but he still didn't appear, neither did Callum, Amy or Ned. Waiting for ten minutes, there was still no sign. Dao, looking concerned, pedalled back up the hill. Murmurs spread throughout the group.

'Did you see them?'

'Was Amy okay on her bike?'

'Cece, did Alex go with them?'

'I, I don't know. One minute he was there, then I turned and he was gone.'

Suddenly a bike flew over the top as Callum raced down the hill, followed by Ned, Amy and finally Dao and Alex.

'What happened?' I asked eagerly.

'Amy was having trouble with her bike, so we stayed to sort it out, took longer than we thought,' he replied.

'Amy, take mine,' Ned gestured, 'your gears are messed up, you'll never get up that hill!'

'Thanks Ned,' Amy replied quietly.

With the group reunited, we proceeded with the roundhouse tour.

'Roundhouses were built hundreds of years ago,' Dao explained, 'consisting of a wooden beam structure, coated in a thick layer of mud and earth, giving them the Chinese name of "earth house" or roundhouse as they're known today. They were built when people fled during the wars, the gigantic roundhouse acted as their personal castle. Often five to eight families would co-inhabit each one, but the village people still live in them today. This one is abandoned, so you can have a sneaky look around,' he gestured to the deteriorated entrance. 'Oh, but watch out for the floorboards, some are rotten, especially on the first floor.'

So essentially, we're playing a game of roundhouse Russian Roulette, fabulous.

By midday I was relieved to see the minibus arrive, ready to drive us back up the hill. I was exhausted, so appreciated the lift. I used the few hours around lunch to lie down and regain some strength.

Afternoon

Missing out on yesterday's visit, Dao kindly took Alex and I on our own private tour of the tea plantations. The cool mountain breeze carried the fragrant earthy scent as we walked between the rows of tea bushes. It was beautiful, overlooking the thousands of plantations in the valley below. The moment was captured in a single photo, Alex with his arm around my waist, half in affection, half supporting me from collapsing. My face is sickly pale, but we have wide happy smiles, grateful to be alive, together and surrounded by the beauty of Fujian.

FORTY-FIVE

Gamble Town.

30th October
5:30a.m.

Alex shook me gently.

'We're almost here Cece, time to get ready.'

The few hours on the night train were hazy, I barely remembered getting into my bunk.

'Mmm okay thanks, did you sleep?' I mumbled as I looked up.

Alex's eyes were shadowed by dark circles. 'Mm, not really, but it's okay. We're in Macau!' he said with a jaded enthusiasm.

I smiled sympathetically.

6a.m.

We were herded straight onto a two-and-a-half-hour bus to Macau's border. The next few hours consisted of security checks, scanners, passports, forms and hauling rucksacks on and off until we all collapsed with fatigue on the other side of the border crossing. From there, we took two short coach rides to a grand building which turned out to be the Galaxy Casino. A crystal chandelier hung above an illuminated fountain in reception, everything was lined with gold. We couldn't help but feel shabby, entering with rucksacks, sweaty clothes and belongings that would not have totalled to the value of a single casino chip.

Dumping our bags and freshening up, we were taken to one of the largest casinos in the world, the Venetian. And my, was it impressive. A mega complex of gambling tables, bright lights and flashing screens. Chips, cards and dice everywhere, being sorted, shuffled or rolled; each representing thousands of dollars to be won or lost. This was Macau, a gambler's paradise. We played a few games of roulette, doubling our money but losing the winnings on the final go. *Should have chosen red.*

Old Town

The afternoon was spent in the Old Town. Our enthusiastic guide, Fen, greeted us with an American twang.

'Hey guys, how are you doing? Welcome to Macau, land of gambling and Portuguese landmarks!'

He led us through crowded streets, past old Catholic churches and elegant yellow and white rimmed buildings. In our free time, Alex and I sat on the steps in front of the remains of St Paul's, people watching and munching Portuguese custard tarts (Macau Po tarts). Taking them out of the brown paper bag, they were still warm when we took our first bite. Layers of salty, buttery pastry melted in your mouth followed by the warm sweet custard and caramelised sugar top.

To finish the final leg of the journey, we took a wavy one-hour ferry back to Hong Kong, *where it all started*. After a quick bowl of veggie noodles in Temple Street, we collapsed onto our bunks.

31st October

I woke to Alex kissing my cheek.

'Morning, how did you sleep?'

'Morning, I can't actually remember falling asleep!'

'Haha, yeah. I went to brush my teeth then two minutes later I came back, for our final night together, and you were fast asleep.'

'Haha, Alex I'm sorry.'

'It's okay, I knew you were super tired, and it probably would have been too hot for us both to share one bunk anyway.'

'True, but you should have woken me!'

'Oh, I tried but you were gone, the amitriptyline had knocked you right out!'

'Nice, real sexy, haha.'

Packing up, it dawned on me that this was the final day together before we'd be separated again for two months.

The Dragon Trip parts
12p.m.

It was hard to say goodbye to the remaining members of the group. We had been together for a month, all day every day, we'd become a little family. 'Safe travels' and 'stay in touch' were repeated so many times between us it echoed down the hallway as people left the hostel. I gave Geena one final big hug, feeling like her little sister as she wrapped her arms around me.

And then, it was just the two of us.

'Just come with me, I'll put you in my rucksack, we can both move to Cambridge together.'

'Come with me to Chiang Mai for the final adventure!'

'You know I'd love to, Cece.'

Airport

'So, this is it,' Alex said solemnly.

'I'm so happy you came on this trip.'

'Me too, I was so worried last year about not being able to join you, but it worked out. I love you so much Cece.'

I threw my arms around his neck and whispered into his ear, 'I love you to the moon and back.'

I savoured every second, walking as slow as possible until the guard gestured me through the gate - I had to steal my last glance. I'll never forget the forlorn look on his face as I blew him one last kiss.

Flying above the clouds, he never left my mind. The sun dyed the sky pink as I approached Thailand.

Time for a new adventure to begin.

PART FOUR

Thailand, Cambodia and Vietnam

FORTY-SIX

Chiang Mai and the scooter.

1st November

The Box Hostel was made up of two levels of cargo crates, renovated with bunk beds and minimalistic furnishings. My bed was on the second level which stretched out onto a little balcony overlooking the ground floor. A spiral staircase led to a boardwalk with a few tables and chairs, where travellers lazed at all hours of the day.

I promised myself I'd have a chilled 'Cece CVS prevention day' so sat on the balcony reading, in the slightly uncomfortable heat. I didn't get far before my mind started to plan the next month, which reminded me what my dad had said about cutting the trip short and coming home early. I pushed it to the back of my mind and rang Alex instead. I envied him a little, being at home while I was alone in another completely different country. It was nice to hear his voice, but it made me miss home and its familiarity.

'Hi, have you just arrived?'

A perky American girl had just popped up onto the balcony. She was well-dressed with flawless hair and makeup, which was impressive considering the heat.

'Hi, yes, I arrived last night,' I replied.

'Cool, I'm Meggie, I've been here two and a half months.'

'Wow, a Thai expert then!'

'Yes, I guess I am,' she laughed, 'I'm going to scooter it to the Grand Canyon this afternoon.'

'The Grand Canyon, in Thailand?'

'Yes, well the Thai version. It's meant to be really pretty, or so I've heard. Wannna come with?'

'You mean on the back of your scooter?'

'Yeah.'

This is meant to be a chilled day, you should stay at the hostel Cece, this could go seriously wrong.

'Sure, I'd love to.'

Just ignore your rational mind then.

'Cool, well the hostel lady is going to let me practise on her scooter, then I'll go and hire one.'

'Okay so you've never ridden one before?' I asked dubiously. 'Because I have zero experience on a bike, I've never ridden one before.'

'Well no, but I was learning to ride a motorbike back home.'

'Oh okay.'

'I mean you should hire one too, it'll be fun.'

'Cece, this doesn't sound good,' I could hear Alex saying, *'Thai police catch foreigners without a licence all the time. You have to pay your way out and the roads are busiest in the cities. Wait until a National Park in Vietnam.'*

'Ah, well I've never ridden one before, maybe going on the back of yours would be better?' I hesitated.

'Okay I guess.'

I watched her downstairs practising. She was a complete beginner, juddering forward with shaky balance and wobbly feet; her lack of control was unnerving. *This is ridiculous Cece, you can't get on the back with her, you'll crash. Go downstairs and say you're too tired to go.*

Thirty minutes later

'So, you're ready Cece, got your swim stuff? Meggie said, her eyes gleaming with enthusiasm.

'Yes sure, in fact, I think I'll hire one after all.'

Seriously?

'Okay amazing, that's a huge relief! To be honest, I'm not that confident and don't want to drive with your life on my wheels, haha!' she shrilled.

Why are you going with this girl? She is clueless! You've never even looked at a bike before, let alone ridden one. Yes, but at least I'll be in control. Push your comfort zone Cece.

At the garage

Meggie forgot her purse, so I paid for both bikes. We were given two goofy helmets and the keys to the scooters.

'To turn on, you press this and pull brakes,' the lady explained. 'Turn throttle to go. Break like bike. Okay? You go.'

Is this all the instruction I get? Why am I doing this?

I pulled the throttle and lurched forward. *Shit*. I edged out of the shop, pushing the bike with my feet to keep balance. Meggie was already on the main road revving her engine. Clouds of dust circulated as cars, bikes, tuk-tuks and scooters whizzed past, beeping their horns at the clueless white girls blocking the road during Chiang Mai's rush hour.

On the road, I lifted my feet. *Fuck.* I fell sideways, just stopping myself from tipping into another bike that skimmed past. *Ah, this is scary. Come on Cece, get a grip. Pull the throttle, legs up and go; otherwise you'll lose her.* I tried again and got fast enough that I could just about balance. At a lightning speed of six miles an hour, I was riding the scooter. I managed to speed up to thirty as we drove along the road, but the traffic kept overtaking. *Surely there can't be anything left on the road to overtake me?*

After half an hour, we seemed to be further into the city than when we had started. Not only that, but the sun hung mockingly low in the sky, reminding me that the privilege of daylight would soon run out.

'Meggie,' I shouted at the traffic lights, 'where are we? Shouldn't we be there by now?'

She turned, cigarette in one hand and phone in the other.

'We had to go through the centre to avoid the police, and then there were roadblocks, so we had to dodge them.'

'Ah okay, good thinking, but how long left now?'

'Bout half an hour.'

'Okay great,' I said trying to hide my concern.

At some points in the journey, I literally thought I might die. It seemed that every possible diversion and road work was thrown our way. We crossed three lane motorways, mega roundabouts and sudden sharp bends. I've never prayed so hard for left turns. To top it off, Meggie couldn't seem to understand that indicators, or 'blinkers' as she called them, were actually used to tell the traffic where you were going and not just used as a flashy feature. I had to scream 'blinker' at her to prevent the traffic from bulldozing into us.

Two hours later, a wind-swept, white knuckled Meggie and Cece finally arrived at the Grand Canyon, which wasn't much more than a man-made swimming pool.

'Oh, it's closed,' Meggie said with disappointment.

'Well it is 7p.m. now. The sun has set, everyone has probably gone home,' I joked.

'Hmm, do ya wanna get something to eat?'

'I think I might vom if I eat now, perhaps when we get back?'

She made a fake laugh, 'Okay yeah cool, awesome, amazing.'

Despite several wrong turns, locals lobbing beer bottles at us and trying to see through sunglasses in the dark, we made it back to the hostel in just over two hours.[17]

We were greeted by a relieved hostel girl, Khun.

'You're alive! I so worries, I finish my shift but I wait for you come back!'

'Aw bless you, thank you that is so kind of you! We are okay, it just took way longer than expected. Khun, you should come to dinner with us as a thank you!'

'Yea, thaynks,' Meggie squeaked.

---

[17] *There were so many bugs flying around we'd lose our eyes if we didn't wear sunglasses!*

Dinner

'Well that was amazing, I think I'll ride the four hours to Pai this weekend. Cece?' declared Meggie.

My jaw dropped. *Was she mad?* We'd scraped by this time. If it took us two hours to ride a thirty-minute journey, the road to Pai would take us all day! She also seemed to forget the point when, just before the canyon, she lost her balance and almost flew into the oncoming traffic.

'Well this was nice, thank you Meggie, but I think I'll conclude my first biking experience here for now.'

There is no way I'm going to Pai with this crazy lady.

'What? You mean this was your first time on a bike?'

'Yes, like I said to you before, I was a complete beginner.'

'OMG that's so brave of you, wow!'

I looked at her and wondered if she had actually listened to anything I had said this whole time.

2nd November
10a.m.

Sat at a smoothie bar, I couldn't help but feel a little repulsed by the number of loud travellers. It was a sea of crop tops, wife beaters and papaya shakes. *It's a little hypocritical, as I am also backpacking and hoping to see the same touristy sights, but not to this level of 'gap-ya-ness'.* Crass American voices resonated between the walls of the café, boasting about the amazing experiences they'd had that had 'like todally changed their lives'. I'd met many people while travelling, but none as eccentric and outlandish as these. Travellers who had been on the road for so long that their brains had become smoothie bowls after drinking nothing but beer, and their bodies had burnt to wrinkled crisps after countless days in the sun.

12p.m.

Tried my first Thai massage, *well-earned after yesterday's four-hour scooter epic!* I was welcomed by a smartly dressed, giggling Thai woman. My feet were washed and I was asked to change into a pair of loose brown trousers and a baggy top. I was then taken to a cool room with empty beds, covered in gold and burgundy linen. She started from my feet and worked upwards, pulling, pushing, bending and slapping. At one point she pulled my arms around my back and crossed my legs until I felt like I'd been pulled inside out. *More of a yoga work out than a relaxing massage, but good none the less.* I was given hot sweet tea to drink before leaving, but after a few sips saw a little fly swimming inside, so left the rest. Leaving the place, I noticed the words, *'run by ex-prisoners'* printed above the door. A small part of me was pleased I hadn't seen this before the full-body massage.

The cooking class
4p.m.

Continuing with my touristy day, I hopped into a tuk-tuk to be whisked away to a local market. There I met a puffy faced Thai chef, Nuntida, owner of a cooking school. I marvelled at the different kinds of basils, curry pastes, small aubergines and various other vegetables. We bought a few ingredients before heading back to the school to prepare the starter, wonton soup and deep-fried flower wontons. I was then taught how to make papaya salad, pad Thai, green curry with homemade curry paste and mango with sticky rice. It was a pretty relaxing afternoon apart from Nuntida's son running around recklessly between the canisters of gas and sizzling woks. At one point, he came so close to my spatula that he almost became a fried wonton himself! *I don't think Nuntida intended for him to be part of the menu today.*

Arriving back at the hostel, I bumped into a sheepish Meggie. She'd ridden her bike again but had been caught by the Thai police without a license, and therefore been fined five hundred baht. She had also crashed into another bike and had had to pay a further one hundred dollars. *I'm never riding a scooter again in Thailand.*

271

FORTY-SEVEN

Forget and focus on the final destination.

3ʳᵈ November

I had been waiting on the roadside of Phaya Thai, Bangkok for almost an hour. It was hot, dusty and my rucksack was crushing my shoulders. Every passing vehicle coughed up billows of fumes which stung my eyes and added to the unpleasant muggy heat. My eyes were tracking every large bus that chugged past. *Urgh come on fifty-nine, come on, where are you? Ooh is this fifty-nine? Yes, it is! Just in time before I melt into the tarmac! Oh wow, you've just driven past me. Fudge.* I looked around for help but only a fruit seller, smugly shaded by his wagon of melon, shared the roadside.

Several hours later

After eventually making it to the centre of Bangkok, and circling the same street several times, I arrived at my next hostel. I'd booked a twelve-bed dorm, but was delighted to find I'd been upgraded, at no extra cost, to a private room. I'd heard of these things happening to solo travellers, but they'd been lucky rumours up until now. The room was small but neat, a double bed filled the entire diameter and strips of aluminium lined the red walls; making the single dorm seem a little like a coke-can-campervan.

Making the most of my twenty-four hours in Bangkok, and with only a few hours of sunlight left, I headed to Wat Pho. A temple complex filled with towers covered in coloured tiles, gold tipped roofs and hundreds of orange draped monks. I held my breath when I entered the grand room with the world's largest reclining buddha. It was enormous and brilliantly gold. I felt like a child staring up at the skeleton of a dinosaur, a little terrified but in complete awe of its size.

6p.m.

As the sun set, I headed to Khoa San Road's night market, a few streets down from my hostel. Brash vendors sold mango with sticky rice, sunburnt males swaggered around with scorpions on sticks and the same elephant hippie pants flip-flopped along the street. Joining the spectacle, I queued up at the busiest street food stall, *it was only thirty baht for a plate of pad Thai.* As I perched on a step, eating my seventy-five-pence supper, a cockroach crawled out from the drain, only to be squished by an oblivious tourist's sandal. *Hmm, let's hope I'm not eating pad cockroach.*

4ᵗʰ November
5:15a.m.

Ohhh, why so early?

My bus was at six, I didn't have time to moan. I quickly dressed, brushed my teeth and returned to my room to pack. *Wait, the door is locked? But I didn't lock it. And the key, where is the key? Damn it, it's inside. Shit, I've locked myself out!*

I rushed downstairs looking for help, only to have two dopey girls plod up the stairs with a box of hundreds of keys. *It's now 5:40a.m. and they don't have a master key.* After trying a few, they rang their friend, speaking frantically in Thai. *It's now 5:45a.m.*

'Um, sorry but my bus is at six an...'

'Yes, we know,' they snapped back.

Surely I can't be the first person to be locked out by their own door?

At 5.50a.m. the door finally opened. *Okay Cece, you have 10 mins to pack and be on the bus.* I shoved everything into my rucksack, collected my deposit and ran.

1p.m.

Seven hours later, we made it to Chumphon - the ferry terminal and gateway to the islands. *Koh Tao, here we come!* A string of passengers walked out onto a narrow wooden pier,

273

stretching over the bluish-grey sea, to board a large catamaran. I sat mid-level which was outside with a breeze, avoiding the lower indoor levels and precarious top deck. Within the first few minutes the sky had turned a dark ominous grey and the wind was whistling. The boat was thrown up and down by deceivingly large waves; it was like a roller coaster without seat belts. I clung to the bench and prayed it remained connected to the deck. Sea spray hit the side of the boat as it crashed into the water and soaked anyone remaining on the outside. *I can't do this for two hours.* I suddenly felt nervous and very alone. My grandma had hated boats, she got terribly seasick. Towards the end, cancer gave her vertigo whenever she stood up, nauseatingly making the ceiling spin; she had described it as 'seasickness on land'. Two silent tears trickled down my sea sprayed cheeks. *I miss you Grandma.*

For her, I was determined to get through the voyage without surrendering to the seasickness she had suffered. I put my headphones in and didn't take my eyes off the horizon. It was hard to keep focused as everyone around me was either heaving into plastic bags or running onto the deck to violently vomit overboard. Every time someone was sick, I turned up the volume, trying not to lose sight of the horizon. I was completely soaked in salt water, the wind had whipped my skin raw and my body was bruised from the constant impact of the boat hitting the waves.

Two hours later, I made it to Koh Tao alive. *Thank you, Grandma.*

4:30p.m.

After going for a ten-pound wax, I sat on a balcony overlooking the pink clouded sunset and ate shrimp pad Thai with a coconut shake. It was a beautiful evening, but I couldn't help but feel incredibly lonely. *You'll feel better in the morning, you always do Cece, this place is beautiful, you won't get ill here, don't worry.* I headed back to my hostel and crawled into my little pod-like rectangular bunk, numbered A5. *I feel as small as a sheet of A5.*

Checking my emails before bed, I received one from Dad confirming my flight home had been brought forward to the 2nd December.[18] I would only be losing a few weeks, but it meant home was less than a month away. *You can make it that far Cece, you can do this.*

---

[18] *It was only when I returned home that my father revealed to me that he had driven all the way up from Oxford to Birmingham to change the flight! Due to an error in the airline's booking system, it was impossible to change the flight over the phone. To this day I continue to thank my parents for the incredible lengths they went to during my trip. After all, it was as much a challenge for them as it was for me.*

FORTY-EIGHT

A window into the extraordinary world below the surface.

5ᵗʰ November

I woke to the relief of no stomach cramps, which was surprising considering yesterday's epic journey! I was looking forward to this week. I had planned to stay in Koh Tao for at least seven days to allow myself some time to rest and recover. I wasn't the biggest fan of lying on a beach and watching the world go by, but I needed to stop doing so much to prevent anymore CVS attacks. I knew myself too well - as soon as I was in a new place I would want to explore, so by staying on a small island, I would have no choice but to relax.

Morning

It was hot, sticky droplets of sun creamy sweat trickled down my skin as I lay on one of Koh Tao's pristine white beaches. KT was the smaller of three adjacent islands that most travellers visit, and so I had hoped it wouldn't be too spoiled by commercial tourism. It was undoubtedly scenic, with ancient palms reaching high into the sky until they bent from the weight of young coconuts, creating that iconic beach silhouette. The warm seas had a sparkling clarity that made the ocean inviting, even on a rainy day.

I got a little bored watching other couples having fun and relaxing, I longed for Alex, or even just a friend to enjoy the beach with. On a swinging bench opposite me was a girl of my age, I watched her for a while to see if she was with anyone else before branding her as a 'solo traveller'. *Right come on Cece, time to make friends.*

'Hey, are you alone?' I asked.
'Um yeah.'
'Oh cool, me too!'

Lana was from the US, but she had spent a year studying in Northern England. We got chatting and hired paddleboards for an hour. Living by the sea for a few years I had tried the sport a couple of times, but it was Lana's first go. Every few minutes I'd hear a splash or a thud as she fell, but always followed by a fit of giggles - she was a good sport. It was fun but I missed Alex. We had become quite good at paddleboarding and I wanted to share the moment with him. *I guess funny stories and photos will have to do.*

Afternoon

I chilled on a tree swing with my first mango lassi (a thick yoghurty drink), while catching up with Alex on the phone. It was nice being in a place that he had visited, just a year ago, during his own travels. It felt familiar, as he had told me about this island many times before. Without warning, a monsoon hit and the beach became a messy grey puddle. I ran for cover under a straw shelter and we continued chatting about his new flat and our soon to be lives in Cambridge and London. The rain continued and the water flooded the shelter until I had no choice but to scurry back to the hostel in slippy flip-flops.

6th November

Lana and I were taken to five different sites during our snorkelling boat tour. The current was strong and it took a while to get used to the snorkel gear without swallowing a litre of sea water with every wave. Jumping off the boat at Shark Bay felt like we were in the deep sea. As we swam down, a huge shadow appeared, engulfing the coral below. In minor panic, I looked forward to find a giant sea turtle gliding through the water. He was beautiful, his large shell speckled with browns, greens and greys and two black sage eyes looking out to the open ocean.

At Mango Bay, black tipped reef sharks darted in between the corals with a flick of their fins and shoals of millions of fish swam through the water like flocks of birds in the sky. It was a little window into the extraordinary world below the surface.

Evening

I met a rather sunburnt Lana outside a small bar at the end of the beach. Several ladyboys loitered coyly around the palm trees, enjoying the last few minutes of peace before their shifts at the bar or cabaret began. A few locals were practising fire-twirling on the sand, whistling and cheering each other on as they swung balls of fire inches from each other's skin. The light from each rotation illuminated the water to make it seem like giant fireflies were hovering over the sea. It was almost hypnotic. Beyond the shore I noticed a pair of lovers embracing in the moonlit ocean, the waves caressed them softly as they whispered and giggled. *I want to be held like that. To feel the gentle warmth of the ocean and be encased by two loving arms: Alex's arms.* The island was beautiful, but I couldn't help but feel it would have been so much nicer to have experienced it with someone you loved. *Focus on what you have here Cece, don't think about what you have left behind.*

'For you,' Lana smiled as she handed me an ice-cold glass.

I hesitated. I needed to be careful with how much alcohol I consumed, especially after the Shanghai's post-night out disaster. *Alex won't be here to look after you this time.*

'You want it?' asked Lana.

I didn't want to trigger any more attacks, but I'd been feeling well over the past few days and felt hopeful my body could take it. *After all, Cece, this part of the trip is meant to be relaxing - when will you have the chance to be in this moment again?*

'Sure, thank you,' I said, taking the glass.

FORTY-NINE

There are so many minutes in your life, but only a few of them actually change your life, change your path. People can die, live, marry, divorce, reunite, part, experience great happiness or great sadness all with the turn of a minute hand. Is it up to us how we use them? Or is it pre-destined? Who knows? All I know is that when I am ill, the idea of time and that it cannot be wasted, is brought to a stark reality. When I'm well, I embrace every situation that comes my way and never think twice. Take every opportunity as it comes. But every minute is precious, so use it wisely - you never know which one will change your life.

Unknown time

As we walked back from the bar, I noticed the couple were still in the water, but they had drifted further down the beach, away from the moon's spotlight. I turned my head to have one last look at the romantic scene when splashes of white froth disturbed the calm water around them. I stepped back to get a better look. The girl appeared to be struggling away from the man who was encasing her. It was faint but I could just about hear her screams over the waves. This wasn't a couple in love.

'Cece, what are you doing?' questioned Lana.

'I'm going to help the girl,' I said stripping off my shorts.

'Wait, hang on,' she said clutching my arm.

'There's a man there too, I think she's in trouble.'

'Cece don't go, you don't know them.'

'She needs help. I'm going in,' I shouted.

When you entered the water, you knew something wasn't right. The alcohol had gone to your head. As soon as you were waist deep his hands pulled you in and touched your breasts. His right hand lowered to the lace between your legs. Lana was never there. You were

279

the girl in the embrace, you were encased in his arms, you were the girl struggling.

'Please let me go,' *you pleaded.*

You turned to see his face, but he covered your eyes.

'Cece, you ran away from me all those months ago,' *a deep voice whispered.*

'Who are you?' *you whimpered.*

'You know who I am, you left me at that taxi in Kuching, without a goodbye. You deserted me, you left what we had behind, you left me alone. Well, I came to find you, all these months I've been searching. I'm not leaving you now.'

'I'm sorry. I'm so sorry Dalir,' *you whispered.*

When you pulled away, he pulled you in tighter and kissed your neck.

'No, no, I can't Dalir, you need to let me go.'

He grabbed your legs that were trying to swim away and hoisted them around his hips.

'No, let me go, please let me go Dalir.'

'Just let me have you Cece,' *he moaned.*

When you tried to pull away, he grabbed you tighter.

'Please Dalir.'

'Cece, don't play that game with me again, I know you want me. You've wanted me since Kuching, the signs were always there. You only ran away because you were afraid of what we had.'

'I never wanted *this*, Dalir, never!'

I awoke to the cold moon streaming through the half-closed door of the hostel. My sheets were twisted around my legs and I was breathing rapidly. Disorientated I checked my phone:

[06/11, 22:23] Lana: Thanks for a nice evening girl, good idea only getting one drink and calling it early, I catch my ferry tomorrow morning after all. Lx

I collapsed back into bed, lying rigidly on my back. My whole body was covered in a cold sweat. *It wasn't real. It was just a dream Cece, just a dream.* I continued to lie there, eyes wide open.

Haven't you done enough yet? You've pushed yourself far enough – you are going insane. Why would he return to your mind now? Isn't this a sign that you've done enough, you shouldn't push yourself anymore. Things only get worse when you do too much. It's time to go home. You don't need to do anything else. You have nothing to prove to anyone.

Yes, I do, I must complete the journey, I must do it for Grandma.

She wouldn't want you to suffer. You're not strong enough. You have a chronic illness; you should be at home resting. This is too much for you. It's time to go home. Time to leave.

But I must complete the journey, I missed Grandma's funeral for this, I must finish it, otherwise I missed saying goodbye to her for nothing. I must finish it for her.

You are not strong enough to finish the journey. You were never strong enough.

'Oh Charlotte, you never give up do you? You know I think you could do anything you wanted to in this life. You are so brave.'

Grandma's words echoed in my mind.

'Yes, I am strong enough,' I whispered.

I'm not giving in. I'll make it to the end, no matter how sick I get.

An hour later

Go back to sleep, it's okay. Just close your eyes. He's not here, it's all in your head, go back to sleep.

7ᵗʰ November
6a.m.

My eyes shot open and I sat bolt upright. I looked around the dorm, scanning people's sleeping faces. *He's not here Cece, it was just a dream.* I covered my eyes, holding my head in my hands and exhaled deeply. *I'm tired of this. Tired of travelling alone.*

9a.m.

I lay rigid in my bed until nine - time to get up. I walked wearily to the port to meet Lana before she took her ferry back to the mainland. Seeing her smiling face confirmed that last night was just a dream.

'I feel so fresh today,' she said, 'I should have early nights more often, you're a good influence Cece!'

I forced a smile.

'Anyway, I better get going,' she said giving me a tight hug.

'Safe trip back home and thanks for the past few days Lana,' I hugged back.

Once my only friend had left, I felt very lonely. The beautiful island suddenly seemed deserted and I felt lost and quite alone.

FIFTY

The try dive.

8th November

I needed to do something to take my mind off things, meet new people and get out of the hostel. Unlike most other travellers, I didn't come to Koh Tao for the diving but, as I was spending a week here, it seemed like a waste not to try it. After all, it was one of the cheapest places in the world to learn. Needing a distraction, I signed up to a trial dive.

8a.m.

My instructor was a tall, rugged blonde scuba dude from South London. He was cold at first, *clearly unimpressed to be up so early*, but warmed sensing my nervousness. Due to the monsoons, it was low season, so it was just him and I on the boat along with another small group who were completing their PADI. Everyone looked so tall and strong like they were made to dive, that godlike surfer physique. Oxygen tanks, life vests, tubes and pipes were loaded into the boat. The O tank was so heavy and, along with the weight band, I could barely stand up. I felt so small and feeble, my lungs surely weren't big enough for this sport. I even put my wetsuit on back to front!

'Oh don't worry, the Chinese do it all the time,' laughed Luke.

'Oh cheers, that makes me feel tons better!'

'Haha, you're welcome,' he said smugly.

Luke had been diving for over a decade, he'd been baptised into the water at the tender age of seventeen, being put in a crate full of great whites.

'Okay so a nice easy introduction then?'

'Yeah ah ha, not the ideal first dive I know!'

Like most divers on the island, Luke spent his spare time drinking and smoking weed. This was ironic considering the pre-dive contract I'd filled out stated 'strictly no drugs or alcohol'. Filled with confidence, I was placed on the edge of the boat, my back facing the sea. Luke had run through the hand signals and how the mask worked, but in my stressed mind it was all a jumble.

'Right, I'll go first', he said, leaning backwards into the sea.

It looked simple, but I was terrified. The boat driver helped me shuffle into the correct position as I was struggling from the weight of the tank. *Fuck, I don't want to do this. I don't think I can do it.* Into the water I somersaulted. The mouthpiece was difficult to breathe out of, you had to suck really hard to get the air and I started to panic. Water filled my mask and I raced back to the top, spluttering and removing everything from my face.

'Are you okay?' Luke asked, looking surprised.

'Yes, yes thanks, just had some water in my mask that's all,' I said trying to act calm. *Lord, we haven't even started diving yet and I'm already failing.*

We swam to a shallower part so Luke could demonstrate the basic safety skills: how to get rid of water from your mouthpiece, how to retrieve the pipe if it got lost and how to get water out of your mask, which was the trickier of the three. *How on earth can you get water out of your mask when you are already submerged in water?*

'You push two fingers on top of your mask and blow out with your nose,' Luke explained, 'the air forces the water downwards to clear the mask.'

Simple enough, but I wasn't convinced I would be able to do it several metres underwater. We descended and the pressure increased, making it more difficult to breathe. It was going okay until water leaked into my mask, I tried to blow it out but ended up choking myself. Between the splutters, I couldn't get enough air out of my mouthpiece so started to panic. *I need to go up, fuck I need to go up. Hand signals hand signals, damn what are they?* I grabbed Luke's fin, praying he'd turn around, and signalled to go back up.

Our ascent to the air couldn't have been slower, I felt suffocated with the whole weight of the ocean crushing my lungs, it was terrifying. When we finally reached the surface, it took me a while to calm down.

'It's okay, everyone freaks out when they get water in their mask for the first time. And, normally, most people are in a swimming pool and not the sea when it happens.'

'Sorry I just freaked out and panicked, then I couldn't breathe.'

'It's okay, take as long as you need. I think trial dives are possibly the worst way to try diving, it's scary because you don't have enough time to practise, ah ha.'

At that point I wanted to get out, I wanted to quit, to escape to the safety of the boat and sit with the kind old driver.

'Okay take your time and we'll go back down.'

Down again? I don't want to go back down. No Cece, you can't quit. Not like that, you can do this.

I pulled myself together and tightened my mask. We descended further this time, the water getting darker and darker as we moved further away from the surface. He had to pull me down as the weights weren't heavy enough for my small frame. Sensing my anxiety, he sweetly gave me his arm to grip, *which was very much appreciated.* Visibility was poor but Luke pointed out vanishing anemones and rare fish that glimmered like shards of glass in the sand. We reached a depth of seven metres in the end.

Returning to the surface, the boat driver hauled me back onto the boat like a drowned mouse; I had completed the dive. It was terrifying but I was proud of myself for sticking with it.

It had started to rain by the time we reached the shore and I shivered violently changing back into my clothes. Luke offered to drive me back to my hostel, which was sweet until I realised it was on the back of his scooter. *Too late, you already said yes.* I've never gripped a stranger's waist so tightly as we flew over the saturated island hills. By 11a.m. I'd ticked off two more items on my bucket list - ride on the back of a bike and try scuba diving. The latter, I probably wouldn't be trying again anytime soon.

FIFTY-ONE

He noticed the small details, appreciated the little things in life.

9th November

I met Danielle in the bunk in front of me when she moved into the dorm last night. She was an intense twenty-three-year-old Canadian, with a Victoria's Secret model figure and a contagious enthusiasm for life. Sharing a love of healthy food, we stopped off at a cute plant-based restaurant for lunch. They served huge 'Buddha bowls' filled with edamame beans, cucumber, mango, lettuce and brown rice with a creamy ginger tahini dressing. Dani lived in Dallas with her two-year boyfriend but was hoping to move back to her hometown in Canada, to set up her own café with her sister.

In the afternoon, the island was hit with torrential rain, but we weren't going to let that stop us exploring. We set our sights on hiking to the island viewpoint. The path was muddy, littered with leaves and criss-crossed with fallen trees. Climbing the hills in our black-hooded-waterproofs, we reached the top looking like sweaty seals. From above, the island looked like an earthy colour wheel, with each section blending into the next. The landscape's dark dewy vegetation stretched into the light-yellow sand, running into the clear water on the shore that gradually drifted down to the deep blue ocean. With the rain unceasing, the walk back was treacherous. The streets became one giant gutter. So much water had accumulated on the hillside that we weren't sure if we were in a river or on a path. We were lucky a landslide didn't occur and take us all the way down to the sea!

Evening

After the afternoon's epic, we planned to have a more relaxing evening in the island's centre. We visited a small Japanese restaurant for crab and cucumber California rolls topped with thin slices of mango, before heading to an outdoor bar to watch the sunset. Unfortunately, the rain returned, and we soon took cover under the shelter of an adjacent indoor bar. There, we met Jai - a fun guy who worked as a dive instructor by day and a tourist pub crawl first aider by night *(while everyone else brought a hip flask, he brought the plasters and alcohol wipes).*

'As the weather is pretty shit, why don't you just tag along with me on the pub crawl for a few hours? It's quite fun!' Jai suggested.

With nothing better to do, we joined Jai and his group on their voyage to the next pub. To protect the pub crawlers from being drenched by the monsoon, we walked under a large sheet of blue tarpaulin that was stretched over everyone to look like a Chinese dragon. Throughout the night, we helped Jai with his mission to get as many people dancing, *safely of course,* as possible. By the time we got to the final bar, everyone was dancing on the tables.

Towards the end of the night, I lost Dani and Jai and, surrounded by a sea of drunks, felt suddenly alone. At points, a few people kept trying to put their hands around my waist. The physical contact jolted my memory and I tore away. I pressed myself against the wall of the bar, letting the cool sea breeze calm my rapidly beating heart. *Oh, why has he returned to my mind?* At some points during my travels it seemed like everyone wanted one thing and, if you were caught up in the intoxicated swirl of human desire, it was impossible to escape. *I'm tired of this. I'm tired of feeling so vulnerable. Not only do I have no control over my body when I'm ill, but it seems I have no control over what other people try to do to it when I'm well either.* Never before had I experienced the societal disadvantage of my sex until now. These three and a half months had made me understand why I should have been wary travelling as a female alone.

Once I built up the courage to head back through the crowd, I found Dani and we returned to the hostel.

10ᵗʰ November

Dani and I joined Leon, another one of our dorm mates, for yoga. He was a tall blonde twenty-five-year-old German, with a warm heart and spiritual mind. He had become addicted to diving and, despite having only been in Koh Tao for three weeks, had already completed the advanced course on the island. The way he spoke about diving was like he was reliving every moment. He described the experience so slowly that no detail was missed, from entering the water to feeling the freeing sense of calm below the surface. He had also trained as a yoga teacher in India, which explained the way he hugged me every time we ran into each other.

'Ah Cece, come here,' arms wide open like a wise emperor. He'd wrap his arms around my small body and rock me from side to side while chanting 'mmmmmm', as if meditating.

I liked his gentle, slow approach to life, he took his time eating, walking, speaking and travelling.

'I normally spend a few months in each place, I like to get to know a city, see the locals, watch their routines; see the lady who gets her groceries every morning or watch the policeman who takes a cheeky rum every Saturday at 11a.m.' he explained.

I smiled, I liked the way he noticed the small details, appreciated the little things in life as well as the big experiences. It was a shame we had only just met as he was leaving that afternoon, coincidently on the same ferry as Dani. *Goodbye yet another two friends.*

11ᵗʰ November

My final day on Koh Tao was a little sunnier, but I was sad my friends had left. As I was walking into town, a scooter grumbled to a halt next to me. The rider took off his helmet to reveal the familiar face of Jai, the pub first aider.

'I'm just going for breakfast, want to join?'

Relieved to see a friendly face, I gladly accepted.

He showed me a little juice bar in the corner of town where they sold, according to Jai, the best smoothie bowls on the island. I chose a Malibu smoothie bowl; pineapple and banana whizzed with coconut milk and topped with a spoonful of sweet granola, goji berries and seeds – *the best pick-me-up I've ever tried*.

After breakfast, I jumped on the back of his bike for a trip to the highest viewpoint on the island. We clambered up the rocks, only to be rewarded with a rainy downpour and misty outline of the island.

'Haha typical,' shouted Jai, 'here, let's shelter behind these rocks.'

We sat there chatting until the rain cleared. I liked Jai; he was a short Californian with a beard that made him look thirty as opposed to his true age of eighteen. He loved to talk about his 'fucking rad scuba adventures' and his trucking life back home, helping his Dad drive hundreds of miles across American highways. He was a cool guy and I was grateful a scuba instructor had given up his free day to show me the island.

2p.m.

We headed to the beach to walk along the entire seafront, something neither of us had done yet. We messed around on the tree swings, hanging upside-down and laughing at each other when we fell into the sand and 'ate dirt', as Jai put it.

I jumped into the sea to wash off the sand that had collected in my bikini, while Jai was convincing a few others on the beach to join the pub crawl.

When I returned, Jai asked a little sternly 'Don't you need to pack Cece?'

'Um, yes I guess,' I replied.

'I thought so, let's go.'

'Are you okay, you seem in a hurry?' I asked when we were over the hill.

'Yea, one of those guys was weird, we only spoke for a minute before he asked if you had a boyfriend.'

'What? What is wrong with people on this island! He wasn't even drunk! Sometimes Jai, I feel like you're the only nice guy in this town!'

'Haha, I'm just a sensible medic Cece.'

'Well, thanks for looking out for me.'

'No problem,' he grinned.

12th November

I packed my things ready for the ferry back to Bangkok.[19]

It was strange to leave the island. It was the place I had spent the longest amount of time without travelling further than a few miles. I had enjoyed the time to relax and not worry about moving on. But this feeling of being stationary was bittersweet, because I had to say goodbye to many friends who came and left.

You cross paths with hundreds of people in your life but there are only a few people with whom you share your journey. When you travel however, you journey alone. Your path is your own. You may have moments in parallel with others, but you must ultimately part in the end. It's the inevitability of this separation that makes travelling so hard.

---

[19] *I sadly never had the chance to say goodbye to Jai, and thank him for his kindness, as he ironically hit his head during the pub crawl the night before and was in bed recovering the morning of my departure.*

FIFTY-TWO

Catching sunrises.

13th November

I caught my flight from Bangkok to Siem Reap in Cambodia, avoiding the border scams everyone else had experienced when taking the bus.

My hostel was colour blocked with large rectangles of red, blue and orange making it seem like a Lego house. The courtyard featured an inviting turquoise pool, surrounded by sunbathers and cocktail sippers perching on stools within the water. I was tired and with nothing else to do but wait until check-in, I spent the rest of the afternoon reading in the sunshine, trying to acclimatise to being in yet another new place, alone.

Evening

By the evening, I had re-gained some energy and decided I had to keep meeting new people, even if it was sad saying goodbye to them. *This is the only way you are going to enjoy your last few weeks Cece, keep going.* I met Robin in my female dorm. She was a tomboyish Swedish girl with an interesting style and a discreet gait, dragging her right leg a little as she walked. She wore thick-rimmed glasses that magnified her eyes, dark denim shorts, a loose Hawaiian shirt and a baseball cap that half covered her masculine bowl haircut. Robin invited me out with her friends for dinner in Pub Street, so I eagerly accepted. Having already spent a month in Kampot, I took her advice and ordered an amok, a yellow curry with tofu cooked in banana leaves. Being on Pub Street, cocktails were only two dollars, although so artificially sweet I could barely drink a few fingers worth of my 'Angkor Sunrise'.

I chatted to Robin's Spanish friends for a while, before making my excuses for an early night. Sometimes when travelling, it feels like you are constantly investing so much energy into relationships that will only last a few hours. Whether you spend two or twenty-two hours together, you always separate in the end and have to start again. I know this is what makes travelling so exciting, but in my fourth month, I was a little exhausted of these short-lived friendships.

14th November

I started tackling the medical claim for the drugs I received in Hong Kong. There was a lot of admin to go through which was difficult on a phone but, back in the UK, my parents kindly helped with the forms I couldn't process on a five-inch screen.

Afternoon

Robin and I hired bikes and headed to the Angkor Temple's ticket office. It was only six kilometres, but it took a while to get into the rhythm of Cambodian roads. The traffic was manic and created a terracotta cloud of dust that wrapped around your mouth, eyes and nose like an air-borne anaconda. Locating the office, we purchased one-day passes and headed back to the hostel to plan our temple route.

After a quick bowl of two-dollar Khmer fried rice, we hit our bunks, ready for an early start to catch the sunrise tomorrow.

15th November
4:30a.m.

We sleepily crawled out of our pods as the alarm rang, our eyes wide with excitement.

'It's Angkor time!' I whispered.

We hired bikes again for our temple transport, *much more fun than the twenty-dollar tuk-tuk alternativ*e. Head torches wrapped around the front our of bikes, we made our way through the quiet streets. With only a few tuk-tuks on the road, presumably headed to the same destination as us, it was strangely therapeutic to cycle at this time of the day. Reaching the main temple at 5:50a.m. we quickly locked up our bikes and headed towards the huge crowd of people lining the river in front of Angkor Wat. It was amazing how many people had sacrificed their precious hours of sleep to be present at the sun's unveiling of this man-made wonder.

The supposed sunrise, however, turned out to be a disappointing mass of clouds getting lighter and lighter until the temple was visible. It should have been frustrating, getting up so early to see a non-existent sunrise but, to be honest, at 6a.m. it was just funny.

For the next seven hours it was cycle, temple, cycle, temple. Giant blocks of intricately carved stone, moss covered sculptures and empty doorways stood proudly amidst the ruins. Giant tree roots clawed at the walls, clutching the stone as if it were stealing the temple's beauty away from the eyes of the beholder. I preferred the smaller, more discreet temples. There were fewer people, so it felt like you were discovering the ancient remains for the first time.

1p.m.

We made the long thirteen-kilometre cycle back to the hostel. Robin went back to sleep, while I put on my little black bikini and sat in the pool sipping a creamy pina colada as a reward for the day's exertion.

FIFTY-THREE

A good life, but a hard one.

16th November

Still tired from yesterday's early start, I spent the morning by the pool and fed my obsession with smoothie bowls with another pink pitaya.

1p.m.

Artisans Angkor, a Cambodian social business, recruited male and female orphans from eighteen upwards, training them in traditional Khmer crafts such as silk weaving and wood carving. The headquarters in Siem Reap provided free tours, so I booked to join the silk weaving.

Our guide, Ahir, started the tour in an allotment of mulberry bushes.

'The silkworm's diet consists solely of mulberry leaves as we find this produces stronger silks. Next, we can see the cocoons being unravelled in hot water, first the raw silk, then the fine silk used for the luxury garments. Threads are then dyed different colours and woven by expert weavers.'

He gestured towards a room full of busy women, hidden behind huge looms. The room was silent apart from the sound of wooden pedals and levers in motion. Everyone was focused, their eyes unwavering as we passed.

'You see here, time is money, every thread is a thread closer to a piece of silk,' Ahir explained.

'So, how many worms are used to make a single piece of fabric?' an American tourist asked.

'120,000 worms are needed to make one metre Sir, just one metre of silk.'

It was an incredible process to watch, but I couldn't help feeling sorry for the women; spending their entire day at a loom, mind numbingly moving their hands and feet in the same way and at the same speed to create a piece of fabric that cost more than their salary.

'How many years will they normally spend here?' I asked Ahir.

'It ranges from nine months to ten years.'

'Wow, and they practise the same craft for the entire time?'

'Yes, one craft. If they have the potential to create the artistic patterns, then they can be the creators of the fabric designs, but only a few can do this.'

'And what happens afterwards if they leave?'

'Some will go back to their hometown and grow their own mulberry bushes and even create the thread.'

'Ah okay, so this is an opportunity for a good life?'

'Yes good, but a hard one,' he replied solemnly.

The tour culminated at the Artisans' shop where we were encouraged to buy something to support the organisation. I couldn't afford much, as most items were a minimum of sixty dollars, but I did find two raw silk hair scrunchies, for my sister and I. Ahir stood graciously, head bowed, at the shop entrance as we all forgot about his excellent tour and went off to selfishly spend. I looked back at him and thought his salary probably wasn't much better than that of the weaving women.

'Ahir, orkun cheraown. Thank you for the tour, I really enjoyed it,' I said gratefully as I placed five dollars in his hand. It wasn't much but I hoped it was enough to show him that I had listened. His face softened and his eyes became glassy as he looked down at the green note in his hand.

'Thank you, thank you,' he whispered, holding his head low.

Evening

While having a casual drink with Robin, two burly Brazilian men joined our table. They were drunk and getting more intoxicated with each beer they consumed, which was every ten minutes. They were obsessed with two things, travelling and their bodies. Whilst comparing sights we'd seen in Cambodia, I felt a hand on my bare thigh. I tried to subtly wiggle my leg away, but the Brazilian's grip became firmer. *This is not happening to me again.* With a big smile, I picked up his hand, and placed it back onto his leg. He then moved it back and gave a dirty chuckle. With more force, I picked it back up and dropped it into his lap.

'Oh sorry, I actually have a boyfriend,' I confessed.

He pulled a sad face and moved his hand up to my waist. I shuffled along the bench in the opposite direction.

'Don't worry, I'm not going anywhere, you don't have to put your hand on me!' I said.

'Ah no, but I like.'

'Okay well I don't like.'

He chuckled again and kept trying to move his hand back to some part of my body.

'Listen!' I jokingly shouted, 'I'll stab you with my pina colada straw if you keep doing this!'

'Look dude, she has a boyfriend and clearly feels uncomfortable with you doing that, so back off!' Robin exclaimed.

I gave her a grateful smile. The Brazilian kept his hands to himself after that.

9p.m.

When the guys went to the bathroom, Robin and I took the opportunity to escape.

'Come on, let's ditch the drunks and head to Pub Street, their minds are all brew, they'll never know where we've gone!'

'Great plan and thank you for saving me earlier, that guy was being really weird.'

'No problem, he was an idiot, let's go,' she said taking my hand.

So like birds escaping their cage, we fled the hostel. We hid in a crowded rooftop bar but after one drink I was tired and could feel my meds kicking-in.

Heading back through the crowds, a pair of large hands grabbed my waist and yanked me back. In panic, I grabbed onto Robin's arm. I turned to see the two goofy Brazilians swaying, eyes half closed and their faces slapped with a stupid drunken grin.

'We fouyndd you,' one moaned.

'We need to leave,' I whispered to Robin, 'please, can we go?'

We power walked back to the hostel leaving the guys stumbling behind us. I locked the door and hid under the covers. *You're safe now.*

17th November

I woke with stomach cramps, which wasn't surprising considering the number of things that had happened recently. I stayed in my female dorm, trying to sleep off the pain.

FIFTY-FOUR

I'd run up the hill and wait for her to open the wooden door.

18ᵗʰ November

Two dragon flies, black dots in a perfectly blue sky, darted excitedly above me. It was early evening and a young Cambodian was hacking the top off a coconut for a guest. Three consecutive strikes on the top released a small triangle, to reveal the sweet refreshing water. A wide grin spread across the boy's face.

'First time he cut de coconut,' a bar worker smirked.

I smiled sheepishly and returned to my book, a little embarrassed someone had caught me watching. I spent the day resting by the pool after yesterday's attack, sitting in the sun's warmth and watching the hostel's comings and goings - making the most of my last day in Cambodia.

7p.m.

The airport became hot with anxious travellers, fretting and fanning their faces with passports. The power had been down for almost an hour and no one knew what was going on. When the electric lights were finally switched on, a cheer filled the room and queues started to re-form. Every flight in the terminal was delayed, but at least the air-con was back on.

Vietnam

I arrived in Hanoi at 11.30p.m. After a battle to get a taxi, I made it to the city centre and wearily carried my rucksack up to the third floor of the hostel.

19ᵗʰ November

I woke feeling exhausted and had stomach cramps. *Damn it CVS, again?*

Unfortunately, I had only booked my room for a single night, so had to check out at 11a.m. then move to the new room at 2p.m. I had no energy to protest, so sat like a crumpled zombie in the lobby until my new bed was ready. Around midday, I ran out of water so ventured outside in search of a shop. I immediately regretted it. Streets were manic, a never-ending stream of hooting scooters speeding up side streets and screeching round corners. Pavements were non-existent so you had to walk through the roads and pray nothing hit you. I was pretty drugged up due to the pain, so genuinely feared for my life as I hobbled across the street. I knew culture shock affected me when I moved to a new country, but I'd never felt as scared and shaken as this. *I can't take two more weeks, I'm so tired.*

Hiding behind the curtain in my bunk, I began to cry. Tears streamed down my cheeks as I tried to muffle my cries. I felt helpless, in a lot of pain and completely alone. I wanted familiarity, to see my family, to see Alex, but most of all to see my grandma. I so wanted to ring her and tell her about all the things I'd seen and done. Things that would make her proud. I wanted to run up the hill, tap on the brass knocker of Donnington House and wait for her friendly face to open the wooden door and welcome me in like I was the best thing in the world; just like she had done when I was a child.

But that privilege disappeared months ago. I would never be able to run up that hill and knock on the door, because no one would open it for me again.

FIFTY-FIVE

The streets of central Hanoi.

20th November

Lars was a thirty-three-year-old engineer from the Netherlands. Despite his prematurely greying hair and sun weathered skin, he was quite handsome. He was travelling for six weeks in Vietnam as an extended break from work. Spending most of yesterday recovering in my curtain-drawn bunk bed, he made the effort to introduce himself and check up on me every time he entered the dorm, offering to get me supplies or medication. I'd never met a stranger who was so openly kind to someone he didn't know, he was funny, charming and immediately became my Dutch big brother.

This morning we went down to breakfast to find a grand display of sliced watermelon, guava, dragon fruit, bananas, fried noodles and rice as well as pancakes and toast.

'Pancakes! I'm definitely going for them!' I said.

'Ah that is a good idea, I think I will go for them as well,' Lars replied.

Over plates of pancakes with hot honey and lime, we discussed the day's plans.

'Hey Lars, what's the keyring on your rucksack?'

'Oh, haha, you noticed it. Well, it's a bit silly considering I'm over thirty, but my mother worried about me going on the trip, so she gave me a little puppet as a kind of good luck charm.'

'That's really cute, my mum did the same but with a guardian angel.'

'Yes, the ironic thing was that as soon as I landed in Vietnam, the body fell off. So all I'm left with is a puppet head, aha.'

'Let's hope that's not a bad omen then!'

'Haha, exactly!' he laughed. 'So Cece, are you ready for our walk?'

'I certainly am, love walking, best way to see a new city!'

'Okay great, it will be quite a long walk, is that okay?'

I was still recovering so shouldn't have done anything too strenuous but, longing for a friend, accepted the offer.

'Yes, I'd love to, long walks are great.'

Oh, fabulous Charlotte, it's Kinabalu all over again!

Midday

We covered almost every street in central Hanoi, each one having its own speciality. Streets selling wardrobes, lights, tiles, taps - anything you wanted. You could build an entire house just walking through the city. After a few hours, we stopped for lunch on the roadside where a collection of make-shift kitchens were serving street food. It was busy and we were lucky to get a space, everyone from smart businessmen to gardeners were sat at the mishmash of tables, united by food. We sat with locals on tiny red plastic chairs, eating a plate of stir-fried noodles that cost no more than seventy pence.

Post-local lunch, we headed to Hanoi Zoo. For only thirty pence, we were able to see elephants, tigers, lions, griffins and even hornbills! I got so excited when I saw my favourite Borneo bird hopping around, Lars thought I had seen a unicorn and burst out laughing.

'Hey, Cece the excitable, there are fairground rides too.'

'Haha, nice, but I think they're for children.'

'Exactly, so you'll be able to go on them!'

'Hey, I'm twenty-three!'

'Yeah yeah, try and convince them you're over twelve!'

'Well, you'd have to hold my bags and chaperone me because they'll probably think that you're my father!'

'Oh, you little madam!' he exclaimed.

'It's okay old man, I'll walk slowly so you can keep up,' I shouted, darting towards the monkeys.

3p.m.

On the way back to the hostel, we passed a few lakes whilst sharing some tangy pomelo. Taking caution over the slope to avoid falling in, I peered over the edge of the lake to see the fish, but before I knew it, my body was lunging towards the murky green water. My heart jumped as two hands grabbed my waist and pulled me back, saving me from my algae-fate. I turned and suddenly realised, looking at Lars' cheeky grin, that he had jokingly pretended to push me into the water!

'Ohh you! I genuinely thought I was falling in, that this was the end.'

'Hahaha oh no, you have to be careful you see. Good thing I'm here!'

'If it weren't for you, I'd be fine, thank you very much!' I said, pushing him away, 'Right Grandpa, onto the coffee shop you were telling me about?'

'Yes! Onwards, follow me!'

The previous day, Lars had discovered a little café, selling traditional Vietnamese coffee. The entrance was narrow, just wide enough to fit a till and staircase, but the first floor opened onto a quaint balcony with yellow walls and dark green shutters.

'I was going to say watch out for the low ceiling,' Lars started, 'but then I realised you needn't worry with your height!'

'Watch it Papa, don't want you to have a heart attack at your age going up these stairs!' I said sarcastically.

We sat and watched the busy crossroads below in the afternoon sun. Lars had a traditional egg coffee, which consisted of half a cup of Robusta coffee with a sweet creamy custard top, while I sipped an iced coconut coffee - a shot of espresso over coconut cream ice.

Evening

Lars took me for my first Phở, a bowl of rice noodles, prawns, spring onions, coriander and fresh mint in an incredible broth flavoured with ginger, cinnamon, onion, and star anise. A flavour explosion, it was like Asian Christmas in a bowl. We wandered along the lantern-strung streets before he headed off to catch his night bus to Ninh Binh. We'd become good travel friends throughout the day, so arranged to meet again in Hoi An, when our routes would cross again.

Today had redeemed my rocky start to Vietnam, I was excited for the next few days. I returned to my hotel to pack, ready to board a bus at 7:30a.m. to Cát Bà island, to see Ha Long Bay. *The Vietnam adventure is properly beginning.*

FIFTY-SIX

Giants of the ocean.

21st November
5:30a.m.

My stomach was slightly knotted, but I assumed that was from going to sleep still a little hungry. I nibbled some slices of guava and dragon fruit at breakfast, hoping it would settle things before the bus journey. *Mistake.* My tummy bloated up and the cramps set in. *No! Go away CVS, you can't come back again!* I slumped into my coach seat and closed my eyes, praying it would go away. *I've had enough of being ill.*

After a three-hour bus, we were placed on a ten-minute speed boat and then another bus to the centre of Cát Bà Island. As soon as I saw the first rocky peaks floating in the ocean, the excitement rushed through me; *this must be Ha Long Bay*. The scenery had helped as a distraction, but leaving the final bus the cramps cranked up a notch and I was hit by a wave of exhaustion from the lack of food. My rucksack was pulling me to the floor and by the time I reached the hostel, I was ready to collapse and sink to the centre of the earth. *I'm so tired of fighting this illness*. I lay on my bunk and closed my eyes.

4p.m.

Most of the day had already disappeared and my bus was picking me up to return to Hanoi in less than twenty-four hours. I hadn't come all this way to be ill and just lie in the dark in another hostel, I needed to book some sort of tour for the morning. The cramps had eased after a good dose of paracetamol and a lie-down, so I ventured into town.

Faded posters of Ha Long Bay covered almost every shop window and wall, '*$60 full day*', '*Party boat tour 2 nights*', '*$40 half day, drinks included.*' The last thing I wanted to do was sit on a seasickness inducing party boat with a load of keg-headed tourists. As a last hope to find something, I made my way towards a dodgy looking ferry office on the pier. After many repeated phrases and a little help from Google Translate, I'd booked myself onto a morning tour 8a.m. - 12p.m. for just eight pounds. *Success!* It wouldn't be Ha Long Bay, but the one next to it, Lan Ha Bay, which apparently was the same if not better as it was a lot quieter with fewer tourists. Relieved, I went to lie down on a bench, the cramps had started up again and I needed to regain some energy before walking back up the hill to the hostel. *Life would be so much simpler without this illness.*

22nd November

Breakfast was served on the hostel's grassy roof-top terrace; my stomach was tender after yesterday's mild episode, but I managed a bit of bread and butter to give myself some energy for the tour. I was put on a mini-bus full of tourists and driven to the port on the other side of the island. Everyone else boarded a large ship, whilst a Vietnamese guy, Trung, and I were directed to a tiny fishing boat, about a tenth of the size. *With its peeling paint and creaky floorboards, it was probably ten times its age too.* A small island woman captained the tiny vessel. Bundled up in several jumpers and scarves, she welcomed us on board. Her face was weathered from the years at sea, but her eyes were still dark and youthful. Our guide was only twenty-one, but very friendly and knowledgeable. With their broken English and my limited Vietnamese phrases, the three of us got along really well. It was perfect - a local's tour.

The boat quietly motored through Lan Ha Bay, with barely any other boats in the sea, it was a hidden bliss. Vast karsts and sharp pinnacles protruded out of the water, riddling the blue ocean with grey cobbles. An hour into the ride, we moored up to a floating pontoon where Trung and I had the chance to hire kayaks in order to explore some of the intricacies of the Bay which were out of reach to larger boats. We kayaked in between the boulders, getting as close to the rock as we could without touching it. He was thirty-one and happily married but had yet to see his country's national treasure. So, he had taken the bus all the way from Ho Chi Minh, just for the four-hour tour. *That's commitment to the Bay.* We passed floating fish farms, made up of networks of planks and big floating barrels that enclosed nets filled with fat grouper.

'The people on the farms look poor. But they are very rich. Yes, very rich because grouper sells for big price,' our guide said knowingly.

'Also, these large boats with the thousand lights, they for night fishing, for large squid. Each ship worth twenty-million dollar, so they catch lot of squids.'

We looped back through the Bay to Monkey Island where we scrambled up sharp shards of black granite to reach the viewpoint. The view was incredible, Lan Ha Bay stretched far into the distance. Rock formations rose like giants of the ocean, an army wading through the mist, slowly making their way to land over the centuries.

'So you now live with me on Monkey Island, we build a house?' the cheeky guide asked when we were back on the boat.

'You want to live on Monkey Island together?' I asked.

'Yea, we build a school because you teach math?'

'Haha, love it, how about a monkey school considering it's Monkey Island? Then we'll teach the monkeys maths?'

'Yes, then you marry me?' he said with a grin.

'We'll see how the school goes first,' I giggled.

Back on land, the guide popped me on the back of his bike for a hair-raising ride across the island to return to town. I rewarded myself with a local delicacy of a fried turmeric, rice flour and coconut milk pancake, stuffed with beansprouts and crisp prawns, before making the journey back to Hanoi. The trip had been short, but this morning had made up for everything.

FIFTY-SEVEN

Our lives were completely different, but our minds were the same.

23rd November

I had wanted to visit the famous rice terraces of Northern Vietnam ever since I booked the trip, so as soon as I arrived back in Hanoi I signed up to a three-day trek in Sa Pa.

The majority of the first day was spent travelling. From a spluttering pick-up truck to a five-hour sleeper bus, with a few stops at grubby petrol stations, we proceeded north. The roads became steeper as we headed into the mountains. The coach rattled along, twisting and turning making my stomach curdle from travel sickness. I should have tried to sleep but I was so captivated by the mystical landscape that I couldn't close my eyes.

Arriving in Sa Pa, we were greeted by women dressed in traditional bright patterned skirts and head scarfs, trying to sell us purses or jewellery. Herded through the streets like cattle, we were placed on yet another minibus. *None of us had any clue where we were going or what we were doing.* Fifteen minutes later, we arrived at our final destination - a quiet hostel in the steep outskirts of the township. We were given a simple lunch while being briefed on the itinerary and assigned trekking groups. I was put with two Spanish women in their forties, three twenty-year-old Aussies and our local guide, Ly. From there, we walked down through the villages into the rice terraced valleys of Ta Van, where our homestay for the night was located.

Along the way, a group of females from different tribes joined our trek. They chatted with the only English they knew, 'Hello, what's your name? Where you come from?', offered support over the muddy roads and donned us each with a crown of flowers. Reaching the end of the hike, however, these sweet country ladies turned into crafty saleswomen, bombarding us with bags, scarfs, bracelets and anything else that was woven or embroidered.

'Please, you buy!'

'Handmade!'

'Lady, look nice on you, you buy!'

It was awkward; we weren't expecting to be transported to a night market in the middle of the countryside. It became clear to all of us; *these women hadn't just joined for the ride.* There was one sweet lady who'd spoken to me from the start, she must have been about eighty-five and had trudged all the way by my side. I felt so bad that I bought one of her purses in sympathy, it was handmade, and she even gave me a free ribbon bracelet to acknowledge my purchase. *Probably because I overpaid her by a ridiculous amount, but if it helped her family, then that was all that mattered.*

Ly, our guide, was a funny young lady. She looked ten years older than me but was only twenty-three with a husband and two children. Girls married young in Sa Pa, as early as fifteen. Villagers either farmed on the rice fields or went to earn money in tourism, working in hotels or as tour guides. Ly was a smart girl, but with minimal funds for education, she had resorted to picking up English from tourists in order to craft her own career. Our lives were completely different, but our minds were the same. For the rest of the trip, we became Vietnamese twins, Ly and Cece.

We learnt all about village life, how their clothes were made from hemp fibres, how the year revolved around rice cultivation and the social structures of the valley tribes.

'There are many tribes throughout these valleys,' Ly explained, 'you normally stay in your tribe from birth, unless you marry a man from a different tribe, then you must go and live with his family. Here, we see example of family house.'

Giving us a tour of a traditional mud house, Ly challenged us to turn the corn grinder.

'Come on, Cece, you try,' she beckoned.

It was an old stone mill, with a stiff handle that I could barely get one revolution out of.

'Oh, my dear, if you can't grind corn, you'll never get a husband in Sa Pa,' she laughed.

Late in the afternoon, as we were deep in the valley, the mist lifted to reveal the glorious terraced-lined hills. Purple clouds clustered between the mountains and the early moon reflected in the water-filled rice shelves. *Beautiful.*

Evening

We concluded the day with a group meal of fried sweet potato, fresh crispy spring rolls, garlic salmon, buttery greens, rice and fried battered bananas for dessert. We played a few games of cards before heading to our dorms in the hills. Just before bed, I sat in the cool night air with my hands wrapped around my mug of medicine, savouring its warmth. Everything was still and quiet. The entire valley was pitch black apart from a few twinkling village lights in the distance. *Good night Vietnam.*

24th November

I stepped onto the balcony, breathing in the fresh mountain air and gazing at the valley below. Wild buffalo roamed the fields and ducks waddled across the puddles as mud-caked little boys ran, chasing after them. It was a simple, but seemingly happy life. *Living in such beauty must be quite something.*

I was stopped dead in my tracks on the way to breakfast. A fat buffalo with huge horns and a frisky tail stood in my tracks. *Oh my gosh, how on earth do I get past you then?* We stared each other down for a while until I realised, this beast wasn't budging. When its head was turned, I quickly slid past its rear, praying it wouldn't step back and defecate or crush me. I made it past with only a whip of its muddy tail!

9a.m.

The trek was much harder than yesterday's walk, so all the more fun. Up and down we hiked, through bamboo forests and muddy footways. We even cut through a rice terrace, which was like tightrope walking on a thin sliver of mud within a bog.

'If you fall in, it will take all of us to pull you out,' warned Ly.

We all successfully scaled the terraces and concluded the hike at Tien Sa waterfall, an immense rock face streaming with water that towered above the village.

As I approached the edge, Ly whispered 'Cece, be careful, tourist die here because they fell.'

'Oh, okay thanks, I'll be careful!'

'Yes, it was very bad, but keep it quiet, we don't want more people trying to climb it.'

I think Vietnam's health and safety motivations are slightly different to the UK's.

Afternoon

Having the afternoon to ourselves, the three Aussies and I ventured into misty Sa Pa for a quick look around; it was so foggy we could barely see a few feet in front of us. Giving into the cold, we warmed ourselves up in a coffee shop, sipping ginger tea and nibbling a few Vietnamese biscuits.

25th November

After some speedy honey pancakes, we were off on our final walk to Cat Cat village at the bottom of the valley. A large waterfall cascaded down the rocks, spilling into the river that powered three large waterwheels; the river was a life source for the local tribes. The village was alive, sparkling Vietnamese beauties glided over bamboo bridges, pastel parasols in hand shading their delicate faces from the sun. Villagers in tribal costumes danced traditional routines, elegantly twisting and turning on the tips of their feet. Little girls, grubby faced but dressed in head crowns and beaded dresses tottered around trying to sell bracelets to wandering tourists, their big black eyes widening as a sales tactic. It was strange to watch these little girls as young as two or three, start their long careers as Vietnamese valley girls, *bartering from aged two to a hundred*.

A little girl, perhaps only four years, carried a baby on her back swaddled in blankets, jigging him up and down to soften his cries. It seemed a female childhood in Sa Pa was non-existent; children were trained to be mothers and providers. As Ly had said, they needed to start young; in a decade, she would have her own family to care for. Marriage, children, embroidery and rice fields - repeat the cycle. The only difference from one girl to the next was the colour of her headscarf. From birth, unless your family had money for education, your destiny was set, you were planted, watered, grown and harvested; another grain of rice in the Sa Pa valley. Yet through her hard work and determination, Ly had begun to diverge from this cycle, like many of her generation. Carving out a new path of opportunity for her daughter and the next generation of valley women.

Evening

Six hours later, our little family of women had returned to Hanoi. After a big group hug, we continued on our separate ways. I was sad to leave the friends I had made over the past seventy-two hours. I couldn't have imagined a more hilarious or kinder group of girls to share the experience with.

FIFTY-EIGHT

Candles floated like little fairies dancing on the ripples.

26ᵗʰ November

'Hello lady, hello. You, over there,' a man shouted.

I've just stepped outside Da Nang airport, a little dazed from the early flight.

'Hello, you come here,' the man continued. *Is he shouting at me? Oh lord, what have I done now? I've only just arrived!*

Alarmed, I point to myself and mutter 'Me?'

'Yes you, come here.'

Panicking, I stumble forward but my foot slides down the curb edge. I try to recover it, but the twenty-five kilos on my back pulls me to the floor. I'm facing the dirty ground and my knee is cut open.

'Ow, shit. What do you want?' I try to say without wailing.

'Taxi?' he asks mischievously.

For goodness sake, a bloody taxi, why the hell did you shout at me then?

The man attempts to apologise, but bursts into laughter with his colleagues across the road.

Struggling to get up, I shout, 'No' and walk off, embarrassed and annoyed.

Well that was a fine way to arrive in Da Nang, Cece.

I eventually source *myself* a Grab from Da Nang airport to Hoi An - land of the lanterns.

Hoi An

Old yellow painted streets are lined with vendors selling potato patties, rice pancakes, sugar dusted mangoes and countless shops selling silk scarfs and fans. Over four-hundred tailors are dotted around the city, displaying smart

313

mannequins dressed in fine suits and elegant evening dresses. Tiny wooden boats sail along the river and candle lit boxes float on the water, like little fairies dancing on the ripples. Hundreds of brightly coloured lanterns of all shapes and sizes are strung above the crowds, providing decoration by day and light by night.

I met Lars, from Hanoi, for dinner in a tiny lamp-lit café. We drank iced spiced lemon tea and tried cao lầu, the local delicacy of thick textured noodles with herbs and veggies in a sweet soy sauce. Sitting on tiny wooden chairs, we caught up about our past week, his tales of Ninh Bình and mine of Sa Pa.

'Hey girl, what happened to your leg?'

The cut on my knee had started to scab over.

'Urgh, taxi drivers,' I said, trying not to laugh as I told the ridiculous story.

27th November

Breakfast at the hostel was a fresh selection of passionfruit and mini fried bananas, along with my usual pills and concoctions. I'd met a nice Scottish couple in the dorm, so we all headed to meet Lars at the local fresh market. From there, we discovered a local's favourite spot for Bánh mì. A line of hungry lunchtime customers queued outside a tiny shop where seven ladies were hastily preparing sandwiches. Open the warm baguette, drizzle with oil, spread the chilli paste, fill with salad and cram in all the toppings possible; their hands moved so fast they looked like they were trying to fly.

Afternoon

Walking back to my hostel, a petite lady appeared to my left.

'Lady you beautiful, you figure perfect, like Vietnamese, beautiful. You know I am tailor; I make beautiful clothes for you.'

'Thank you, that's so kind of you.'

'Yeah, yeah, I make some just for you. Tiny waist, I think you Vietnamese from behind, come with me!'

'Um, okay,' I said.

And so, seduced by a tailor, I started to follow her. I was taken to an indoor market, riddled with rolls of fabric, industrial sewing machines and women curling tape measures around mannequins. I was presented with books filled with hundreds of designs, as women from all over the shop came to measure every part of my body.

'This one?'

'This look nice, miss, playsuit very pretty.'

'Or this one, young lady?'

I drew a quick sketch of the business dress I had in mind and was told to return in the evening for a fitting. At 5p.m. an elegant navy dress with little capped sleeves and a bow around the waist was presented for me to try on. It fitted perfectly. *If only Grandma had been here, she'd have loved this - a personal tailor-made dress.*

'Okay lady, you like, you now buy more, in grey, black?'

'Thank you, that is kind of you to offer, but I don't think I'll have enough room in my rucksack,' I said, leaving before they could convince me to order anything else!

28th November

Despite a good night's sleep, I woke feeling drained with the familiar pain in my stomach. I swallowed paracetamol with some warm tea at breakfast, and then returned to lie on my bed, letting exhaustion consume me. I had arranged to go cycling with Lars, but that wasn't happening anytime soon. I felt bad bailing because out of the days he had known me, I'd had CVS most of the time. *I won't be surprised if he finds a better 'non-flaky' friend to do things with, one without a chronic illness.*

29ᵗʰ November

I woke again with cramps, despite the attack finishing early last night. I couldn't bail on Lars a second time. Determined to stave them off, I swallowed some more paracetamol, anti-sickness meds and lay down for another hour. My stomach was tense and unsettled, but I wasn't throwing up or in much pain. *I'm getting on that damn bike today. No stupid illness is going to stop me.*

It was a grim day, but heralding from countries where drizzle is the norm, we embraced the rain and cycled on through the rice paddies. Lars loved photography, capturing candids of locals pruning fields, carrying plants or hacking weeds in the sticky heat. Whereas I just loved being outside, flying through the fields on a bike, feeling well and free. At least with my illness, I really appreciated the 'well days'.

We finished the day at the noodle place again and had a last look at the floating lanterns on the river, before I headed back for an early night. *I don't want to be ill again tomorrow.*

30ᵗʰ November

The cramps returned for a third day in a row. *I just want to go home now, I've had enough. I can't deal with this illness anymore.* My body had started to break down, it was like those weeks in Japan all over again. I needed to stop moving, stay in one place and rest, but my flight home was fast approaching. I had no choice but to push through and get to Ho Chi Minh, where my final flight would depart from.

FIFTY-NINE

*Our hearts went out to the people we had met, praising them for
their kindness and unyielding generosity.*

30th November
8p.m.

The hustle and bustle of Ho Chi Minh's busy streets
continued below, but from the hostel rooftop, it was all white
noise. I stood under a string of fairy lights, tired from the
journey, looking out at the multitude of high-rise buildings
that were changing the city's skyline - a city once known as
Saigon. Perhaps owing to its previous American influence, Ho
Chi Minh was far more cosmopolitan than Hanoi, with wide
promenades, glitzy shopping malls and fancy restaurants. My
hostel was situated on the corner of District One. With plain
white walls and minimalistic décor, it had a Scandinavian feel
and price. At thirteen pounds a night for a female six bed
dorm, it was expensive for Vietnam, but as it was my last hostel
of the trip, I thought I would splash out.

1st December

Arriving in a new city, I should have been sightseeing,
but by this stage in the trip I was tired and just wanted to walk
without agenda. Sitting by the riverside, I finished reading
another mountaineering book on my Kindle whilst deterring
the many Vietnamese men who tried to convince me to hop on
their bike for a city tour.

'Lady you want tour? One hour, very nice!'
'Oh no thank you, I'm fine.'
'Sure? It's very good, I show you all the attractions.'
'No really I'm fine here, thank you.'
Can't a girl just sit in the sun and read?

Lunchtime

Found the cutest rooftop poke café where you could design your own bowl. I chose a base of brown rice and salad, topped with miso tofu, crab slaw, seaweed, mushrooms, marinated aubergine, tangy ginger and edamame beans, topped with nori strips and sesame seeds.

Souvenir searching time. Visiting my final Asian market, I enjoyed absorbing the atmosphere of the bazaar, gazing in wonder at the stalls piled high with dried fruits, local crafts and coffee tins. I picked up a few presents including some coconut candies and coconut husk bowls, which I bartered down from eight to three hundred dong.

Evening

Heading back to shower and change into my little blue playsuit Grandma had bought me, I decided to end the trip how it started, on a rooftop cocktail bar. The lift took me to the fifty-second floor, where I was seated on a high table with single bar chairs. I ordered a creamy pina colada which came in a tall glass filled with ice and a sweet wedge of pineapple.

As the sun set, the city became alive with the lights of cars, motorbikes and thousands of homes illuminating the sky. The roads transformed into rivers of light, constantly moving in a never-ending stream of traffic. Many people consider the river as a city's life source, but in Vietnam it's the roads. Miles of hot tarmac where drivers seamlessly dodge and dart, ignore red lights and swerve around hazards like a ski slalom; where pedestrians play the fickle game of 'flatten or cross' and policemen turn a permanent blind eye. Yet in this wonderful chaos, everyone understands the unwritten laws of the road, and continue onwards in a unified disorder.

I met two travellers at the bar, a large businessman from the States and a New Zealander in her thirties. We were all at the end of our trips, so shared stories of close-shaves, culture shocks and journey delays. We all agreed, however, that no matter where you travelled in Asia, there was always kindness to be found. Our hearts went out to the people we had met, praising them for their kindness and unyielding generosity; no matter the size of their salaries, they shared what they had as if you were part of their family. Perhaps that is the secret to their happiness - be generous, stay humble and always share what you have.

2nd December

Final day in Asia. This is it Cece, your last day, you have almost made it!

I started the morning with some rooftop yoga overlooking the city. Then popped into the café across the street and picked up a final iced coconut coffee. Sipping the sweet coconut nectar, I walked a long way down the river, gazing at individual streets and locals enjoying the sunshine. I headed towards the HCM museum where a group of students stood in a huddle. Sheepishly giggling, one approached me.

'Umm excuse me, please. We are students and we have a project. Yes, we have a project.'

'Okay cool,' I said trying to put them at ease.

'Yes! Please could you answer some question about museum?'

'Yes sure!'

'And it's okay we video you?'

'Okay, but perhaps I should go in the museum first, as I don't know very much at the moment?'

So, after a speedy look around the museum and a little help from Google, I was ready to be interviewed. They asked me several questions about the history of the city and the museum's accessibility to tourists.

'Great, well if that's all your questions then perhaps we should add each other on Instagram, in case you have any more questions?' I said.

'Oh yes!' the interviewer exclaimed, while the others smiled and nodded their heads excitedly.

Two hours later

> *Instagram: 'you have fifty new likes and one follow request'*
> *- crikey, someone's keen.*

Afternoon

Waiting for my Grab to the airport, a Taiwanese lady who had been in my dorm, looked calculatingly at my rucksack.

'Oh, you go to the airport now? How you get there?' she asked.

'By a taxi,' I replied.

'Because I used all my money, I bought a bag and now can't get to the airport haha. Can I share with you?' she asked.

At the poor excuse of spending her money on a commodity, I had little sympathy and was about to say no. But then thought how the people I've met here have been so nice that I should follow in their footsteps and be a kinder person. *It won't cost you anything extra, just be nice and help her.*

'Yes of course,' I smiled.

Su was a reception teacher and her round smiley face and calm voice reminded me of Iris. We chatted about our travels right up to the departure lounge. She tried to repay me for the ride with Taiwanese jelly sweets, but I kindly declined – in the end I was just happy to help her. It was nice to meet a new friend, even at the very end of my trip, and I was glad I had helped her get home. After a quick photo and farewell, we parted at the boarding gate.

Then, it was just me.
Goodbye Vietnam.

SIXTY

19 Flights
1 Earthquake
2 Typhoons
15+ CVS attacks
7 Countries
987 WhatsApp messages
60 Journal Entries
270 Instagram Posts
1 Turquoise Rucksack
8 Kindle Books Read
16 Postcards
0.5 Litres of Tears
100s of Amazing People
1000s of Smiles

4 Months in Asia - Complete

Above Hanoi

Nearing the end of my first flight, the old lady sitting next to me ran to the bathroom. For the next twenty minutes, loud retching sounds echoed throughout the plane. Returning, she sunk wearily into her seat, eyes closed. I placed a wet wipe in her hand, and she took it gratefully. Guessing she was Thai, I typed into my translator app 'do you need anti-sickness meds?' but she looked confused and within a few minutes we were landing. As she left the plane, she tapped my arm and smiled for the first time during the entire flight. I guess that was her way of saying thank you.

3rd December
Istanbul Airport
2a.m.

Sitting on the balcony of a coffee shop, I sorted through the five different SIM cards I had acquired, trying to restore each one to its correct packaging. I watched the crowds browsing through duty free or rushing to the gates. *Was it really this time four months ago that I had been one of these people going in the opposite direction?*

The final plane home

The moon, a bright crescent, illuminates the ink black sky. The people below are sleeping as we fly over the English countryside. *I'm on the final plane home.*

In many ways, I felt empty. I had become so broken and ill during my time away that I no longer recognised my own reflection, I had lost a part of myself. But perhaps, because of this, I had also rebuilt myself. I am here now, alive and smiling because I fought through every day, even when I felt so sick that I hoped it would be my last. I am here now because I never gave up.

I believe, in this life, that the bad things are needed to make you appreciate the good. You can always learn from them; they make you stronger if you can see beyond them. When I was well, my mind was clear. I saw, listened and breathed in everything around me because I was free from pain. If it weren't for the pain, grief and misfortune, I would not have seen so much kindness. Over thousands of miles, I have experienced a lifetime's worth of kindness: Tadasu, Iris, Nanami, the Malaysian couple, those at the shelter and many more. Kindness, I believe, is one of the most important things in life.

We enter and exit this life with nothing. Money and possessions are left behind. We only remain in the memory of another. My journey is now in the past, it is finished. Time will wear away my footprints, people will forget my name, but the acts of kindness will remain forever in my heart.

Gatwick

When I landed in Gatwick, I received Alex's message he had sent as I departed Vietnam.

[02/12, 17:29] Alex: Well, well, well Cece - four months. You've done it exactly! I just wanted to say, before you go, that I am so very proud of you for everything you have achieved over the last four months! You've absolutely bossed it!! You're amazing!!! The best girlfriend anyone could wish for! Literally can't wait to hug you again!! Have a safe flight!! I love you to the clouds and back!! xxx

I savoured the message, reading it three times whilst in the queue for passport control. I guess it still hadn't hit me that I was no longer in Asia, that I'd completed my challenge and that I was returning home.

As I stepped through passport control, I counted the steps, breathing in the last moments of my journey. I had pictured arriving at Gatwick hundreds of times throughout the trip; but now the moment was only minutes away I didn't know how to react. *Past these doors, you'll be reunited with your family.* I longed for Grandma to be there, for her to wave at me with excited eyes as I walked through the gate. But the last wave she would ever give me had been four months ago. *She would be proud of you Charlotte.*

For the nineteenth time in four months, I walked into arrivals. Seeing my parents faces in that moment will be a memory I hold forever. Their faces lit up and my mother excitedly tapped my father on the shoulder, gesturing for him to pull out the homemade sign, *'Welcome Home Charlotte xoxox'.* I ran as fast as I could and fell into both their arms, a smile spread across my face as little tears dripped down my cheeks.

'Charlotte I am so proud of you, completely in awe, I don't know how you did it!' my mother cried.

323

In that moment, I realised the only fundamental of happiness in this life; one that my grandma had found long ago: to be surrounded by those who love you - your family.

'Charlotte you must always remember you are loved. So loved.'
- Ruth Baylis, Grandma, 2nd August 2018

I will always remember you Grandma. The little Welsh girl who learnt to live with nothing. You found your own way, loving and caring for other children until you fell in love and made your own happiness; creating the little family you deserved as a child. You gave me your curly hair and your gift for stories. You gave me your imagination and taught me to dream and to travel. You gave me your strength, your Chikara. I travelled half the world for you, and visited everything I'd promised to, from the mountains of Fujian to the geishas of Kyoto. I wear your name between my first and last, to keep your memory safe forever.

I will tell our story.

In our wildest moments we can be the freest.
On dreamy July evenings, my sister and I would race through
dusty country paths, slicing through green fields, all the way to the
hidden river. The wind whipped our hair as we sped through the
sweet summer air on our bikes. We felt free, alive and wonderfully
wild. No matter what life throws at us, let us always be wild.

AFTERWORD

Reasoning Behind the Journal

Reason One

At some point early in the trip, Alex asked me why I was investing so much time in my journal.

'It must be a book, these entries you write are so long!' he guessed.

'Haha, no, it's just so I can remember,' I replied casually.

But in truth, I did it because it made me feel closer to my grandma, she had such a beautiful way with words, written or spoken. The adjectives and adverbs were chosen with thought and composed into phrases that were simple but described the subject in such detail. I could listen to her stories for hours, because every sentence was crafted with care, every word was devoted to the story. I wanted to write like her, to be able to tell stories like her. I was writing this journal because I did not want her gift to be lost, I needed to harness it. If I could learn to write like her, she would live on.

Reason Two

To recognise all the people that helped me. There are so many people that are so selfless, generous and kind that they will help anyone. I learnt that no matter where you are in the world, there is always someone who will show you kindness. And that, I believe, is something that should be celebrated.

Dear Tadasu,

I hope you are well and getting ready for Christmas?

I have completed my four-month trip in Asia! I am flying back to the UK this evening.

After we parted and I recovered - I continued my journey down the South of Japan and then visited China, Thailand, Cambodia and Vietnam. I have been trekking in the rice terraces, visited Lan Ha Bay, worn a kimono in Kyoto, tried diving, visited Angkor Wat and continued to hike in national parks. I have attached a few photos! Japan, however, was my favourite country and I would like to return in the coming years. The kindness you showed me in Hokkaido still remains at the forefront of my mind and will be one of my strongest memories of the trip. I will move to London in January for a new job, so if you ever travel to England - let me know!

I hope you and your family are well and enjoy Christmas!

Best wishes,
Cece

Hi Cece,

Congratulations on completion of your journey!

You know, I thought that you would make it because I felt something very strong in you.

I'm impressed that you have visited all these countries with your heavy backpack and enjoyed every moment in your journey...I love your diving pictures!

Now Asahidake is beautifully covered with snow, and I enjoy cross country ski as a part of my job in the visitor centre. I'm also a staff member of Japan Para Ice Hockey Team, and I occasionally visit Europe for tournaments and matches. So someday I might have a chance to visit your country.

Wishing you a very Merry Christmas!
Tadasu

Reason Three

With CVS or a chronic illness, you go through life trying to be as positive as you can until the next attack comes along and knocks you off your feet. But when you are well for multiple days in a row, you feel superhuman, because you can forget your suffering. Every day feels like a gift because you can do anything you want without pain or sickness, you feel invincible. I call this the false fitness effect, because when you do eventually become ill again or have another attack, it can feel like you've lost everything you built when well. You must not only deal with the pain, but come to remind yourself of the reality, that you are not like everyone else, that you are not a superhuman with unlimited energy and that you can't control your own body. For you, good days are a gift, not a given.

I was reminded of this feeling on my twenty-fourth birthday. The first birthday without my grandma, the first time I wouldn't receive an envelope with her handwriting. The night before I had been feeling grateful for my life. It had been weeks since my last attack and I was happy. I had the day all planned out: open cards, buy my friends ice cream at work, go for a climb and visit a Japanese bar with my best friend in the evening. I put on a full face of make-up, something I rarely did, and put on one of my smarter work dresses. Just as I was about to leave, the dreadful pain in my stomach returned. Within five minutes I'd wiped off the make-up, changed back into my pyjamas and crawled back into bed. *Please be a mild attack.* For most of the morning I cried as the cramps got worse. I spent the day lying in a dark room alone, popping paracetamol like birthday shots. I concluded the night, vomiting until there was nothing left and collapsing with fatigue. It wasn't the best way to start my twenty-fifth year.

Despite having the condition for over a decade, I am still learning from those around me, those far stronger than me, how to deal with CVS. Whilst I was travelling, I had the tendency to fight my condition, to resist it and push it away, which is sometimes the worst thing you can do. There is no point in fighting something that you can't control, you need to let the attack run its course. Most of the time, you just need to accept that you are ill and accept that today won't be as good as others – but that doesn't mean that your life has stopped, it has just been put in the slow lane for a while. Sometimes, to find peace, you just need acceptance.

I am still learning how to accept my illness and save my energy for the recovery. I am learning how to make the most of my time not only when I am well but more importantly when I am ill. I am learning not to fight but to become a fighter - an accepting, yet relentless, fighter. I am learning how to be a silent warrior - the strongest people of all.

I wrote this journal for the sufferers and the carers of those with chronic conditions; to give a voice to the silent warriors. Warriors who endure hours of lying alone in a dark room, hours writhing in pain, hours of nausea and vomiting, hours of exhaustion but who still make it to the end of the day hoping for a better one tomorrow. I wrote this journal for those who believe a better day is always around the corner if you can fight to reach it. If you are determined enough and never give in, anything is possible.

In recognition of the silent warriors, 15% of author royalties will be donated to CVSA UK - a charity dedicated to providing information and support to sufferers of Cyclical Vomiting Syndrome and their families.

NAME LIST

Named locals and travellers I met along the way

- *Aaron - Swiss hiker (Hokkaido)*
- *Ahir - Cambodian silk farm guide (Siem Reap)*
- *Amy and Ned - Young Northern couple (The Dragon Trip)*
- *Bibi - Xi'an tour guide (The Dragon Trip)*
- *Bo - Chengdu tour guide (The Dragon Trip)*
- *Bonnie - Cantonese healer from The Healing Room (Hong Kong)*
- *Bram - Traveller from the Netherlands (Kyoto)*
- *Che - Knowledgeable Malaysian spontaneous guide (Kota Kinabalu)*
- *Chesa - Filipino Mount Kinabalu climbing partner (Kota Kinabalu)*
- *Dalir - Pakistani paediatrician (Kuching)*
- *Danielle (Dani) - Canadian traveller (Koh Tao)*
- *Dao - Fujian tour guide (The Dragon Trip)*
- *Darren and Rachel - Older Northern couple (The Dragon Trip)*
- *Delima and Hatar - The Malaysian couple (Kubah National Park, Kuching)*
- *Elias - Belgian, Mulu National Park enthusiast! (Mulu, Borneo)*
- *Fen - Macau tour guide (The Dragon Trip)*
- *Geena and Mia - The nurses (The Dragon Trip)*
- *Iris - Kindly looked after me in HK (Hong Kong)*
- *Jai - Pub first aider from California (Koh Tao)*
- *Jan - A Cantonese 'victim' from The Healing Room (Hong Kong)*
- *Jason - Wannabe Aussi traveller (Kota Kinabalu)*
- *Jia - Yangshuo tour guide (The Dragon Trip)*
- *Jim and Lauren - Welsh couple (The Dragon Trip)*
- *Kairo - Kinabatangan Kapitan, guide and ranger (Kinabatangan River, Borneo)*
- *Kari - Excellent photographer from Norway (Hiroshima)*

- *Khun - The Box Hostel staff (Chiang Mai)*
- *Lana - US traveller and snorkelling partner (Koh Tao)*
- *Lars - Netherlands traveller (Hanoi and Hoi An)*
- *Leon - German yoga instructor and traveller (Koh Tao)*
- *Luke - Diving instructor from South London (Koh Tao)*
- *Luna - The Great Wall tour guide (The Dragon Trip)*
- *Ly - Rice terraces guide (Hanoi)*
- *Marianne - Young German traveller (Singapore)*
- *Meggie - American scooter partner (Chiang Mai)*
- *Melanie and Ben - Scottish couple (The Dragon Trip)*
- *Nanami - My paternal grandparents' dear friend (Tokyo)*
- *Noah - Iris' son (Hong Kong)*
- *Nuntida - Thai cooking school chef (Chiang Mai)*
- *Robin - Swedish tomboy and temples partner (Siem Reap)*
- *Sapphire and Yina - Moganshan tour guides (The Dragon Trip)*
- *Saris - Swedish traveller and knee examination chaperone (Kuching)*
- *Sophie - Dutch international student (Kokura)*
- *Callum and Veronica (Vee) - Southern couple (The Dragon Trip)*
- *Su - Taiwanese traveller, airport taxi sharer (Ho Chi Minh)*
- *Tadasu - Visitor's Centre guide and the kindest man in Hokkaido (Daisetsuzan National Park)*
- *The French Girls (les filles françaises) - Feeca (Fee), Liba, Amelia and Mini (Kuching)*
- *Tommy - Essex Lad (The Dragon Trip)*
- *Trung - Lan Ha Bay tour partner (Vietnam)*

ACKNOWLEDGEMENTS

I am where I am today because of my family - my Mother, Father and Sister – Amanda, Paul and Jemima Clark. I would like to thank them for spending hours proofreading my work, for their unconditional love and for their relentless support during my travels and life so far.

Although they are not here today to read this, I know they will still hear my story. So, I would like to thank my maternal grandparents, Wilfred and Ruth Baylis, for their kindness and love, for teaching me how to reach my dreams and to never give up.

My three Exeter girls, Bozhana Miteva, Rebecca Jones and Sarah Scott, for being such dear friends and for believing in me, always.

To Basia Stoecker, who proofread my work and taught me acceptance, openness and introduced me to new cultures through her own personal travel stories.

My paternal grandparents, Sallie and David Clark, for helping me with my vaccinations and for passing on their many stories of Japanese culture - they displayed a beautiful silk kimono in their hallway which I used to gaze at as a child.

To Samantha Hastings for dedicating her time to proofread my work.

Finally, to my best friend, editor and adventure partner, Alex Manaton, who remains the brightest star in my skies.

Printed in Great Britain
by Amazon

54034365R10203